Further Praise for *From Knowledge to Intelligence*

"This book clearly and uniquely es[...] tween knowledge management (KM) and co[...] cutive moments throughout the book provid[...] or the issues addressed in each chapter. A mus[...] for an organization that has to compete!"

—**Babette Bensoussan,** Director, The MindShifts Group, Australia and SCIP Fellow

"This book will reduce ignorance and add new insights to the continual evolution of knowledge leadership, especially on how to develop the capacity for intelligence. By combining their separate expertise in knowledge management/intellectual capital and competitive intelligence, the authors have shaped a most timely and valuable book . . ."

—**Leif Edvinsson,** The world's first holder of professorship of Intellectual Capital

"As a manager in charge of offices in three countries, I have to deal with many of the issues addressed by this book. Both finding, using and protecting my organization's intelligence is a constant challenge. *From Knowledge to Intelligence* has been extremely helpful in organizing my thinking on this challenge."

—**Marie Fioramonti,** Managing Director/PRICOA Captial Group

"*From Knowledge to Intelligence* provides a practical tool for developing strategy by business leaders. The book moves from theory to action steps quickly and offers good recommendations on finding and using intelligence that should help businesses compete."

—**Bruce Gorchow,** President, PPM America Capital Partners, LLC

"*From Knowledge to Intelligence* is a remarkable contribution to the knowledge management and competitive intelligence literature. While clearly defining the differences between the disciplines, it also focuses around their seamless integration. As a practitioner in these areas at a major multinational pharmaceutical company for over fifteen years, the theme of the work rang true to the mark, i.e., the overarching objective of these and other decision support functions is to support management in building and sustaining competitive advantage through evidence based decision making.

Of particular interest was the introduction of the concept of the SPF (strategic protection factor). This concept provides a bold new theoretical risk assessment framework for structuring the delicate balance between the creation and protection of a firm's intelligence and knowledge assets.

This text should be become part of required reading not only for practitioners new to the KM and CI fields, but for advanced practitioners as well."

—**Cliff Kalb,** Former Senior Director, Strategic Business Analysis, Merck; Former President, SCIP

"It's easy to overlook the importance of competitive intelligence in an e-commerce business model. Rothberg and Erickson do a good job in pin pointing where the opportunities and risks lie."

—**Chris McCann,** President, 1-800-Flowers.com

"Valuable information that can help a company win is routinely collected, yet the recognition, organization and distribution of this info to the appropriate decision makers is typically not systematic . . . nor optimal. *From Knowledge to Intelligence* will help you gain competitive advantage through a better understanding of how to use information . . . much of it from data you already possess . . ."

—**Frank Minerva**

"Rothberg and Erickson do a terrific job explaining how to take knowledge management from a walk to a run in your company. They impress upon us the reality that in today's business world with increasing pressure to find and hold a real positioning advantage, knowledge management is as important an asset for success as your company's brand name. And maybe moreso!"

—**Terry D. Peigh,** Senior Vice President, Interpublic Group of Companies

"Rothberg and Erickson provide the most authoritative approach to the integration and complementarities of knowledge management and competitive intelligence. Their approach, embodied in the essence of competitive capital, will soon become a key concept in the lexicon of business literature."

—**John E. Prescott,** Ph.D., Professor of Business Administration, Director of the Doctoral Program, University of Pittsburgh

"When two leading experts on competitive intelligence and knowledge management get together to layout how to exploit knowledge assets, you expect to get actionable insight—and this book delivers. This book provides a practical framework to implement a program to convert knowledge to actionable intelligence that fits the needs of the organization. Using a metaphor of sunscreen protection, SPFs provide a way to quickly understand the balance of risk, reward and costs to leveraging knowledge. An investment in this book will have immediate payoff for those that believe that knowledge and intelligence are power."

—**William Ruh,** Chief Technology Officer, Software AG Inc.

From Knowledge to Intelligence

Creating Competitive Advantage
in the Next Economy

From Knowledge to Intelligence

Creating Competitive Advantage
in the Next Economy

Helen N. Rothberg *and* G. Scott Erickson

ELSEVIER
BUTTERWORTH
HEINEMANN

AMSTERDAM • BOSTON • HEIDELBERG • LONDON
NEW YORK • OXFORD • PARIS • SAN DIEGO
SAN FRANCISCO • SINGAPORE • SYDNEY • TOKYO
Butterworth-Heinemann is an imprint of Elsevier

Elsevier Butterworth–Heinemann
200 Wheeler Road, Burlington, MA 01803, USA
Linacre House, Jordan Hill, Oxford OX2 8DP, UK

Library of Congress Cataloging-in-Publication Data
Rothberg, Helen N.
    From knowledge to intelligence : creating competitive advantage in the next economy/
Helen N. Rothberg and G. Scott Erickson.
        p.   cm.
    Includes bibliographical references and index.
    ISBN 0-7506-7762-7 (alk. paper)
    1. Knowledge management.   2. Competition.   I. Erickson, G. Scott.   II. Title.

HD30.2.R6648 2004
658.4′038—dc22

                                                                    2004050665

British Library Cataloguing-in-Publication Data
A catalogue record for this book is available from the British Library.

ISBN: 0-7506-7762-7

For information on all Butterworth–Heinemann publications
visit our Web site at www.books.elsevier.com

05 06 07 08 09 10   10 9 8 7 6 5 4 3 2 1

Printed in the United States of America

Table of Contents

Foreword

Seek'em (CIKM), A Recipe for Executive Success

"Knowledge has value, intelligence has power." This catchy phrase runs throughout the new book by Professors Helen Rothberg and Scott Erickson. This is sheer poetry in a field where poetry is the last thing you'd expect. But then R&E's book was the last thing I expected. Marrying competitive intelligence with knowledge management? Why?

Maybe, just maybe, it's because, separately, these two disciplines fared less well than expected. My colleagues in CI may not like to hear it, and surely my distant relatives in KM will claim I have no clue, but the truth is, neither discipline achieved what it was set to achieve or what it *could* achieve if done properly. CI always aimed at driving action by influencing decisions—important decisions. By inference, CI's audience should have been "important decision-makers." But what happened to be true in governments has been untrue in business. While CI roles have been institutionalized in 97 percent of all Fortune 500 firms, and thousands of smaller companies all over the globe, CI has failed to become an executive's dominant methodology for identifying strategic risks and *sustaining* sources of competitive advantage. Instead, it has been narrowly focused on competitors, rather than the bases of being *competitive*, which are of course much broader and much more strategic in nature. Then, just like market research, it has been relegated to a supporting role in tactical product projects, being seen as "good to know," not a "*must know* at all cost." It has remained far removed from the halls of influence and the boardroom, where it should be, and has been buried deeply—sometimes six to seven levels from the top—in marketing or marketing support departments. In other words, business leaders have consistently shown a preference for CI to help the sales force generate one more sale rather than saving the whole company from slow and certain death. Go figure. On second thought, this is not so different in government, is it?

Not to be outdone, KM has fared even worse. To laymen like me, and many other managers, KM has become a label on large consultant-pushed initiatives, ranging from feel-good information-sharing campaigns, politically correct "learning organizations," or simply good old-fashioned expensive IT projects, sponsored by CIOs and others who spend money regardless of expected returns. As practiced, KM is actually nothing more than a glorified IT, just as CI in many companies is nothing more than a glorified Internet search function! Now, if you marry a glorified IT to a glorified search engine, can you get *power*?

Yes, you can—if you follow R&E's practical recipe. As the authors say, "At minimum, galvanized knowledge merged with competitive intelligence practices can continuously fortify strategic decision-making. At maximum, it can generate competitive capital, a potentially defendable and sustainable source for earning above-average returns."

The merger of knowledge management systems with competitive intelligence practices is supposed to, according to R&E, transform knowledge into competitive *actions*. There is an urgent need for competitive actions in a world where incumbents do not innovate and turnaround CEOs replace lagging CEOs at an alarming rate.[1] On the one hand, the disinclination of Fortune 500 firms to act is a blessing, as it allows entrepreneurial minds to enter and destroy old and slow dinosaurs with better solutions to customers' problems. On the other hand, managers in their thousands pay for their leader-

1 In 2002 alone, 39% of all CEOs departures, globally, were forced ("CEO Succession 2002: Deliver or Depart," *Strategy+Business*, Summer 2003).

ship's inactivity while the leaders collect their golden parachutes. So it is those managers who should push for better knowledge management using competitive intelligence practices for seeking *new* knowledge (about change). In other words, managers who'd like to see their jobs preserved should push for CIKM (seek 'em and they will come).

One innovative aspect of this book is that in marrying CI and KM, it creates the concept of "SPF"—Strategic Protection Factor— which measures a firm's commitment to protecting its knowledge. As an old hand in running war games, I will be glad if business executives do not read this book. Their lacking in SPF makes it so much easier to estimate their intended moves in the market. On the other hand, my personal knowledge is that firms notable for their secrecy are actually not up to par on the competitive intelligence side. Secrecy creates an insulated culture, unsuitable for an external focus. The authors do well to warn executives to keep the balance in the quest to increase knowledge assets and protect existing assets. It is left to corporate management to carry out their recommendations halfway, as usual.

Finally, a thought about the meaning of it all. When a man or a woman reaches the pinnacle of power, a CEO position in a large multinational firm, does (s)he really need competitive intelligence or knowledge management? The CEO has dozens of people working directly and indirectly for him, providing news briefs and easy-to-digest analyses and a few PowerPoint slides summing up the issues, so as not to waste the CEO's valuable time. Intelligence filters up to the seat of power through dozens of "gateways," where it is massaged, dressed up, toned down, and cleaned up. It has to fit with the style, the basic beliefs, the immediate concerns, and the political pull of the group around the CEO. It should not offend particular division heads, or EVPs, or it will lose support. It cannot be too unpopular. It mustn't go against consensus. Yet, say R&E at the end of their book, "Intelligence gets its power from unfiltered, timely scrutiny of the competitive environment and the firm itself. Whether providing operational or strategic value, intelligence can directly impact how and what the firm does. To facilitate this, executives need to articulate an intelligence vision to get people engaged. And, they need to use the intelligence capability to give it meaning." This is the last and insurmountable obstacle to CIKM. The noisy collapse of the "New Economy" was a testimony to the arrogance and insularity of CEOs and venture capitalists and the majority of well-compensated "stars" among the security analysts who as a loosely arranged coalition to maximize the stock market bubble hastily declared the death of strategy and intelligence and replaced it with technology for the sake of technology. High tech and large tech, Fortune 500 and San Jose startups, all suffered from lack of KM and lack of CI and worse—lack of leaders who seek out CIKM. They were all sure they had the "next big thing." Competition was immaterial, risk analysis was for the birds, and no one could beat or resist their great idea. Will that change in the *next* economy? That depends on changing legislation and regulations regarding the governance of corporations, on a more active SEC, on many more stockholders' lawsuits against executives and directors taken by surprise by market developments, and on public outcry against CEOs, who from the height of their insular HQ consider filtered information to be a clear picture of a world they can't see! The next economy, with all its might and sophisticated IT and sharing tools and knowledge dissemination and virtual collaboration, its shadow teams and active external focus, its global competition and digitized networks, will still depend to the largest extent on the most banal of human factors: the actual *use* of knowledge-turned-intelligence by successful executives who must stay humble in the face of a constantly changing environment.

Ben Gilad
Academy of Competitive Intelligence
SCIP Meritorious Award, 1996

Foreword

Knowledge Wealth and Competitive Intelligence

In the knowledge economy, the value of corporations, organizations, and individuals is directly related to their knowledge and intellectual capital. Unfortunately, the majority of attention in corporations is still devoted to navigating on the financial map—this in a world where the tangible assets often account for only 0.1% to 25% of a company's stock market value. For navigating on this financial map and tracking and managing these assets the organization has a CFO and controllers, software systems such as ERP and the whole profession of auditors. But what intelligence systems do we have for navigating on the intellectual capital map—for tracking and managing the corporation's intangibles and intellectual capital? So far it is mainly CRM–customer relationship management systems. What is needed is an intelligence window into these new value-creating spaces. We need intelligence systems to develop a new map of knowledge assets as well as flow for intellectual capital.

A new and potentially paradigm-breaking focus in the intersection between knowledge and intelligence is the recognition of the importance of understanding the intellectual capital of organizations and cities, regions, and nations. Currently, organizations, as well as societies as a whole, are like eighteenth-century ships, charting their positions with only north/south navigational tools. Knowledge has become the key source of wealth not only at an organizational but also on a national level. And enterprises, particularly those in the public sector, are in danger of undermining their future success by focusing exclusively on financial assets in their accounting procedures. Plotting a course solely based on traditional financial reference points leaves them blind to the opportunities on the lateral horizon. Lost on a turbulent sea of change and without a lateral navigational tool to guide them, they cannot navigate the uncharted challenges the management of intangibles is presenting. It is time for a new approach focused on meaning making, rather than just money making. We need to stop being prisoners of vertical thinking (or bottom-line syndrome) and start to focus on lateral thinking in our corporate longitude. (This more creative thinking might lead to such perspectives of organized intelligence as brain gym and the skill of quizzics—the art and science of questioning skill propounded by the late Stevan Dedijer, professor emeritus of Lund University, Sweden, a great thinker gifted with unusual foresight.)

When the field of accounting was in its origin, more than 500 years ago, the study was about both knowledge and active intelligence. An approach whereby assets are simply recorded on a balance sheet is far too narrow. In order to get a deeper understanding about the principles of wealth creation, in today's context of rapid global dissemination of information, intelligence, and intangibles innovations, it is essential to develop a lateral perspective. A lateral approach to accounting is necessary to include the intangibles and non-financial assets of knowledge creation, networks, and relationships. The wealth of organizations, as well as the wealth of nations, lies in the space in which human capital and structural capital interact, also called the intellectual capital space. We need a Knowledge Navigation system that can plot the corporate longitude of intellectual capital on both the vertical and lateral horizons.

The abuse of management accounting is resulting in anorectic leadership behaviour, trying to starve organizations into the future, especially by cost savings that cut the important nourishment of intangibles such as knowledge, R&D, and learning. Furthermore it results in misallocation of resources by investment institutions. It is like asking what is the cost of good or bad weather, instead of asking for weather forecast. What is needed is a longitudinal system to visualize, design, cultivate, and capitalize with active intelligence on these value creation interactions (see more at www.corporaratelongitude.com).

This book will reduce ignorance and add insight into the evolution of knowledge leadership, especially on how to develop the capacity for intelligence. By combining their expertise and perspectives on Competitive Intelligence and Knowledge Management, Helen Rothberg and Scott Erickson have shaped a most timely and valuable book that provides a clear and practical blueprint of how to turn knowledge into active intelligence to create competitive capital that also develops the capacity to create further intelligence. The book offers an ease of reading mixed with very good insights that managers and executives can put into practice right away.

Leif Edvinsson
The world's first director of Intellectual Capital
The world's first holder of professorship on Intellectual Capital
Lund University, Sweden
Appointed Brain of the Year 1998 by Brain Trust, UK
Creator of UNIC-Universal Networking of Intellectual Capital
See also www.corporatelongitude.com

Acknowledgments

Our editor, Karen Maloney, made this book possible. Her patience, encouragement, and belief that we would find our voice created an environment where we could. To her we are extremely grateful. We also thank the pioneers in their fields, Leif Edvinsson and Ben Gilad, for penning the forewords.

A special thanks to Ben Gilad for introducing me to the field of competitive intelligence and planting the seed for the shadow team concept. I appreciate Marist College for granting me a sabbatical to begin this journey. My family, sisters, and friends have been very supportive through this process, and I thank them. Last, and certainly not least, I have deep gratitude to my friend and coauthor Scott Erickson. If there is such a thing as an intellectual soul mate, I have found mine in him. One could not ask for a more intelligent, talented, and kind person to call a partner.

Helen N. Rothberg

My thanks go to my wife, Jean, for living with me throughout this process and providing encouragement and love when I needed it. Although the puppy-of-the-month club didn't help my efficiency, it certainly made the trip a lot more interesting. Ithaca College and my colleagues have provided me with support during this project, and I appreciate everyone's help and encouragement. And, like Helen, I don't think I could have asked for a better coauthor, one who is intellectually stimulating when it's time to work and full of fun when it's time to play.

G. Scott Erickson

Introduction

In his final column for *Fortune* magazine in 2001, Thomas Stewart reflected on a decade of intellectual capital (IC) thought and practice. One of the great popularizers of both IC and the closely related field of knowledge management (KM), Stewart noted the slowing of momentum in the field but still held out great hope for its future prospects. Once a source of substantial interest in the late nineties, with firms hiring chief information officers and installing substantial KM systems, IC/KM had experienced seemingly slowing commitment in the years directly before Stewart's piece. Some firms failed to see rapid payback. Some never got the hang of it. But many were successful, and Stewart held the faith in his farewell. Noting how IC had changed the discussion (the Balanced Scorecard can at least get a nod in many firms), continued to create interest, and brought key terms and techniques into the mainstream, Stewart claimed both valediction and an unfinished fight.

We also believe in the value of organizational knowledge. Whatever disappointments may have accrued from buying into the IC/KM movement were a result, we believe, not of a problem with the concept but of the tendency to not go far enough. In this book, we deal with the future of knowledge management. What we see is not a failure of IC/KM but a hesitancy of some users to appropriate full value. Indeed, we believe the field to be too humble in some ways, while not providing enough guidance in others.

We authors come from two different fields: one from an intellectual property background who kind of fell into intellectual capital/

knowledge management as it became a topic of interest for practitioners, and the other a competitive intelligence (CI) practitioner and scholar, trained to acquire proprietary information and knowledge from unsuspecting target organizations. In idle conversation, we discovered a number of similarities in the two disciplines, KM and CI, both obviously aimed at managing knowledge assets. We also discovered some critical differences, at least in part because CI has been defined, primarily, by practice. KM, though practitioners are critical, of course, has had much more development in terms of theory.

Our initial work together often resulted in defending "our field" against the claims of superiority from each other. The outcome was a great deal of work over the past five years that gets to the core of each discipline and reveals how both KM and CI can benefit from the insights the opposite field can provide. We took our thoughts to practitioners and theorists through consulting assignments, academic papers, and friendly conversations, and refined the blending of the two disciplines. This book is the result of this process.

In general, we focus here on how competitive intelligence informs KM practice. Knowledge management also has a lot to add to CI, and we touch on that point, but that's another book. We believe a number of things, based on our experience, knowledge-gathering, and analysis.

- KM is too limited in how it defines knowledge assets of value. In particular, competitive knowledge should be one of the core concerns of knowledge management, along with human, structural, and collaborative capital. Awareness and understanding of what your competitor is doing or is capable of doing is available throughout your firm, in people's heads, and is as critical to competitive advantage as any other sort of organizational knowledge. In addition, the modern organization—in large part because of modern information technology tools—shoots volumes of information throughout its interconnected e-network. This information comes from enterprise planning systems, supply chain management systems, and customer relationship management systems, and includes such details concerning what the entire network, from supplier to retailer, is doing that it can become valuable knowledge and more. Expanding the definition of what is a knowledge asset brings these valuable resources into the sphere of the KM system.

- KM is too often a library function, doing a wonderful job gathering and storing knowledge but failing to seek it out. Many, many exceptions to this exist, as firms with successful KM programs use them strategically, but a lot of knowledge is also left on ice, without practical application. CI programs, on the other hand, are generally project-oriented, going after knowledge to address or answer a specific question. Facilitators and teams are formed around key issues, then let loose to find the key information that leads to the best strategic or tactical decision. KM tends to sit back and wait for knowledge. CI identifies knowledge gaps and then goes out and fills them.

- KM can be passive in how it uses the knowledge base. Again, the gathering, codification, and sharing function is absolutely vital and can make substantial contributions to firms practicing KM. But KM is generally used for specific operational questions, as someone accesses the database to address a problem in production, R&D, and so forth. Very rarely does anyone stop and take a look at what is in the knowledge database, trying to establish relationships, gain insights, or other analytical perspectives. Business intelligence touches upon such actions but is generally limited to customer databases. If KM can learn to utilize its full, expanded database—human capital, structural capital, collaborative capital, competitive capital, and operational information/knowledge—and conduct directed analyses upon it, its value to organizations will increase exponentially.

- KM does not necessarily feed decision-makers at all levels. As just noted, the KM system is often used to answer operational or, at best, tactical questions. Knowledge can be used for strategic purposes. As it is, KM should be directed more to higher levels of management, including top executives. If subjected to analysis, particularly analysis directed by top decision-makers, KM can be invaluable.

■ Last, but not least, KM typically fails to have any concerns about protection of knowledge assets. One point that CI practice makes pointedly is that knowledge has value to your competitors. And there are competitors out there employing CI operations, perhaps against you. Although KM theory and boosterism often encourage "more, more, more" when it comes to knowledge collection and distribution, wider sharing of knowledge assets can also leave you wide open for CI incursions. You can spend all that money and all that time putting together a KM system, seeking competitive advantage from your knowledge assets. And with one slip of the tongue by a receptionist over the phone or with one ill-considered comment by an executive making a speech, it can all pass to your competitor, essentially for free.

This book explores how to better manage knowledge assets according to things we have learned from CI practice. We term this an *intelligence approach*. It has two facets. Initially, we'll make a case for doing a better job identifying and building your knowledge assets, *all* your knowledge assets. By recognizing everything that is knowledge, purposefully plugging knowledge gaps, analyzing it appropriately, and feeding insights to decision-makers, you can vastly extend the capabilities of the knowledge assets available to you. Fail to do this, and you run substantial risks of losing ground to competitors who do. We justify this broader view of KM in the first couple of chapters, as well as in Chapters 7–9.

Second, we'll make a case for protecting your knowledge assets. The better job you do of growing your knowledge, the more you put yourself at risk of competitive intelligence incursions. It's a dilemma, but not one that can't be resolved. The key is to understand your environment for building and protecting knowledge. Identify and understand the circumstances, and then you can make decisions that optimally balance the risks of building and not building your KM resources. We define the key risks in Chapter 3 and then move on to a discussion of how to evaluate and react to your own risks in Chapters 4–6.

Finally, we'll give you some ideas about how to implement systems that can accomplish this, admittedly, imposing task. Certain structural steps can be taken to better build and protect knowledge assets. Firms seeking an intelligence approach will also need to install favorable cultures and ethical practices. These ideas are presented in Chapters 10–12, winding up the book. In short, come on this journey with us, and we'll provide a roadmap to potential competitive advantage through better knowledge asset management and protection. We'll alert you to the potential of your assets, the dangers that surround you, and, most importantly, what to do about it.

Part 1: Knowledge Meets Intelligence

1

Generating Competitive Capital

Play nice, share your toys, and win the game.

During the 1990s, the telecom industry began a changeover from analog to digital transmission systems. For suppliers of hardware, the timing of the switch was a delicate decision, as manufacturers faced the traditional problem of when the developing market would be large enough to justify shifting production to the new technology. Motorola was one of the key players in this market and possessed an important advantage over competitors. The U.S. firm held key patents on which other mobile phone makers, such as Nokia, needed to pay royalties if they were to make digital phones. Within its own organization, Motorola held knowledge of Nokia's plans concerning production of digital phones.

But, somehow, this knowledge was never applied. Whether top management wasn't aware of this competitive knowledge or simply didn't realize its importance, Motorola ignored direct evidence of Nokia's increasing participation in the digital market, failing to forcefully enter the market itself until it was far behind its Finnish competitor (Finkelstein 2003). Possessing knowledge is important, but to be truly useful, knowledge must be used. Knowledge must become intelligence.

Knowledge has value, but intelligence has power. This is a key lesson as we move from the New Economy to the Next Economy. The New Economy concerned itself with managing the enterprise, the firm's knowledge assets, and competitive knowledge. The Next

Economy demands that all this be merged into a capability foster-ing the creation of actionable intelligence. At minimum, better man-aging all aspects of an organization's knowledge base can fortify strategic decision-making. At maximum, it can generate defensible competitive advantage through intelligence, a sustainable source of above-average returns.

In discussing this new perspective on knowledge and intelligence, we need to make sure we're all speaking the same language. This is particularly important in this context because we are bringing two distinct disciplines (knowledge management/intellectual capital and competitive intelligence) into the mix. As an initial guide, Table 1.1 lists the terms that describe the evolution of knowledge assets into strategic assets.

Intelligence turns intellectual capital into actionable knowledge for strategic decision-makers in the organization. An intelligence approach expands the definition of knowledge to include opera-tional systems and competitive intelligence. An intelligence approach also recognizes that the strategic use of knowledge requires an understanding of the circumstances of its use—not all firms will want to manage their intellectual capital in the same manner, since they may face different competitive environments. And finally, an intelligence approach requires that top management receive and use key pieces of knowledge. Intelligence merges knowledge manage-ment systems with competitive intelligence practices, leveraging the impact of knowledge on a firm's performance.

Competitive intelligence (CI), by its very nature, is somewhat hidden in terms of practices and impact. But the evidence at hand suggests that its use has an important bottom-line impact on firms that employ it. We'll discuss some of the issues involved in measur-ing CI's results in Chapter 2, but the U.S. Office of the National Counterintelligence Executive has estimated that the amount of trade secrets changing hands runs up to $300 billion annually. That is split between legitimate CI and outright espionage, but it still gives some sense of the magnitude of the practice. Imagine how the competitive arena in your field would change if your competitors

Table 1.1   Knowledge/Intelligence Terms

Terms	Definitions
Knowledge Management	The process of codifying, collecting, and disseminating the firm's knowledge assets
Knowledge Assets	Intellectual capital of the firm: *Human capital*—knowledge resident in employees regarding their jobs *Structural capital*—knowledge regarding organizational systems, structures, and processes *Relational capital*—knowledge regarding managing firm-specific relationships with external stakeholders such as customers, collaborators, and regulators *Competitive capital*—competitive knowledge resulting from market-driven analysis of information internal and external to the firm
Competitive Intelligence	*Field of practice*—supports strategic decision-making and assists executives in identifying whether the firm is competitive (Gilad 1994) *Process*—purposeful and systematic gathering of internal and external information from multiple sources, its synthesis, integration, and analysis producing actionable results
Intelligence	Knowledge in action: Strategic use of knowledge assets, including widespread, purposeful gathering, analysis, and use in making strategy. Also includes protection of knowledge assets. Actionable outcomes: *Tactical intelligence*—CI processes are applied to one or multiple knowledge assets, which results in actions with immediate implications for the firm's operations *Strategic intelligence*—CI processes are applied to one or multiple knowledge assets, which results in actions with implications for the firm's future strategy
Shadow Team	Cross-functional composite of individuals who engage knowledge assets in competitive intelligence practices around explicit competitive issues and generate tactical and strategic intelligence in support of executive decision-makers. A small cross-functional boundary-spanning entity that learns everything about a competitive unit.

acquired and used your deepest and most valuable trade secrets. Imagine how your performance might improve if you acquired theirs.

The firm ranked by The Futures Group as the leading user of competitive intelligence is Microsoft (Curtis 2001). Its prominence wouldn't surprise anyone who follows CI as a discipline or anyone competing with the firm. Microsoft visibly employs a shadow team against Linux and firms using the operating system, has been accused of using other CI techniques against smaller competitors, and has defended against CI actions by Oracle and Palm (we'll discuss and document each of these instances in later chapters). And again, this is not surprising when one watches the firm turn on a dime and obliterate competitive products (WordPerfect, Lotus 123, Netscape Navigator) or change its entire approach to computing by suddenly committing to the Internet in the late 1990s. Again, precise connections to CI can be hard to make and quantify, but any objective view would grant that Microsoft would find it impossible to operate in the manner it does without an aggressive competitive intelligence competency.

This chapter provides the thinking behind an efficient and effective method for bringing knowledge management (KM) and competitive intelligence system practices together. We begin by clarifying the building blocks of both KM and CI practices and their similarities. We then offer a structure and process for generating competitive capital, a step that presages a deeper understanding of how knowledge assets can be used in a more strategic manner.

Knowledge in the Firm: Managing Intellectual Capital

Recognizing and managing knowledge assets is a good thing.

Knowledge walks. Job mobility, layoffs, retirements, and unexpected events are paths for knowledge's journey out the firm's door. In late 2003, both the CEO and the top designer of Gucci left the firm after they were unable to come to terms over the amount of independence they would have as the company moved forward. With Gucci moving to a mass-market model, the firm's controlling partner, Pinault Printemps Redoute, was betting that it had incorporated the knowledge of these key players within Gucci's processes (Friedman 2003; Galloni, Carreyrou & Rohwedder 2003). But how sure could it be that it had successfully harvested and archived those knowledge assets? Unused knowledge can leave or be forgotten if it fails to reach the right people.

Knowledge sleeps. Organizations rarely know the full depth of their members' capabilities beyond current job descriptions or previous job titles. A Los Angeles–based utility company we'll call Western Utilities was planning to extend its business across the Mexican border. It selected a top engineer and business development executive to manage the process. They encountered great difficulty getting the project moving, since neither spoke fluent Spanish nor understood much about the Mexican way of doing business. In the same building, two floors and two levels down was a manager who was having a love affair with Mexico. Although from the United States, he was fluent in Spanish; had been studying Mexican culture, archaeology, and art for many years; and had made multiple trips to the country. Wouldn't he have been a nice addition to the development team?

Knowledge hides. Companies with multiple divisions or related businesses rarely know each other's client bases, products, and process knowledge or the full depth of potential products and services for cross-selling. A diversified New York City media communications company (referred to here as Integrated Marcom) decided to try and bring together various divisions that focused on the pharmaceutical industry. During a meeting break, one of the members from an advertising agency was talking about trying to capture new business with a prominent pharmaceutical firm. It turned out that the participating public relations company had been conducting business with that very firm for years. It knew the contact person, serviced a therapeutic product line, and understood business-winning trigger points. Wouldn't it have been helpful to know this information before pitching the potential client's creative team?

Knowledge is static. Firms can spend a small fortune on knowledge management systems. Ultimately, it only has value if people use it. Otherwise it serves as yet another reference in the company's "library" that gathers dust as few remove its contents from the stacks. This is precisely the issue that confronted Motorola as it faced strategic decisions regarding analog/digital products and competing with Nokia.

Knowledge is a chameleon and a primary component in competitiveness. The knowledge management (KM) movement is an attempt by organizations to capture, codify, organize, and redistribute the firm's tacit forms of intellectual capital or knowing and make them explicit. In other words, the essence of KM is to find, awaken, and harness the ingredients of sustainable advantage.

The building blocks of knowledge management systems are the various forms of knowing, or intellectual capital (IC), resident in the firm (Davenport & Prusak 1998; Edvinsson & Malone 1997). How many small technology firms are beholden to the person who has the product or process patent in his or her head? This is *human capital*, a personnel issue, and refers to the palate of knowledge that employees bring with them: education, job skills, employment experience, travel experience, hobbies, and so on.

Why has it been so hard for other discount retailers to imitate Wal-Mart's model? *Structural capital* is a systems issue: part management science, part organizational behavior. It reflects an understanding of the networks, culture, and processes for producing and delivering goods and services.

How often does an account leave a firm when the account manager decides to change jobs? *Relational* or *collaborative capital* is firm- or employee-specific and is indicative of the ability to manage relationships among and between customers, collaborators, regulators, and others external to the organization.

The goals of knowledge management systems are to capture resident knowledge, make it part of the intellectual capital cache of the firm, leverage knowledge assets through redistribution to other employees, and facilitate the creation of new knowledge. A better understanding of what the firm, as a collective, knows, combined with distributing this knowing to the right places, can be a source of competitive advantage.

Competitive Intelligence: Finding What You Need, Using What You Know

Competitive intelligence manages competitive knowledge strategically.

Intelligence explores. When a gap exists in the knowledge store, the strategic organization will set out to fill that gap. Firms often invest valuable resources in creating products without fully investigating competitor capability and intention to respond. A Northeastern packaged food company, "Food Flavors," was considering entering the salad dressing category. After investing in the creation of a competitive product, a "war-game" simulation was run to discover how the two dominant market leaders would respond. The game revealed that consumers were very loyal to competitor brands and that competitor margins made it impossible for them to gain penetration through a price war. Food Flavors management decided to differentiate the product and launch it under an existing brand with strong brand equity.

Intelligence discovers and protects. Knowledge management, as a discipline, has never really focused on the idea that knowledge assets are valuable not only to an organization but, potentially, to competitors as well. The essence of competitiveness in certain industries revolves around proprietary information and discovery. Competitor access to such information can interfere with first-to-market status and process innovation. A large U.S. pharmaceutical firm, "Drugs, Inc.," investigated competitor FDA approval status for ailment-specific drugs. During this investigation, managers learned that they were consistently beaten to market within certain categories. A competitive intelligence discovery project revealed that scientists, both in-house and those contracted to work on clinical trials, were very willing to share their knowledge with peers at professional conferences.

Intelligence creates and earns. Exploration and discovery can lead to early identification of new revenue streams. Early in the Gerstner reign at IBM, intelligence activities were aimed at information technology vendors to whom IBM was losing customers. The discoveries led to a visibly more competitive IBM with new service offerings (Behnke & Slayton 1998) and subsequent revenue growth.

Intelligence saves. CI activities not only identify strategic avenues for revenue gain but also for revenue savings. An employee of a midwestern ready-to-eat market leader, "Cereal Country," noticed an unusual structure owned by a competitor near the firm's own out-of-state facility. A fellow employee who had previously worked for the competitor identified the facility as a flexible new product manufacturing testing site, allowing the primary firm to react more quickly to the planned competitive incursion. The firm adopted a similar process for testing and launching new products, with significant savings to the bottom line.

Intelligence is knowledge in action. Competitive intelligence (CI) is the ethical practice of gathering, synthesizing, and analyzing information from resources internal and external to the firm. It is akin to doing one's homework using multiple sources and adopting multiple perspectives. CI answers "what if" and "so what" questions or alerts the firm to changes in its environment. CI is both an offensive practice—what can we do?—and a defensive practice—what must we do? Ben Gilad (1994), a CI pioneer, suggested that the primary function of CI is to help CEOs "see the truth," identify whether their organization is still competitive, and test their vision of the firm.

Much as KM systems do, CI identifies, collects, and leverages knowledge. In this case, the knowledge concerns competitors, but the basic structure would be familiar to anyone with a background in KM theory or practice. CI, however, goes beyond the KM model. For one thing, the knowledge sources are broader and more diverse. As detailed in Tables 1.2 and 1.3, CI seeks out not just competitive

Table 1.2   CI Research Checklist*

Type of Information	Sources
Company Financials	Annual reports, credit reports, government filings, Moody's, published articles, state filings, Wall Street Transcript
Market Share	Funk & Scott (F&S) Predicasts, literature search, market studies, Nielsen/IRI reports, Market Share Reporter
Company Background	Annual reports, government filings, credit reports, F&S indexes, investment reports, Kompass directories, newspaper index, published articles, Standard & Poor's, Wall Street Transcript, Corporate Biography
Industry Background	Association reports and studies, industry handbooks, investment reports, published articles and reports, special trade magazine issues, trade magazines, Industrial Outlook Handbook, Standard & Poor's Industry Analysis, Value Line
Competitors	Standard & Poor's, Thomas registers, special trade magazines, industry buyer's guides, Yellow Pages, associations, Leading National Advertisers (LNA)
Industry Experts	Articles, key magazines, biographies, conference listing of speakers, authors of technical articles, patent holders, consultants, university professors, Speaker's Bureau
Management Personnel	Association membership directories, local newspapers, PR departments, college alumni associations, *Wall Street Journal/Financial Times*
International Information	Chamber of commerce, consulates, embassies, international credit reports, International Trade Administration (ITA), country-specific data such as government agencies, associations, and information/trade groups
Advertising	*Advertising Age*, LNA, local newspapers, advertising associations, news clipping services
Government Experts	Department of commerce, Washington Researcher's Guides, federal and state sources of information—by state and industry

* Adapted from Fuld (1995: 49)

Table 1.3 Typical Intelligence-Gathering Sources and Activities

Type of Information	Sources
Publicly Available Information	National, regional, and specialized newspapers, newsletters, want ads, trade journals, academic journals, conference materials, magazines, industry publications, comparative industry surveys, analyst reports, press releases, transcripts of speeches, corporate histories, corporate officer biographies, interlocking board network of directors, SEC filings, census data, patent filings, bureau of land management filings, environmental impact statements, zoning maps and other regional (county and state level) geographic and statistical data, chambers of commerce, sociological and psychographic data, directories of private firms, association and professional society memberships, universities, business school cases
External Sources	Upstream and downstream suppliers, vendors, strategic alliance and venture partners, venture capitalists, consultants, topical experts, lobbyists, politicians, union representatives
Internal Sources	Employees across level and function such as sales force, new business development and product development groups, procurement, corporate library, internal documents, databases and data warehouses
Active Collection	Attending academic and practitioner conferences and trade shows; speeches by industry experts, competitor representatives, government regulators, and so on; mingling at social gatherings; debriefing new employees; interviewing; driving through regional areas where competitors have facilities; facilities tours; phone calls; observation

knowledge in employees' (and others') heads but also from other places, including the following.

- *Publicly available information*
  When competitors monitoring domain name filings noticed Amazon.com's registration of amazongreetings.com and amazoncard.com, they were able to identify a strategic move by

Amazon into greeting cards through publicly available information (Blumenstein & Harris 1999). And publicly available information can be loosely defined. Reuters was absolved of stealing proprietary financial information from Bloomberg because prosecutors decided the Bloomberg information was already widely available in libraries and on the Web (Starkman 1999). Reuters was able to apply the data to its own competing products.

- *Internal sources*
  As part of their job description, marketing and sales employees of Dow Chemical are expected to develop and use internal (and external) networks of human intelligence concerning competitors (Miree & Prescott 2000). And competitor ex-employees have long been a valued source of knowledge, even when nondisclosure agreements get in the way. From Wal-Mart/Amazon.com (Nelson & Anders 1999) to Lucent/Cisco (Solomon & Thurm 2000) to SAP/Seibel (Kerstetter et al. 2000) to Ford/Fiat (Mackintosh 2003a, 2003b), ex-employees and their "inevitable disclosure" of knowledge have been the subject of substantial legal and press attention.

- *External sources*
  A salesperson for Coordinated Resources, a Herman Miller (HM) reseller, knew that a particular firm was the major competitor for a given account. Other salespeople from HM's distribution network had noted on the HM intranet that the competitor's office cubicles had no power source. The CR salesperson was able to use this information to better focus her sales presentation on this important differentiation (Peterson 1999). Boston Scientific allegedly set up a separate company that contracted with other firms in an attempt to copy the stent manufacturing processes of Medinol, a supplier of Boston Scientific as well as others (Tomsho 2001).

- *Active gathering*
  As just noted, Microsoft has a standing "attack team" that is charged with keeping close tabs on Linux, searching out any

and all information concerning the rival operating system (Gomes 1999). Similarly, Microsoft itself has been the target of particularly aggressive information-gathering tactics, including dumpster diving (Simpson & Bridis 2000) and hacking (Heavens 2000).

The diverse sources within each category as well as a general checklist of potential knowledge fonts are detailed in Tables 1.2 and 1.3 (which focus on clearly legal and ethical procedures).

CI is not a library function. It is driven by strategic questions posed by senior decision-makers, competitor profile-building, and continuous situational analyses. What further differentiates CI from other information-driven functional activities is the integrative engagement of "HUMINT"—internal and external human intelligence. Purpose-driven CI activities include gathering published data, collecting information from public filings regarding regulatory requirements and technological innovations, and conducting trend analyses regarding economics, demographics, social movements, and global environments. CI further encompasses the engagement of tacit knowledge from all sources of the firm's intellectual capital. It accesses expertise, information gathered in sales calls and at conferences and trade shows, and additional input from external experts such as consultants. CI combines competitor and competitive situational analyses with scenario planning, war gaming, and knowledge management activities to generate the intellectual capital needed for creating layers of sustainable competitive advantage. Again, Tables 1.2 and 1.3 offer fuller generic research checklists and samples of intelligence-gathering activities.

So Now That We Have All of This Information, What Do We Do With It?

Knowledge management has things to learn from competitive intelligence (and vice versa).

Knowledge implies that learning and experience have been applied to information. Certainly this is a good thing—having knowledge at one's fingertips. The difference between knowledge and intelligence is that "knowing" explicitly becomes appropriate action. This is also a good thing—taking knowledge and doing something with it. In knowledge management, tacit knowledge becomes explicit and is distributed or readied for distribution to those who may think to use it. In competitive intelligence, knowledge is sought and gathered to answer specific questions and to create action-oriented portfolios around specific issues. Thus, the fields of knowledge management and competitive intelligence have at their core the active capturing of information and knowledge—again, a good thing—to discover what is known and to do something with it. In such capture is the risk that reams of information and knowledge get stored, sitting patiently, waiting for a use that never comes. Or that intelligence is generated within silos and never shared with others in the firm who can benefit from it. For anyone who has been engaged in the design and implementation of these systems, the real question becomes: What should I do with all this information? How does it help the enterprise run any differently? Is it really a good thing, this use of time and resources?

The answers to these questions are critical. Knowledge can be created throughout the enterprise yet never come together in a way that strategically benefits the firm. One reality emerging from the 9/11 Commission is that different knowledge-gathering agencies had bits and pieces of information regarding terrorists and their activities, yet this information did not come together to paint a cohesive current knowledge landscape of terrorist activities or to generate proactive intelligence scenarios of what the future held. We will never know whether anyone could have put all these pieces together and predicted what was possible before that fatal day in 2001, but knowledge benefits from being used and fueling analytical insights. Less dramatically, how many competitive opportunities are missed by not having a method for bringing together all the knowledge being "managed"? If this question appears obvious, then the bigger question is, why don't firms do more about it?

What an understanding of competitive intelligence can really add to knowledge management is this aspect of better using knowledge assets. Intelligence brings a new perspective, initially, by including all knowledge relevant to strategic and tactical actions, including competitive knowledge and operational processes such as enterprise resource planning, supply chain management, or customer relationship management systems. By better recognizing all the types of information and knowledge available to an organization, those employing intelligence can leverage knowledge assets of all types even more widely. And, as we shall discuss, users will also be more mindful of everything that needs to be protected.

Second, intelligence broadens the field by identifying gaps in knowledge and then actively seeking to fill them. KM has typically focused only on existing knowledge within the firm and better ensuring that those existing assets are captured and shared. There is a branch of the field that has started to explore the creation of knowledge (e.g., Birkinshaw & Sheehan 2002; Choo 2002), and some practitioners, such as McKinsey, do purposefully seek out knowledge in order to fill gaps in their asset base (Matson, Patiath & Shavers 2003). But systematic programs to continuously collect new knowledge about a particular competitor, customer, product, or other topics are rare in KM circles, nor is project-oriented knowledge collection for making better decisions or solving problems widely practiced. An intelligence approach brings such directions explicitly into the mix.

Third, intelligence also ventures beyond the walls of the firm, seeking knowledge from collaborators, competitors, and others outside the organization itself. Again, this approach is not unheard of in KM, with its Communities of Practice and other techniques that venture outside the organization. But the types of knowledge sought in such efforts are limited. Competitive intelligence is designed to gather pertinent knowledge from all possible sources. Once more, the practice more readily recognizes the value of such knowledge and can gather it either systematically or for a specific purpose.

Fourth, intelligence grows the knowledge of the firm through analysis. Going beyond the issues of unused or unrecognized knowledge, intelligence actually examines the knowledge base, seeking to draw insights through analysis. Very little of what we see in the KM literature or in KM practice deals with examining knowledge assets in order to draw new insights. When knowledge acquisition or knowledge growth is discussed, it has to do with adding to the knowledge stock from someone's tacit knowledge or some other source. The idea that knowledge assets can grow because analysts study existing knowledge in order to uncover connections, trends, and so on, is foreign to the field. Related concepts such as business intelligence or relationship management are based on such an idea—that examination yields insights—but KM has not forcefully developed in that direction.

Finally, intelligence makes knowledge actionable by creating structures to make sure that what the firm knows is delivered into the hands of decision-makers. Knowledge can be a gateway to better strategies. When KM does broach the topic of strategy, it is generally in terms of how better use of knowledge assets can contribute to competitive advantage (Zach 2002). This is important, of course, and we believe that using all available knowledge assets only deepens the importance. But the idea that knowledge, used properly, can actually improve strategic decision-making at the highest levels of the organization (and everywhere below) is only rarely discussed (Davenport & Prusak 1998 is an important exception) and not in much detail. One critical piece of an intelligence system is providing analyzed knowledge to top decision-makers, considerably increasing the strategic impact of all knowledge assets. A strategic approach to knowledge also implies examining the environment within which the firm operates before making decisions. We develop this aspect of strategic knowledge management later in the book, but the main point is that how knowledge is shared, given the presence of CI activities by competitors, needs to be a situational, strategic decision. Valuable knowledge assets can be more easily obtained by a competitor's CI activities if shared too widely. Once again, this is an aspect of knowledge management that an intelligence approach more explicitly addresses. What is the bottom line? Full knowledge, with appropriate analysis, provided to the key manager at the right time defines how intelligence can extend and protect the capabilities of knowledge management systems. But how is that done?

A Simple Solution: The CIS and Shadow Teams

By adapting mechanisms such as the Competitive Intelligence System and Shadow Team, knowledge management systems might be even more effective.

Unnecessary complexity is one of the biggest mistakes organizations make in creating KM or CI systems. The strength of a knowledge-collection or intelligence-generating system does not lie in advanced information technology, and investing in a system does not magically create competitive advantage. Technology is only a tool, not the engine that makes the system work. People make the system tick, people from across an organization's functions, locations, and networks. Their resources include sharing what they know and giving meaning to what others know. Technology can help in managing the process, but it is not the answer in and of itself.

A basic competitive intelligence system (CIS) provides a simple conceptual framework for capturing and distributing information and knowledge throughout the firm and can establish a good foundation for installing an intelligence-based approach to knowledge management (see Gilad 1994 and Gilad & Gilad 1988 for the genesis of this model; and Rothberg & Erickson 1999 for an adaptation). A CIS resembles a knowledge management system but extends it by incorporating the gathering of external HUMINT and publicly available information. Key to the success of any CIS is the ability to secure and actively engage data and knowledge from across the organization's activity sphere including but not limited to functions, networks, locations, levels, partners, and macroenvironment. The purpose of a CIS is to facilitate and support senior-level strategic thinking with appropriate intelligence. Figure 1.1 illustrates a basic CIS.

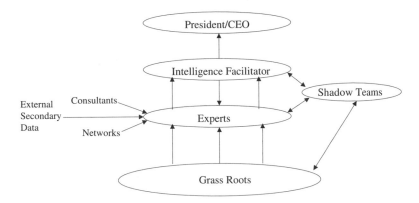

Figure 1.1 Competitive Intelligence System

There are four process requirements (adapted from Gilad & Gilad 1988, and Gilad 1994).

- *Easy grassroots access*
  The CIS must be easy to use and accessible to employees anywhere in the world, at any time. The system will only be successful if employees can readily contribute information and insight. Hassle-free involvement with the system makes it part of regular work activity. Fueled by grassroots participation across the firm's activities, information is gleaned from such rich opportunities as trade shows, client visits, supplier orientations, clinical trials, and union meetings.
- *Experts*
  A CIS depends on a structured network of "expert analyzers" who offer their technical skill, knowledge, and personal experiences. They engage with the CIS by validating information, discovering relationships between pieces of information, and conducting analyses. In short, they commence the process of turning information and knowledge into actionable intelligence. They can also direct actions to acquire additional knowledge necessary to "fill in the blanks." These experts are primarily firm employees but can also often be outside consultants. They can operate individually or in teams.

- *A storage system*
  This tool is capable of centralizing and categorizing information that can be retrieved on demand and distributed selectively. A firm's knowledge management system can readily be adapted for this practice. If one is not in place, software systems designed specifically for CI practices are readily available.
- *Convergence point*
  The final piece is centralized convergence of bits and pieces of data from across the firm and its extended network of collaborators. The convergence point is an individual, the Competitive Intelligence Facilitator (CIF). The CIF is the "decoder of market signals" and is responsive to senior decision-makers such as the firm CEO or SBU president. The CIF pieces together contributions from the firm's bastions of intellectual capital, external networks, and other outside sources. This deciphering and integrating bits of information identifies internal firm blindspots, competitor intentions and capabilities, and industry trends. As part of the executive cabinet, the CIF ensures that objective, impartial information and analysis is available when strategic issues are discussed and courses of action are orchestrated.

HUMINT is the heart of the CIS. Through individuals submitting information or experts who apply their specialized knowledge and networks, HUMINT contributes information and generates competitive knowledge. A simple method for extracting value from HUMINT and fortifying the CIF is to engage "shadow teams." *A shadow team is a small cross-functional boundary-spanning entity that learns everything about a competitive unit.* A competitive unit can be a competitor, product line, supply chain, or alliance prospect. National, industry, or firm characteristics determine the logic behind shadow team design.

The shadow team, a CIS think-tank, becomes an ongoing repository and synthesizer of competitive unit-specific information

(Rothberg 1997). The objective of a shadow team is to learn everything possible about its target, through published data, personnel and network connections, and organization knowledge or hearsay, so it can begin to think, reason, and react like the competitive unit. It vacillates between working on special projects and on creating a storehouse of unit-specific knowledge. A shadow team is charged by senior decision-makers to answer specific questions. It can also operate as a competitor profiler, understanding the management thinking of competitive rivals so it can assist its own management in planning offensive and defensive competitive postures.

The most important action of shadow teams is to bring together knowledge from across the firm. In doing so, they facilitate learning and the creation of new knowledge that can directly impact the firm's competitive posture. Their activities rely on and generate social capital as they use their own internal and external intelligence sources to give life to information and action to intelligence. These actions, whether through war gaming, scenario planning, competitor profiling, or regulatory shift analysis provide decision-makers with unfiltered analyses. This competence, the bringing together of the intellectual capital of the firm and integrating competitive information to answer "so what" questions or to sound an early warning alert, generates *Competitive Capital* for the firm (Rothberg & Erickson 2002). Competitive capital is intelligence resulting from market driven analyses created by structurally embedded shadow teams. Just as other forms of intellectual capital, competitive capital is a knowledge asset, but it can add even further value as an actionable product from CI processes.

If shadow teams become intelligent, they leverage the CIS and their own resources to generate this competitive capital—the bedrock upon which multiple layers of competitive advantage are built. Shadow teams, by their very nature, bring together the intellectual capital of the firm. Their processes and products are *de facto* trade secrets, generating unique, defensible strategic advantage.

From Knowledge to Intelligence with Shadow Teams

Shadow teams create intellectual capital out of competitive knowledge.

Shadow teams bring together organizationwide competitive knowledge and create competitive capital through competitive intelligence processes. Shadow teams gather knowledge from across functions, levels, and locations. They provide unfiltered assessments that are future-focused and offer resolution to existing challenges by working hand-in-hand with the CIF in building competitive landscapes and war room analyses. As organic units operating within and without the organization, they have the ability to go beyond the firm's blinders and identify areas of strengths and weaknesses, opportunities for new markets, or ways of doing business differently.

Through exchanges and combinations of existing knowledge and discovery, shadow teams generate new learning that steps outside of the firm's data warehouse and into its strategic decision-making. It is this specific feature of shadow teams—the merging of knowledge management with competitive intelligence—that provides the firm with a strategic asset. Engaging in competitive assignments, shadow teams generate competitive capital by extending competitive knowledge-gathering activities across the firm's Value Chain.

Competitive capital emerges from discovering competitive capabilities, competitive vulnerabilities, new markets, and new processes. By activating knowledge assets by means of competitive intelligence practices and tools, firms using shadow teams go beyond knowledge and generate intelligence. If incorporated into the processes of the firm, this intelligence enhances strategic decisions. Thus, in pushing knowledge to integrative and active levels, shadow teams, through the CIS, enable the firm to readily employ its palate of competitive knowledge assets in creating sustainable competitive advantage. By adapting this type of framework to all knowledge management activities, organizations can better develop all of their knowledge assets. Applying CI techniques and CI structures to static intellectual capital, firms develop dynamic, strategy-driven competitive weapons. This better use of assets can result in sustainable competitive advantage as the knowledge becomes intelligence.

Shadow/Intelligence Teams Can Turn Knowledge Into Intelligence

Shadow/intelligence teams create intelligence and value.

The result? Firms can employ intelligence teams, similar to shadow teams in structure but not shadowing a competitor, to capture walking knowledge. As employees engage with these intelligence teams, their input is considered part of the collective knowledge of the firm. They contribute their intellectual capital, which is combined with other sources of knowledge and intelligence to create new learning and new action. If new learning and actions are directly tied to firm core competencies and strategy, then the firm has actualized the benefits of its information-gathering activities.

Intelligence teams awaken sleeping knowledge. The utility firm seeking new business in Mexico could have been more successful with the use of an intelligence team. As a member of the intelligence team, or as a contributing expert, the employee who was knowledgeable of the Mexican culture would have been integrally involved. To start, the team would discover the formal and informal methods for conducting business in Mexico, and perhaps other HUMINT existing in the firm or its extended network that could identify contacts in the host state. The team could explore which competitors were already in the market, how they were positioned, and who their contacts were. Further, the team could identify the cultural imperatives specific to the region where the firm wanted to do business. In essence, the intelligence team could have integrated the intellectual capital of the firm with external competitive information to create a roadmap for succeeding in this new venture.

Intelligence teams discover hidden knowledge. A chance discussion among employees from different divisions of Integrated Marcom revealed resident knowledge of a targeted pharmaceutical firm. In this type of firm, large clients can serve as the unit for intelligence team organization. The team would work across the menu of companies within the firm's structure, bringing together all forms of intellectual capital. In addition, careful analysis of the client would also provide profiles of key decision-makers, sector competitive and competitor analyses, and a full menu of client support analyses. When preparing to pitch a large client, intelligence teams would be involved, identifying sources of HUMINT, key strategic issues, and personal preferences of client decision-makers. While this is a rather tactical operation for an intelligence team, the loss of a large account can threaten the independence of the firm, and so tactical decision support can be just as important as strategic in some situations.

Intelligence teams explore. When Food Flavors needed to discern whether it could be successful in a competitive category, it was the shadow teams organized around competitors that were brought together to war-game. Having a cross-functional composition, each shadow team understood the competitor's capabilities down to its P&L statements, advertising agency expenditures, and emotional commitment to its brand. In this instance their actions resulted in competitive capital that shaped the firm's decision to compete in a tight category under a brand with existing equity. The organization's deep knowledge and understanding of its competitor had evolved into a concrete asset.

Intelligence teams discover and protect. Drugs, Inc, had structured a shadow team around ailment classifications. The team was charged with investigating a rival firm's FDA approval status. During this investigation the shadow team learned that they had an additional challenge—competitors were beating them to market. They launched a counterintelligence investigation and discovered that scientists were openly sharing information with professional colleagues. Additional investigation revealed that other employees also shared sensitive information with suppliers and representatives from competitor firms. A program was created to generate awareness for protecting intellectual property and competitive information throughout the organization. The shadow team created competitive capital by identifying competitor CI processes and by then creating a new process for managing the security of its firm's sensitive information.

Intelligence teams save. When the unusual facility was discovered by an employee at Cereal Country, the knowledge was passed on to the shadow team structured around a specific competitor. HUMINT investigation revealed the employee who had previously worked for the competitor and had some knowledge of that type of facility. Additional surveillance of the site and discussion with engineers in manufacturing revealed that this competitor's product testing facility was far superior to the other firm's. Cost benefit analysis further revealed that the competitor's new product introductions resulted in millions of dollars of savings when compared to the company because of this facility. The shadow team generated competitive capital by identifying a new flexible manufacturing process for new product introductions (countering the competitor's advantages), resulting in sizable cash savings.

Intelligence teams create and earn. Louis Gerstner called IBM's teams "virtual intelligence teams" (Behnke & Slayton 1998). The mission of these intelligence teams was to assess competitor actions and strategies. Their goal was to discover why IBM was losing market share. The team leader was responsible for ensuring that corporatewide strategies accounted for competitor marketplace capabilities. Although IBM had ongoing CI activities, they lived in different functional areas. It wasn't until the creation of intelligence teams that communication, information sharing, and collaboration were integrated. Intelligence teams brought together external information such as market research, press clippings, competitive analysis reports, consultant studies, and so on. They captured personal knowledge about competitors from executives and linked a wide range of strategic decision-makers worldwide. The intellectual capital generated by these teams improved IBM's competitive position—laying the background for the creation of new technologies, processes, and business groups (including Global Services). In addition, and even more impressively, these intelligence teams contributed to a cultural shift at IBM where knowledge sharing became more greatly valued than knowledge hoarding.

Bringing Together Knowledge Management and Competitive Intelligence

Thinking, talking, doing.

Sustainable competitive advantage has become less reliant on the physical processes of conducting business, such as manufacturing, and more on the management of knowledge and intelligence across the firm's Value Chain. Essential to finding pockets of opportunity and discovering the firm's true capability for competing is tapping into the knowledge inside the heads of employees and the wealth they can generate by combining intellectual capital with the tools of competitive intelligence. This process provides the firm with both the means for recognizing its internal capabilities and its ability to position, in an active sense, in its competitive market. Well-known techniques such as SWOT analyses identify such internal and external fits unidimensionally. Typically, they identify the opportunities and threats in the external environment from the macro and competitive perspectives. The current strengths and weaknesses of the firm are matched to these challenges. But the CIS, and shadow teams in particular, shift the SWOT analysis into a multidimensional model, where dynamic competitor strengths and response capabilities and the firm's own strength in responding are also taken into account.

Shadow teams create competitive capital by merging what is known and what others may do into what we should do. Alternatively, shadow teams assist the firm in thinking through strategic moves in unfiltered, cross-parameter ways that more clearly simulate the actual competitive environment. By applying the lessons of shadow teams, organizations can make better use of their other knowledge assets and generate tactical and strategic intelligence for decision-makers.

The core of the intelligence process is taking existing intellectual capital throughout the firm, identifying other knowledge needs, conducting analyses that point to specific actions, and feeding the results of the analyses to appropriate decision-makers. While it is the goal of knowledge management systems to capture the thinking, it the mission of the CIS to activate it—in other words, what does this knowledge mean when pieced together to tell a story or when posed to answer specific intelligence questions? Shadow teams can simulate the doing through war gaming and scenario planning. But ultimately, senior management is responsible for the doing—welcoming intelligence generated by shadow teams and using it to fine-tune strategy.

Activating knowledge assets and engaging competitive intelligence help the firm make money, save money, and manage risk in charting its future. While we cannot know what will be, we can work toward predicting what *can* be. Intelligence incorporates all of the firm's assets and addresses tactical issues, such as how to manufacture test products, pitch a new client, or figure out why competitors are first to market with product offerings. In its ultimate use, intelligence provides an opportunity to simulate alternative competitive futures, identify areas for growth in a backdrop of competitor capabilities, and help direct how the firm can best invest its scarce resources for creating layers of advantage.

There are many challenges inherent to building knowledge management and CIS models. Issues such as culture and structure will be considered in a later chapter. But a key in both instances is the recognition that people, their individual and collective knowledge and ability to generate actionable intelligence, are the greatest asset of the firm. It will take senior management recognition, participation, and the rewarding of activities to get people to share what they know and engage in creating firm-based intelligence to truly achieve the type of sustainable advantage demanded by the Next Economy.

Executive Moment

Much of what has been talked about in this chapter sounds like and is common sense. To determine whether your firm is on the path to generating competitive capital, ask and honestly answer the following questions.

- Do you know all of what you need to know before making a strategic decision?
- Do you know where to find what you need to know?
- Do you know what to do with the information once you find it?

Internally, think about the following.

- Mapping the decision according to whom will be affected by and who can affect the decision
- Bringing representatives together to gather reactions and intelligence
- Asking representatives if they know any others who should be considered
- Gathering intelligence from this outlier group

Externally, think about the following.

- Mapping the decision according to what external issues support and do not support the decision. Identify external environment, competitive, and competitor areas for data gathering.
- Review how this information has been used—what integration and analyses have been conducted, does the information used have integrity, has the information been turned into intelligence?
- Use intelligence to adjust strategy.

Using this approach raises yet another set of related questions.

- Do you know what your people know in terms of competitive knowledge?
- Do you have structures in place to allow interdisciplinary communication for all types of knowledge?
- Do you analyze all of your storehouses of knowledge?
- Do paths exist to funnel knowledge and analysis to the decision-making levels of the organization?

At issue here is whether there are KM systems and processes for cataloguing human resources and other knowledge assets, accessing them, and facilitating the sharing of resources. If you do not have any KM systems, then the answer to these questions rests with how well you know who works for you. Even managers who have close relationships with their employees do not always know the full cache of their knowledge assets.

If you do have a KM system, the issue then becomes whether people use the system, whether it functions as a storage facility or library, and how friendly it is for people who use it to share and develop its contents. How often do the products of this sharing reach your desk?

Finally, does the firm engage in CI practices? Is competitive knowledge shared across the firm's Value Chain, or does it just exist in the marketing and sales departments? And most important, as a senior level decision-maker, do you have a mechanism for having specific strategic questions investigated in an unfiltered and timely way? Do you have a mechanism to guarantee that such analyses reach you regardless of their implications? If the answer is no to any of these questions, but especially the last one, read on.

2

Turning Knowledge into Active Intelligence

It's in the way that you use it.

—Eric Clapton

It is not enough to "know" something. It is not enough to know who knows something. It is not enough to know how something works. It is not enough to capture what is known, who knows it, and how it all works. To stay competitively astute, it is not enough to have all this knowing and very little doing. What is essential is the doing: How does what is known and captured get used? KM systems only fulfill a piece of what the firm needs to orchestrate its future. They capture, organize, and distribute. CI systems provide the pathways for knowledge to become intelligence that is actionable. They respond to initiatives and, more importantly, answer "so what" questions. They are also future-focused.

Getting a grip on the value of competitive intelligence to a firm is difficult. Although we know intuitively that better understanding of a competitor should lead to better decision-making (and can demonstrate it with anecdote after anecdote), quantifying the impact of CI is much more difficult. Obviously, a number of variables contribute to returns at major corporations, and participation in CI (or not) is only a single variable and hard to separate out. Further, CI practitioners tend to be somewhat secretive, sometimes hiding their very existence, let alone results. That said, CI practitioners often note the growth in intelligence activity, with membership in the Society of Competitive Intelligence Professionals (SCIP) mushrooming from several hundred to 8,000 over a ten-year period reaching into the late nineties, as well as the fact that virtually all Fortune 500 firms have some CI capability. If it didn't pay, why would so many successful businesses employ CI practices?

But on a more objective level, there have been attempts to quantify the impact of CI. One study looked at sales and EPS of firms using CI versus those not using it, and it found a substantial difference (in favor of CI) on both measures (Cappel & Boone 1995). Even so, some of that methodology is questionable and certainly not convincing in terms of causation (if bigger firms use CI more than smaller firms do, then, yes, their sales will be larger). Probably the best indicator of the importance and monetary value of CI comes from trying to put a dollar value on losses rather than gains. In a recent survey, Fortune 1000 firms reported $45 billion in annual trade secret losses to competitors (ASIS/PriceWaterhouseCoopers 1999). And in its annual reports to Congress, the U.S. Office of the National Counterintelligence Executive (NCIX) estimated losses of $100 billion to $250 billion (2001) and $300 billion (2002) annually due to foreign economic espionage/competitive intelligence activity. If those losses create anything approaching equal value to those on the other side winding up with such knowledge, we're talking about a major issue for executives. And, of course, economic espionage and CI are not only cross-border phenomena—such actions likely take place at least on the same level domestically.

This chapter further explores the relationship between KM and its quest to harness the intellectual capital of the firm, and CI and its quest to employ all that can be known inside and outside the firm in pursuit of competitive advantage. By combining the two disciplines, we believe managers can come closer to harnessing some of those hundreds of billions of dollars for their own firms.

KM and CI: Amplifying the Differences

Competitive intelligence and knowledge management do have some important distinctions.

In the last chapter, we focused on the similarities between KM and CI while beginning a discussion about how firms can benefit from a combination of the two disciplines, particularly by employing some CI techniques in KM systems. In this chapter, we provide a deeper discussion of the benefits accruing to firms that are able to combine the concepts to establish competitive advantage.

KM and CI systems are both organized around the collection, organization, and use of knowledge. What distinguishes the two practices is the type of action associated with each of these activities.

Collection: Mining to Getting

Capturing the intellectual capital of the firm drives KM practices. The goal is to collect knowledge that is tacit and make it explicit. People are asked to contribute personal knowledge such as resolving a problem on a production line. Collection is defined by what lives in the firm. Competitive intelligence is more ends-driven. Finding what needs to be known to build analyses and facilitate strategy drives CI practices. So while CI collects what is known across the firm about competitive issues, it also steps outside the firm to learn more from consultants, published sources, and business partners.

Let's use an illustration of a hypothetical pharmaceutical firm interested in discovering where a competitor is in a clinical trial process. Using KM practices, the firm would have flagged employee knowledge concerning the underlying technology, likely production processes, and efficacy of similar drugs developed internally. Using CI practices, shadow team members would also purposefully seek out information from seemingly unconnected internal databases and employees, and the team would engage a series of external sources as well. Cross-functional in nature, the team would seek out organizational knowledge across the firm's Value Chain, including supply, manufacturing, and distribution partners. It might research patent filings or funding proposals from the National Science Foundation. Members might visit the Web sites of professional scientific organizations for presentations (some of which might concern clinical trial results, for example) from annual meetings. Prepublication copies of medical journals would also be pursued for similar information. Further collection could come from attending legal proceedings or searching regulatory filings. While KM practices mine internally, CI practices mine internally and externally, with a purpose, and using all available knowledge sources.

Organization: Cataloguing to Analyzing

Once information enters a KM system, it is codified and catalogued. Key words determine where and in how many categories information is placed. The same piece of intellectual capital can be logged in a research file for engineers and in a positioning file for marketers. More than 50 percent of firms in an *InformationWeek* survey of knowledge managers report their key objective in KM processes is leveraging search and collaboration capabilities (Kontzer 2003). Raytheon, for example, instituted a Six Sigma program to ensure that collected quality management information was reused and shared. Other firms use KM systems to share knowledge across locations with a client to solve a problem. In the same *Information Week* article, Kontzer noted that U.S. engineering group Montgomery Watson Harza's largest client is in the United Kingdom. To solve a wastewater filtration problem, a project manager, using the firm's KM system, brought together the foreign client and the domestic experts virtually. In two hours he identified a solution that saved the client from spending $10 million on a new system. In both cases, the core issue was to not duplicate knowledge discovery if it already existed but to make it available to those who could benefit from it.

Search and collaboration are also key ingredients in a CI system. However, CI takes the process further. Information and knowledge are gathered from internal and external sources. Then a CI director or shadow team analyzes what is discovered, turning pieces of recorded competitive capital, purposefully sought out HUMINT, and published information into meaningful scenarios, portfolios, and early warnings about changes in the competitive arena. Such analyses are created for strategic decision-makers and, when appropriate, can be made available to other divisional groups. Further, if a shadow team or other piece of a CI operation identifies a missing piece of information, the CI system is designed to go out and get it by means of any and all CI techniques.

Palm Pilot's awareness of Microsoft's impending threat in the handheld market provides a case for thinking through how KM and CI would approach this challenge. In KM, any information that existed within the firm's intellectual capital on Microsoft and its operating systems, if lucky, would have been coded and catalogued. Such information might have included sales reports and engineering white papers on capabilities, or identification of people who had worked with or in collaboration with Microsoft. The CI approach would have a shadow team bring all of these disparate sources of intellectual capital together, actively explore the firm for additional, task-specific HUMINT, do public source investigations, and speak with manufacturing or distribution partners. CI practices would then go even further and try to deliberately collect information to give the analysis on Microsoft's competitive capability more depth. And this is exactly what happened. In an effort to gather valuable inside information concerning the details of Microsoft's operating system for handhelds, Palm placed an employee at a customer demo session that Microsoft was conducting as part of the product rollout (Tam 2003). This provided Palm with essential information for developing and competitively differentiating its own product and its operating system. While a KM system organizes information into a variety of functional categories, CI systems access these mines, extend their yield through active investigation internal and external to the firm, and then analyze findings to answer "so what" questions. They activate what is known into what it means competitively.

So CI also takes the step of analyzing the knowledge resources available. Whereas KM systems are established to make knowledge identifiable and accessible, they do not necessarily prioritize the knowledge or try to identify patterns or predict future directions. By employing a CIS such as that described in the previous chapter, a firm has a structure in place to bring expert opinion and dedicated, informed analysis to bear on a competitive issue. For specific KM applications, there is no reason that analysis can't add to a firm's understanding of the knowledge and its fullest applications. In a sense, further learning takes place that builds the intellectual capital to even higher levels. Organizations that can more effectively employ their knowledge resources can further separate themselves from others in terms of competitive advantage.

Use: Distributing to Doing

KM systems can go a step further than creating a mine or library and become an active part of the firm's information service. Individuals can be alerted when new information is catalogued into the system based on predefined preferences, product links, and research needs. Knowledge can be delivered to the right place at the right time in order to solve problems or provide assistance. This same capability exists in CI systems. The major difference here, beyond those already discussed, is that CI systems provide components of or stimulus for competitive actions. Knowledge becomes intelligence through action. Actions take form in influencing strategy-making or the execution of strategic or tactical moves. Shadow teams, whether building scenarios, performing strategic group analyses, or conducting war games, turn what is known into what needs to be done (reactive moves) or what can be done (proactive moves). They convert competitive information into intelligence products that are more likely to make their way into the path of executive decisions. And again, there is value in adding other forms of intellectual capital into the mix.

In his address to the 1999 Society of Competitive Intelligence Professionals (SCIP) CEO Roundtable, John Pepper, then CEO of Procter & Gamble, commented on the turbulent business environment and spoke of the need for intelligence to "develop from collecting, analyzing and disseminating knowledge and information to the point of helping organizations acquire and use information and knowledge to create winning strategies" (Pepper 1999: 6). Mr. Pepper continued to describe how P&G's "Global Knowledge Network" would be used in a new CI structure that embedded CI activity into strategy development "in the line." Specifically, the move was from static to actionable competitive analysis, including scenario planning and response modeling using shadow teams, and incorporating all of the firm's knowledge into the strategic planning process.

And let's not forget learning. As noted earlier, KM and CI practices can provide more information to knowledgeable people and foster learning. Through sharing, collaborating, and analyzing, the firm's knowledge assets increase. Competitive learning through the application of CI is driven up the corporate ladder. CI products are generated specifically for the use of senior level decision-makers, although their execution is felt at all levels. As shadow teams become think tanks and scenario enactors, executives learn more about competitor response capabilities, the impact of regulation and disruptive technologies, and the nuances of early warning systems. And as decisions are made and actions are taken, further learning takes place. Everyone from the CEO down to the salesperson trying out closing tactics finds out what works, what doesn't, and how competitive strategy should be formulated in the future (as all this learning is added to the competitive capital of the firm). In short, learning can feed the intellectual capital of the firm, and executive learning can impact the firm's competitive advantage by energizing strategic thinking and implementation.

KM or CI, It's Not "Or" But "And"

CI has something to add to KM.

Knowledge has power when converted into intelligence. Intelligence is actionable, with knowledge being applied to strategic decisions and execution. On its own, KM is an underperforming asset. The challenge is to have people use knowledge while it's still meaningful—today's knowledge can be yesterday's news. This is the core value added by CI processes and systems, improving the quality of timely knowledge by stewarding its shift to active intelligence. CI can provide KM with a vehicle for assertively integrating the firm's knowledge with activity.

Unlike KM processes that focus on orchestrating existing forms of the firm's intellectual capital, CI engages multiple forms of knowledge internal and external to the firm. CI doesn't just rely on what is known inside; it relies on all that can be known from all sides. It actively seeks out information and knowledge to fill gaps, discover patterns, or predict outcomes. KM relies on capturing, codifying, categorizing, and distributing data. CI mines such information, driven by edict or question, combines it with multiple points of external data, analyzes it, and delivers it to an appropriate decision-maker. CI doesn't just collect information for the sake of having it. Instead, it seeks what needs to be known at the moment it is needed for use.

KM's mission is to capture and manage the firm's knowledge assets. Whether defensive—as a response to losing information when people leave—or offensive—to leverage what can be used—it is a passive activity. CI practices are aggressive by nature. They actively pursue information, analyze and integrate what is discovered from the universe of sources, and produce predictive and actionable products. The KM imperative is to capture; the CI imperative is to utilize. KM is an iterative process that grows through its use and evolves as users expand their thinking, practice, and contribution. CI uses practices that could access and move KM process from passive collection into active strategic contribution. CI techniques regarding competitive information, for example, push KM past disparate sources of information on competitors or what they have done and toward an understanding of competitor capabilities and predictions of what they might do.

And KM has something to add to CI.

Contributions between the disciplines of KM and CI run in both directions. In capturing the intellectual assets of the firm, KM processes create a wellspring from which CI practitioners can draw. CI practitioners pursue HUMINT when competitive questions or ongoing analyses identify the need for firsthand information. HUMINT, then, is deliberately sought during CI investigations. HUMINT is not collected, however, as a matter of course for securing the intellectual capital—in this case the competitive capital—of the firm. While project-driven CI has obvious applications, organizations can also benefit from having a structured system to collect, codify, and leverage existing competitive knowledge. Account managers, for example, are significant wellsprings of information in media communication companies. The account manager knows the purchasing history, personal preferences, and strategic needs of various clients, including their options as to other media companies and their offerings in each area. If the account is put up for bid, the successful or unsuccessful account manager can acquire in-depth knowledge of the various competitive proposals. Having an account manager log this competitive information into a KM system makes it available for use whether the account manager leaves the firm or wins the lottery. The standard logic for KM usage applies to competitive information, too.

Although information captured by a KM process may not be immediately actionable (or even up-to-date), it can still have rewards for CI practitioners as a first stop for discovery, even in a time-sensitive investigation. KM can also provide value to CI by creating libraries of frequently requested intelligence resources, competitor reports, and market analyses, enabling a CI operative or shadow team to spend more time on analysis and less time on searching.

In short, KM can facilitate CI processes by capturing tacit knowledge and making it explicit before it leaves the firm or remains undiscovered, can assist in avoiding duplication of effort by sharing reports, and can facilitate analysis by creating an arena for collaboration and easy access to disparate sources of information and knowledge. CI, on the other hand, extends KM practices by moving the collection process outside of the firm, both for human and published sources. It contributes knowledge from active field collection. It adds analysis and learning to the mix. Last, and most salient, CI influences competitive advantage by transforming knowledge into active intelligence that impacts strategy making and execution at the executive levels of the firm.

Case in point. Shell Services International has created a combined CI and KM capability. Management of competitive knowledge enables the CI team's ability to focus more of its efforts on core CI activities, allowing the team to provide analysis with greater influence and value to senior level decision-makers. At the same time, the firm monitors and catalogues tactical efforts, the end-products becoming part of Shell's knowledge management capability. By further leveraging CI products such as *ad hoc* requests and ongoing market analysis, organization members have the opportunity to quickly access timely reporting and enhance their own ability to engage in focused data collection and intelligent decision processes (Breeding 2000). As such, CI and KM practices feed each other, better enabling both to enhance the organization's strategic capabilities.

And "So What?": Turning Knowledge into Intelligence with Layers of Advantage

Unique, defensible competitive advantage can be created by combining KM and CI.

In his seminal work *Competitive Strategy*, Michael Porter (1980) introduced the idea that the purpose of strategy was to bring the firm unique, defensible competitive advantage: the ability to earn above average returns in its strategic group. Ben Gilad (1996) suggested that competitive advantage was fleeting and needed to be "layered" so that firms can remain ahead of "me too" competitors. Hamel and Valikangas (2003), recognizing that competitive environments are turbulent, indicated that firms need "resilience," a strategic ability to change even before the need becomes obvious. What these influential thinkers have in common is the recognition that organizational success is tied to managing the competitive environment. We believe that the integration of KM and CI is central to managing this environment.

Organizations must be able to access the intellectual capital of the firm, monitor information in the environment, and convert both into analyses that reach strategic decision-makers. Michael Porter was the first to suggest the use of business and competitive intelligence in conducting industry structural analysis. Ben Gilad extended this notion by propagating the use of intelligence not only to diagnose current competitive situations, but also to predict future shifts and provide early warning capabilities. Focusing on the nature of the firm, Hamel and Valikangas indicated that organizations need to be able to reinvent their business models and strategies as circumstances change. In essence, their insights suggest that the creation of competitive capital will help the firm remain the master of its future.

Competitive capital is found in firms that accumulate and manage their competitive knowledge resources. Intelligence, in all forms, comes from the strategic management of knowledge, understanding the environment within which knowledge is collected and used, and making the knowledge actionable, especially by strategic decision-makers.

Firms gain by merging knowledge management systems and practices with competitive intelligence systems and practices. The resulting actions can be tactical or strategic in nature. Propelling knowledge to intelligence can create layers of competitive capital.

KM and CI systems are created to assist the firm in building and sustaining competitive advantage. Achieving and sustaining this level of competitiveness requires that the firm simultaneously stay on top of its current business, ahead of competitors for future business, and in the forefront of defining what future business can be. This is the concept of layers of advantage, and layers of advantage come from layers of intelligence built from a foundation of knowledge assets. Layers of intelligence include action, strategy, and prediction. Tools such as shadow teams can help build layers of intelligence by engaging in market-embedded analyses that draw from the full spectrum of the firm's KM and CI practices to answer questions that cut across the firm's need to "do the thing right" (tactical) and "do the right thing" (strategic).

Action: Supporting the Fortress

Maintaining current competitive advantage is a tactical issue, focusing on the present or short term. In this venue, intelligence is concerned with what is going on. From a competitive standpoint, maintenance typically includes identifying and analyzing actions such as market development, pricing strategies, and client management. From a broader perspective, knowledge about internal and external logistics, operations, human resources, and so on, would feed the process. This layer of intelligence can be reactive—learning everything about a competitor entering the firm's lead product category—or proactive—launching a new pricing strategy anticipating a competitor's entry into a product category. This action layer of intelligence is focused on how to compete in the current business arena.

Cereal Country, discussed in the previous chapter, discovered that the test manufacturing facility it identified was saving its competitor millions of dollars in new product launches. The firm adopted a similar operational strategy for its own new product introductions.

Strategy: Planning Moves from the Fortress

The next layer of intelligence is strategic and involves the development and execution of strategy. This strategic layer is future-oriented. With a proactive orientation, firms engage in analytical activities that will impact strategic decisions. In developing competitive capital, shadow teams might explore topics such as product development and positioning, response scenarios to disruptive technologies and regulatory shifts, and targeting new markets (such as moving from prescriptive to OTC drug segments). From a broader perspective, identifying strategic shifts such as new applications of information technology to processes or an industrywide move to outsource transportation and fulfillment would be topics of interest. The key point is that knowledge accessible by a firm can yield insights as to competitive shifts and how to deal with them. Intelligence, through collection and analysis, can provide an understanding of not only competitive actions but of the underlying competitive strategies. Intelligence can also provide a better base for strategic decisions of how to deal with competitor intentions. The strategy layer moves beyond the concept of how do we compete to how will we need to compete.

Food Flavors, also in the previous chapter, was launching a new salad dressing. The competitor was the category leader. The shadow team surmised through war gaming that their response to a challenger would be aggressive. This influenced the strategic decision to launch the product under a known brand of a related category leader. The higher brand equity of the existing name significantly strengthened the defensive capabilities of the market entrant.

Prediction: Beyond the Need for a Fortress

The prediction layer of intelligence moves beyond the concept of how will we need to compete in the future to how can we change the rules of competition. It moves through strategy and into reconstruction. This layer of intelligence bypasses move/countermove and strategic gamesmanship. Instead, prediction identifies opportunities to compete in a unique realm, in a unique way. Its intent is to create a new competitive arena. From a competitive standpoint, this level of intelligence implies knowing and understanding a competitor so well that a shadow team could actually predict the strategic and tactical moves the competitor might make. The shadow team develops empathy. From the broader perspective, an organization would hope to hold enough knowledge and understand it to such a degree that it is able to establish some probabilities about the future environment within which it will do business.

Nokia has held a dominant position in the multimedia handset industry for a number of years. Getting wind of Microsoft's development of software for this market, and fearing for its own margins if Microsoft was successful, Nokia launched a strategy to ensure that it would continue to be the industry standard (Pringle 2002). If Nokia had simply acted, it might have reactively engaged in competitive pricing. A more strategic approach might have been to launch a preemptive legal action riding the coattails of other antitrust issues Microsoft had faced in Europe. Instead, it changed the rules of competition by using Microsoft's reputation against it, forming a coalition of hardware vendors who didn't want to be dependent on Microsoft as a single operating system provider. Nokia effectively created an alternative standard to which Microsoft would have to adjust. In the words of the great Chinese general Sun Tzu in *The Art of War* (2002): "To subdue the enemy without fighting is the acme of skill."

Layering intelligence through integration of KM and CI can bring the firm to the apex of sustainable competitive advantage. How else can a firm become "resilient" unless it actively engages in learning about its competitive environment? How else can change effectively occur before it has to without unfiltered, timely analysis that harnesses the KM and CI capabilities of the enterprise? In other words, how else can the firm reinvent itself or its markets without relying on rich, integrated intelligence? The implication here is that, on some level, all three layers of intelligence—action, strategy, and prediction—need to occur simultaneously to create a seamless perpetuation of competitive advantage. The depth of this practice, the creation of intelligence itself, can become the firm's most valuable competitive asset.

Sharing What You Know: A Challenging Oxymoron

Knowledge assets can be defined even more widely, raising even more questions.

At the core of any KM or CI system are the people internal to the firm who are willing to contribute what they know. Should the full contents of a KM or CI system be open to all employees in the firm? How does one determine who should have access to what and under what circumstances? Some firms have very formal structures in place. At one firm, a senior CI executive suggests that recorded information, reports, and literature reviews can be catalogued readily. Analyses, depending on their scope and use, are shared with some selectivity. Sensitive information critical to firm competitiveness is privy to senior executives only. Extremely sensitive information is not recorded at all but only shared orally. The firm seeks to define and understand the relevance of knowledge and intelligence to its competitive advantage so as to determine the boundaries of access.

Further, in an age of Web-based systems for managing the business, a firm needs to give some thought as to what entities have access to its operating knowledge. Supply Chain Management (SCM), Enterprise Resource Planning (ERP), and Customer Relationship Management (CRM) systems pass operating knowledge among a slew of upstream and downstream collaborators. While not knowledge that is normally included in KM discussions, this information is vital to the competitiveness of many modern businesses and would be of obvious benefit to potential competitors. Once again, how does one determine who should have access to what and under what circumstances?

Consider an example. Part of the foundation for outsourcing procurement and manufacturing logistics requires the sharing of sensitive marketing information. JC Penney's surrender of its procurement, manufacturing, and warehousing functions, and, most recently, marketing forecast functions to the Hong Kong firm TAL is a case in point (Kahn 2003). TAL controls Penney's dress shirt category. It also supplies products for J. Crew, Calvin Klein, Banana Republic, Tommy Hilfiger, Liz Claiborne, Ralph Lauren, and Brooks Brothers. Where does the knowledge of one client's marketing strategy end and the other begin? How much information sharing is competitively smart?

Protecting What You Have: "Who's Zooming Whom?"

CI also poses a protection dilemma for KM operators.

This question raises the issue of yet another important intersection between KM and CI. If knowledge assets are of value to the firm, wouldn't they be just as valuable, perhaps more so, to a competitor? KM advocates typically support the widest possible collection and distribution of a firm's knowledge assets. The logical conclusion is that this includes the entire Value Chain, and, hence, not only the core firm but many, if not all, of its collaborators. But this sharing takes place in an environment showing increasing levels of competitive intelligence activity. KM, as a discipline, should at least broach the question of whether full and unquestioned distribution is ideal or even desirable. But just as CI poses a potential threat, it may also provide answers.

According to Douglas Bernhardt (2002), a CI consultant and educator, CI functions as the firm's sword in supporting the quest for competitive advantage, and the shield, serving the first line of defense in protecting proprietary assets and strategic ambitions. The importance of protection, or "counterintelligence" activities, cannot be stressed enough. Our discussion thus far has focused on the need to assemble the intellectual capital of the firm for easy access, thereby creating new knowledge and enabling competitive analyses. KM practices make the firm's knowledge base more explicit, whereas CI activities revolve around collecting published, internal, and external information. Both practices can increase the firm's competitiveness but can also render it vulnerable to losing competitiveness through infiltration because of naïve protective practices.

The implications are that the effort to create protection mechanisms for the firm's intellectual and competitive capital should be as strong as the efforts to create KM and CI systems. This goes beyond the idea of firewalls and protected intranets. One approach to managing the firm's intellectual and competitive assets revolves around decisions to patent innovative products and processes. As suggested by cases such as the Amgen patent hearings, however, the question becomes whether disclosure in exchange for legal protection is truly the best protection mechanism. Amgen found its courtroom awash in representatives of competing biotech concerns (Bennett & Mantz 2000). And patents, of course, are published as well. The noteworthy "Yale Study" suggested that factors such as secrecy, moving quickly down the learning curve, exploiting lead time, and sales or service efforts were seen by practicing managers as more effective protection mechanisms than were patents (Levin et al. 1987). This research centered on intellectual property more than the wider field of intellectual capital, but the point is the same. And as we discuss softer knowledge assets, the questions of protection are even less straightforward. In short, as shadow teams integrate KM and CI systems and work toward helping sustain layers of competitive capital, the firm needs to protect this valuable source of sustainable competitive advantage. We'll discuss how to establish an effective protection scheme later in this book.

Final Thoughts

KM and CI are parallel practices that enhance each other's capabilities. Together, they help the firm generate intelligence to sustain competitive advantage. As the firm supports the creation of these practices, both of which rely on people contributing what they know, it needs to take into consideration the costs and benefits of sharing knowledge and intelligence within the firm and across the Value Chain with partners. Finally, as much effort should go into protecting the competitive and intellectual assets of the firm as goes into capturing and generating them.

Executive Moment

We discussed the need to engage both KM and CI practices in decision processes. Our assertion is that by doing so, layers of advantage can be created and sustained. With this in mind, consider the following.

- Do you use your existing knowledge assets to their fullest potential?
  - □ Is knowledge sought out for specific purposes?
  - □ Is your knowledge analyzed?
  - □ Is knowledge combined to provide learning opportunities?
  - □ Does knowledge lead to action?

These questions revolve around a firm's knowledge-gathering habits, the when and how of people coming together to share what they know. Is knowledge accumulation driven by specific needs? Is there an opportunity for brainstorming? Do people gather informally to bounce around ideas? If ideas emerge through serendipity, are they captured? Do people formally or informally follow through on ideas? When brought together to resolve specific problems, what happens to the outcome? Is it captured and distributed for others to learn from? Do people find out what happened with their recommendations and whether they worked?

- Do you use competitive intelligence to its fullest potential?
  - □ Do you practice competitive intelligence?
  - □ Do you catalogue and distribute competitive knowledge, even if not for a specific purpose?

How often do you augment your working knowledge of a competitor, process, or client with competitive knowledge? Many executives believe they have a good understanding of how their arena works (and they actually may), but how often is it validated? Does anyone talk to the sales force outside of the sales function to gather client and competitor understanding? Are scientists asked about what they've learned at professional conferences? Also, is there a method for leveraging the scores of reports, white papers, contracted studies, and internal analyses on competitive and competitor information? Or are different departments or functions duplicating their efforts?

- Does your firm possess competitive capital?
  - □ Can you identify competitor activities?
  - □ Can you discern competitor strategies?
  - □ Can you anticipate future competitor strategies?

When you plan, whether in marketing or R&D or production, do you primarily focus on what you are doing, or do you also consider how competitors can or will respond? This takes a deep understanding of capabilities and intentions. In other words, do you use some version of a shadow team or informally poll a cross-function of people for their perspectives?

- Do you understand all the knowledge resources present within (and without) your firm?

Have you ever taken a knowledge asset inventory? Is there a human resource information system? Do people within the firm know how to discover who knows what? Is your staff well versed in using the multitude of publicly available reference materials, reports, and search engines? Do you gather knowledge from your suppliers, channel partners, and industry associations?

- Do you recognize the threat that CI poses to your knowledge assets?

Many firms invest copious resources in capturing knowledge and creating intelligence and then do very little to protect these assets. Does your firm have clear policies that are communicated to every employee about confidentiality, engaging with solicitors, and/or interacting with external partners? Are there clear policies about sharing information internally? Are people generally made aware of the fact that CI activities are not just something in which to engage but also something about which to be concerned?

3

It's a Risky Business

Even sunshine burns if you get too much.

—"Anonymous"

The sun is good for us. It sustains our life on this planet. It provides vitamin D, impacts our moods, facilitates photosynthesis, creates warmth, and, when channeled the right way, gives us power. It also provides a tan—for many a noble goal in and of itself. In northern and southern climates, the sun is something to be soaked up when present because the full extent of its powers is cyclical. In equatorial climates, where the sun is always in full force, it is something to be managed. And for the fair-skinned, it is something to consistently protect against. The sun is a necessary ingredient to nourish existence. Managing it according to the conditions of the environment determines whether it is beneficial or not.

Knowledge is good for organizations. The ability to turn knowledge into intelligence and facilitate strategic decision-making is a key to achieving competitive advantage. Knowledge, whether collected for archiving (KM) or sought around specific competitive issues (CI), is a primary component in creating actionable intelligence. Knowledge is at the forefront for achieving advantage in the New Economy. It nourishes the organization. It becomes power as intelligence, a resource to harness and exploit.

Business models are evolving and taking advantage of the union between knowledge and digitization. Firms employ information technology to capture and use knowledge throughout the Value

Chain. As part of an industry's landscape, those firms not reaping the economies and insights from knowledge can fall quickly behind. Conversely, those who are the first to implement may pull ahead.

Thus, one can assume then that the more knowledge captured, developed, and used, the better—right? The more rays we absorb from the sun, the better—right? Not right. While we propose that CI practices are essential for releasing the potential of knowledge, they are also practices designed to discover the knowledge of others. If you are doing it, you can bet others are doing it, too. This presents a paradox. Not developing KM practices can put the firm at risk if competitors are developing them. If one's competitors are busy establishing competitive advantage through better use of knowledge, standing still can leave you far behind. On the other hand, developing knowledge assets in a CI-intensive industry puts the firm at risk of unwittingly sharing the fruits of its labor. If you go to the trouble and expense of developing knowledge assets only to lose them to a competitor because a key employee leaves or a document is misplaced, you are wasting resources chasing a unique competitive advantage that never comes. To develop knowledge resources or not to develop knowledge resources? What's the firm do?

Procter & Gamble is one of the most advanced knowledge management companies in the world. The firm launched an intranet knowledge collection and sharing system, called Emmperative, in 2001 (Nelson 2001). The system offered accessible corporate knowledge, from market research data on Vidal Sassoon to Web-design expertise used by Millstone coffee. P&G also is known for its close collaboration with retailers, especially Wal-Mart. P&G has explored "smart package" products that transmit real-time information from the store shelf (Dalton 2001) and, as a major supplier, will be a part of Wal-Mart's Radio Frequency Identification (RFID) tag experiments for tracking inventory. So the firm is intimately involved with operational data from its clients and is privy to marketing and promotional plans as well. Finally, P&G is working to streamline its supply chain, sharing knowledge with its upstream partners as well. "A shopper buys a roll of Bounty paper towels, and that would trigger someone cutting a tree in Georgia . . . . That's the holy grail," according to a P&G supply chain manager (Nelson & Zimmerman 2000).

But these KM applications are not happening in a vacuum. P&G faces highly competent, highly competitive foes in a number of markets. One of its principal competitors, in many different product categories, is Unilever. The two firms were involved in a widely reported dumpster diving incident recently, and their competitive intelligence rivalry goes much deeper. Patent tracking, listening in on train conversations, posing as cab drivers for transportation services employed by the other firm, infiltrating internal marketing conferences, and other such CI/espionage activities (some of these would cross the line of what is considered legitimate and ethical CI) have been employed in the rivalry (Curtis 2001). Indeed, the firms know one another so well that new products have a very short term of exclusivity. The research done in the R&D departments is so similar and secrets are so hard to keep that any product introduction can be shortly answered by a competitive version that was already in the pipeline. When Unilever first started selling Persil Power, P&G knew of the cleaning power of its manganese compounds but also knew of the damage it could do to clothing, having researched the same ideas and abandoned them. P&G actually shared the knowledge with Unilever, at least trying to keep its competitor from making a huge mistake.

How does a firm like P&G make decisions about how much to develop its knowledge resources? How do managers decide how much competitive intelligence they need to practice, including counterintelligence? How can you decide what to share and what to keep secret, what to protect and what to distribute freely? P&G's approach seems right for it, but is it appropriate for all firms? Our answer to the last question is "no." And the answer to all of the rest is a definitive "it depends." Environmental circumstances affect intelligence, and the optimal knowledge strategy will depend on the conditions facing an individual firm. In this chapter, we'll explore what some of those conditions may be and how strategic decisions can be made about the optimal development and use of knowledge assets and about obtaining intelligence.

The Risks of Developing Knowledge Assets in a Competitive Intelligence World

Sharing everything with everyone everywhere may not be an optimal strategy (but neither is keeping it all to yourself).

There are two types of ultraviolet rays—UVA and UVB—whose effects vary by geography. The goal is to select the sunscreen or SPF that is appropriate for skin type and geographic region, balancing their impact to achieve a healthy and glowing tan. The same is true for intelligence-generating practices. There are two types of risk: Knowledge Management, or KM Risk and Competitive Intelligence, or CI Risk. Both need to be taken into consideration, responding to the needs of the firm and the demands of its competitive environment, in developing a knowledge strategy. Without a knowledge strategy, without SPF, you can get burned. The tricky part is that these risks move in opposite directions as knowledge assets are employed.

Figure 3.1 graphically depicts these two competing risks factors. The horizontal axis represents KM use and asks this question: What is the optimal level of knowledge collection and sharing? How much knowledge sharing is best? It considers the level to which knowledge assets are developed and distributed across the firm and its collaborative networks. The vertical axis represents risk, including both components (KM Risk and CI Risk).

The KM Risk component is found in knowledge management practice. In Figure 3.1, it is illustrated by the downward sloping curve, signifying less risk as more knowledge is developed and used. Ideally (indeed, it is often an implicit assumption of standard KM theory and practice), an organization would like to develop its knowledge assets to the fullest and reap the greatest advantage. Further, if the firm doesn't develop its knowledge assets while com-

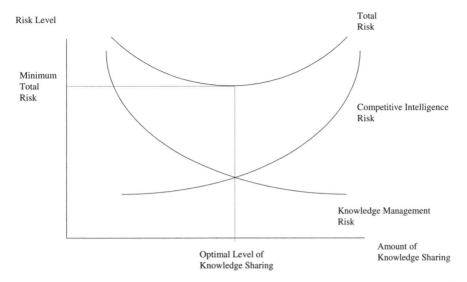

Risk Level

Total
Risk

Minimum
Total
Risk

Competitive Intelligence
Risk

Knowledge Management
Risk

Amount of
Knowledge Sharing

Optimal Level of
Knowledge Sharing

Figure 3.1 KM Risk and CI Risk

petitors do, then it could be at a considerable disadvantage. Competitor firms can benefit from the lag, reaping the benefits of using knowledge assets while others gear up to do so. Every firm has a potential, or ideal, level of knowledge development, the greatest possible level of collection, codification, sharing, and analysis of its knowledge assets. If it fails to reach its potential, it runs risks of being left behind by those competitors who come closer to their ideal level. In general, the KM Risk curve in the diagram demonstrates that the less a firm engages in developing its knowledge assets, the higher the risk that competitors will gain ground. Alternatively, as knowledge assets are developed (move further to the right along the curve), the KM Risk decreases.

This ideal of total knowledge asset development, however, is hampered by the realities of CI practices. The second risk component asks this question: What is the risk of CI activity against the firm? As knowledge assets are developed and distributed, what is the threat of infiltration? The CI Risk curve in the diagram illustrates the risk of losing proprietary knowledge to CI efforts. It moves in the opposite direction of the KM Risk curve. As illustrated in Figure 3.1, as knowledge is developed and applied by the firm, and is further distributed throughout the organization and to collaborators, CI Risk increases. Alternatively, as we move out the horizontal axis (more knowledge sharing), the CI Risk curve slopes upward, indicating greater risk. The more firms develop and share their knowledge, the more it is available to be discovered. The more competitor firms in an industry engage in CI practices, the more likely those discoveries will be made. The less rigorous a nation is in protecting the intellectual assets of its firms, the more likely the secrets will be accessed. In short, the very practice that we have been suggesting, merging KM and CI practices, provides more CI opportunities against the firm in question, fueling this risk dilemma!

Because the risks move in opposite directions, a firm needs to develop a knowledge asset management strategy based on understanding these risks. The level of these risks will vary according to national, industry, and firm variables. In essence, every organization needs to evaluate its own situation, and we will provide a guide for doing so. We recommend a framework adapted from Dunning's (1981) eclectic theory for market entry (also, Hill, Hwang & Kim 1992). As was the case in that structure, an eclectic or individual approach works best because every firm's situation will differ. These units of analysis—national, industry, and firm—provide a framework for determining KM and CI Risk levels and thus the firm's total level of risk. Each factor and its role in risk management strategy will be discussed in more detail in the second part of the book. What they imply here is that the risk challenge is a holistic process, as essential to a firm's competitiveness as developing intelligence capabilities themselves. Understanding your firm's total risk position provides prescriptions for strategically using and protecting knowledge assets. Moving from knowledge to intelligence requires recognizing an organization's situation as well as when the risk curve has shifted, and responding skillfully.

From a prescriptive standpoint, the organization will want to operate at the minimal risk point on the Total Risk curve. This curve is also depicted in Figure 3.1 and represents adding together the KM and CI Risk curves. Operating to the right of the minimal total risk point (too much use of knowledge assets) will subject the firm to too much CI Risk relative to the gains from knowledge management. The firm is too open, to the point it risks losing proprietary control of its own resources. Operating to the left of the optimal point (less use of knowledge assets) will subject the firm to too much KM Risk relative to the gains from keeping the knowledge proprietary. The firm is too secretive, to the point of not developing its knowledge resources fully while competitors do.

The shift from knowledge to intelligence involves discerning the optimal point of knowledge development and the point minimizing CI and KM Risks. Layers of advantage cannot be developed without a sound knowledge asset risk management strategy. Even if a firm leads its competitive group in developing knowledge assets, the advantage can be short-lived. Success will lure other firms to do the same, and they will also try to discover best practices as to how it is done. This fuels CI practices, and eventually the knowledge lag advantage is gone. The competitive arena dictates that firms continuously monitor and make adjustments to their total level of risk. The environment, and the firm's sensitivity to it, determines how much SPF—Strategic Protection Factor—is needed.

Which SPF Is Right for You? The Art of Balancing Risk

Minimize risk by understanding your knowledge situation.

Strategic Protection Factors, our version of SPFs, are ratings that represent the combined level of KM and CI Risks. Each SPF has explicit challenges and strategic prescriptions. Each has levels of KM Risk and CI Risk that determine the overall risk faced by the firm. By understanding the risks faced, organizations can bring the appropriate strategies to bear on their situation. The matrix in Table 3.1 illustrates how the risk curves come together and what they mean for developing, sharing, and protecting the firm's knowledge assets.

Table 3.1 Strategic Protection Factors

	Knowledge Management Risk (Sharing) Low	Knowledge Management Risk (Sharing) High
Competitive Intelligence Risk (Protection) Low	Low CI/Low KM **SPF 5: Just in Case** *Brilliance as Hit or Miss*	Low CI/High KM **SPF 15: Play It Safe** *800-pound Gorilla and Symbiosis*
Competitive Intelligence Risk (Protection) High	High CI/Low KM **SPF 30: Protective Coverage** *Glass House*	High CI/High KM **SPF 45: Total Block** *Cold War*

The horizontal of the matrix concerns the location of the KM Risk curve from Figure 3.1. As noted, this type of risk relates to the challenges of not developing knowledge assets to their fullest potential (when competitors might). For any given level of knowledge development, KM Risk might be high or low, depending on the specific environmental and firm-specific factors facing that organization. The curve will always decrease as more knowledge is developed by a firm, but these factors will affect its position. If low, it will be closer to the origin (lower and to the left). If high, it will be further from the origin (higher and to the right). The continuum ranges from a situation in which knowledge assets have little value (low KM Risk) to situations crying for a deeply rooted collaborative system engaging the firm and its network of partners (high KM Risk).

Whether the issue is that knowledge is difficult to make proprietary, difficult to share, or is so individual as to make a "system" impractical, extensive knowledge sharing doesn't necessarily benefit a firm. So not all businesses require a deep level of knowledge assets or collaboration in order to carve out advantage. Such situations would be classified as low KM Risk (little risk from not developing knowledge assets). At the other end of the dimension are firms that need to collaborate across the organization and its networks due to their business environment. Firms trying to achieve operational excellence may need to partner upstream in supply chain management. Firms vying for market power with a new innovation in a mature industry may need to partner with smaller innovators or channels downstream. For a variety of reasons, managing knowledge fully and well may be an absolute requirement for success for such an organization. In such cases, we would consider the firms to have high KM Risk.

The vertical labels in Table 3.1 represent the position of the CI Risk curve from Figure 3.1. The curve demonstrates the threat of losing intellectual property or other proprietary knowledge assets. As with the KM Risk scenario, "low" CI Risk suggests a curve close to the origin, low and to the left, and "high" CI Risk suggests a curve far from the origin, high and to the right. In all cases, the curve will be upward sloping. On the firm level, CI Risk is simply the danger of losing proprietary knowledge assets to a competitor (who is presumably conducting CI activities). It implies the required level of protection for such knowledge assets. Here we suggest a continuum stretching from competitors behaving relatively independently of each other (low CI Risk) to one of dynamic competitive rivalry where firms are jockeying for position and watching each other closely (high CI Risk). Firms that pay little attention to one another do business in industries where the action of one does not create a ripple of response across others. Whether methods of competition are so different that competitive knowledge is unimportant or a firm has such a dominant position that its competitors aren't bothersome, protecting the firm's knowledge assets is not a high priority because competitors are not looking for them. In industries where the stakes are high, however, such as those in maturing life cycles or where investment levels are specialized and high, competitors constantly monitor one another for preemptive, proactive, and reactive purposes. Protecting knowledge assets is a primary concern because the stakes are high—advantage is hard to come by and may be found only in knowledge. Where a firm falls on the protection dimension is a function of the challenge of shielding knowledge assets in the face of competitive rivalry.

SPF 5: Just in Case, Brilliance as Hit or Miss

Low KM Risk/Low CI Risk.

Brilliance as hit or miss is a situation where an individual or a special circumstance is the sole source of advantage. The impact of competitors discovering knowledge assets is moot because they are tacit and not transferable. Similarly, the knowledge may have given an organization significant first-mover advantage (or similar strategic/tactical action) that has made copying immaterial. This is not to say that there is no competitive rivalry. Instead it suggests that market success depends less on proprietary knowledge assets and more on a singular vision. Artists become successful because their vision aligns with a societal pulse at a given point in time. They do not need (and usually do not want) the input or skills of others— they rarely collaborate with other artists to create their works. Notoriety is part talent, part timing, and part blind luck. Certainly within the artistic community there is competition, but knowing what other artists are working on will not necessarily improve a competing artist's ability to create a name for himself or herself. There are too many other factors that influence that occasion. Similarly, knowing what the first-mover does, down to the minutest detail, doesn't really help unless a competitor has something substantial that allows them to go beyond it.

Figure 3.2 shows how this situation can be illustrated by the risk curves. The KM Risk curve is low, with little danger of being left behind by a competitor who makes better use of knowledge techniques. Similarly, the CI Risk curve is low, with little danger of losing proprietary knowledge assets to a competitor. The optimal strategy, in this situation, is to go ahead and make moderate use of knowledge management, where it helps, because both types of risk remain relatively low.

Drivers for Brilliance are reputation, timing, and supply. A cabinetmaker will be in demand because of a reputation for fine work or for charging the least. Supply factors, such as how many cabinet-

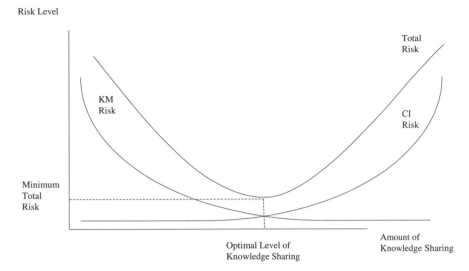

Figure 3.2   SPF 5: Brilliance as Hit or Miss

makers there are in the region, and economic factors, whether people or developers have the capital to remodel or build, can also drive demand. An inventor can create a product that captures the imagination. Angel investors will decide if it gets built. Pricing will determine who initially buys it. Timing, tastes, and happenstance determine if it hits or misses. Actors, musicians, artists, designers, and others with singular gifts face similar circumstances. In late 2003, for example, the CEO and the top designer of Gucci left the firm after having difficulty agreeing on new contracts (Galloni, Carreyrou, and Rohwedder 2003). The key question was whether Gucci had managed to institutionalize the knowledge and abilities of the two leaders or whether the company was to take a big hit in terms of the lost talent. In all likelihood, this type of creativity was probably hard to capture. Gucci may be able to find other talented individuals, but we believe it unlikely that typical knowledge management techniques would be successful in such a case.

Brilliance may also be characteristic of cottage or fragmented industries. Here again, reputation, timing, and supply will influence how busy any individual or establishment is. There are no category leaders in nail salons. Their success depends on the quality of the manicure, its price, the store's location, and how many options people have within a neighborhood. CI Risk revolves around comparative pricing, which is easy to discover.

Brilliance is not limited only to creative individuals, early-stage entrepreneurs, and small businesses. Large firms whose success is based on a unique vision may be in the same situation, particularly if their competitive advantages are hard to copy and/or they have established a large lead in terms of first-mover advantage. Many service industry organizations, whose operations are right out in the open, can be subject to this sort of environment. Consider Southwest Airlines. The secrets of its success, in terms of operations and marketing, are not hidden, including a single model of aircraft (lower training and spare parts inventory costs), nonhub routes (lower gate costs, quicker turnaround times), few amenities, and good labor relations.

Any number of competitors have sought to copy the model, from JetBlue, AirTran, and the majors in the United States (Song, Ted) to European firms such as EasyJet and RyanAir. None have yet had the same level of success, in large part because the knowledge is difficult to copy. Indeed, a case can be made that Southwest's preeminence is based on the singular talents of its one-time, long-time CEO Herb Kelleher, who was able to instill a culture in the company that allows it to keep a friendly, motivated labor force and enthusiastic customers even with a low-cost, low-service structure. And now that it is the largest discount carrier, it will be difficult for others to copy its success, at least in the United States. So while the firm does share its knowledge assets (cooperating with Dollar Rent A Car, for example, in sharing their computerized reservation systems, *Economist* 2002), the sharable knowledge is limited. And it has little to fear if exposed to CI efforts, since most key knowledge is already out in the open and its advantage is supported by a tacit asset— its culture.

SPF 5: The rays of the sun have a hit or miss effect on brilliance. They can be shining brightly yet at an angle that provides little more than indirect light,

*or they can warm the surface and promote growth. In this situation, one can
safely bask in the glow of the sun, with few concerns for protection, in the
hope that brilliance develops.*

Brilliance is the knowledge asset. This type of knowledge can sometimes be inseparable from an individual or a set of circumstances.
As a result, those possessing it can safely try to develop their genius
with little fear of losing it to a competitor. Strategically, it is still
important to know the competitive landscape, how others are positioned to use knowledge, and what their capabilities are. Some decision will still need to be made as to the optimal level of knowledge
asset development, but the stakes are not so high. Decision-makers
also need to keep in mind that, at times, success may have less to do
with strategy than with a match of talent and circumstances that
works "just because."

SPF 15: Play It Safe, Symbiosis or Dancing with an 800-Pound Gorilla

High KM Risk/Low CI Risk.

The 800-pound Gorilla is a firm that dominates its market. More
often than not, this occurs in mature industries with tight structures.
Operational excellence is important to the bottom line. Here, knowledge assets need substantial development, across the Value Chain
and network partners. Not developing these capabilities puts a firm
at a disadvantage (high KM Risk). With a tight industry structure,
brands and competitive positions staked, CI Risk is less formidable.
With few major players, it is easier to monitor the strategic group.
New entrants can be rare. If they do enter, they are positioned to
fulfill a niche the Gorilla doesn't satisfy or, symbiotically, to help the
Gorilla stay in bananas. In the symbiotic case, they enter with full
disclosure of knowledge assets. Competition turns on finding a way
to secure an efficient and reliable supply chain, extend distribution
channels, or increase market power through acquisitions, alliances,

or diversifications. At this point in an industry's life cycle, the goal is to keep the customers you have, sell them more stuff, and perhaps gain some of your competitor's share. Doing so requires competition to occur on many points, including price, quality, and convenience. Understanding the customer and securing value-based operations drive knowledge asset development.

In this industry's Value Chain, success comes from aggressively developing knowledge resources. Developing or maintaining the dominant position as the 800-pound Gorilla is one defensible strategy. Another is to be a partner in supplying the Gorilla bananas. Once this symbiosis occurs, competitor activity, although something to be monitored, is less of a concern. Even if a competitor obtains key knowledge, it will have a hard time duplicating the dominant firm's position. The symbiotic partnership requires both parties to share sensitive competitive information with each other. They become tight components in each other's Value Chain. This reality helps protect the relationship from competitor intrusion. Thus, the CI Risk, the need to protect activities from external incursions, is a moderate concern. The focus is on the source that supports competitive advantage. Similarly, competitors of the Gorilla have CI concerns, but they are moderate compared to the risk of falling further behind the Gorilla in terms of knowledge sharing.

As Figure 3.3 suggests, the conceptual foundation of this situation is found in high KM Risk and low CI Risk. Both are illustrated. With this scenario, the optimal point is associated with significant knowledge asset development, specifically because CI is not a risk until these assets are considerable. Firms choosing to operate at the optimal point will find their strategic choice exposes them to some risk, certainly more than was the case with the hit-or-miss situation, balanced between KM and CI.

As an example, consider retailing and how it has been dramatically changed by the emergence of Wal-Mart, an 800-pound Gorilla. The discounter is the largest retailer in the world and threatening to become the overall sales and market capitalization leader, regardless

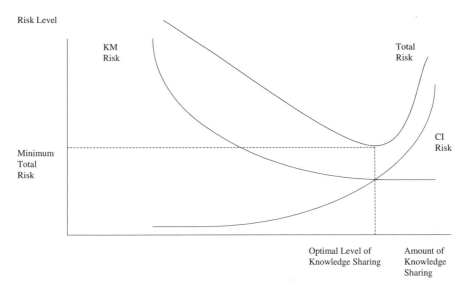

Figure 3.3   SPF 15: 800-Pound Gorilla and Symbiosis

of industry. Its evolution was born of human capital—the genius of Sam Walton, who charted the course of the firm through good common sense and competitor analysis, including an early strategy to locate in underserved markets. He also had the foresight to understand the early advantages of technology as a management tool. Wal-Mart's dock-to-dock inbound logistics management system and associated inventory management tactics are also foundations of its success. Wal-Mart developed structural capital to create an efficient supply chain management process that saves it the expense of warehousing inventory and enables it to customize product delivery by store. It has gained so much power in the industry that its suppliers are required to adhere to Wal-Mart's latest desires for increasing efficiency, regardless of cost. If you are Procter & Gamble and sell 17 percent of your goods to Wal-Mart, you have to seriously consider doing what you are asked (Boyle 2003). Wal-Mart also constantly examines customer needs and wants, creating a pallet of offerings that attract customers across demographic and psychographic groups. Delivering on this success takes relational capital, a network of partners who supply and transport Wal-Mart's merchandise. Wal-Mart's dominance comes from the development of its deep knowledge assets. But at this point, Wal-Mart is so far ahead of competitors and has such formidable barriers to entry that in spite of its expansive KM use, it has little to fear from CI activities of competitors (even though it takes such efforts seriously and does protect itself).

As a result, competitors need to do the same with their knowledge assets if they are to stay in the game. Some have tried to establish a similar end-to-end organizational knowledge system, even going to the extent of trying to lift Wal-Mart's information technology people. Amazon, for example, is well known for its ambitions to copy the Wal-Mart information-driven operations structure (Wingfield 2002), including attempts to hire away key information technology executives (Nelson & Anders 1999).

Similarly, JC Penney has had to transform its business model to respond to the Gorilla's challenge. As noted earlier, the firm has developed deep relational capital with a symbiotic partner (Kahn 2003). TAL, operating out of Hong Kong, has become a shirt supplier to many major retailers. For JC Penney, TAL not only manages upstream operations such as just-in-time shirt inventory management, but has also moved downstream, forecasting demand and even designing shirts. The success of this relationship rests on the development of knowledge assets, structural and relational capital, and a collaborative business model. While JC Penney needs to keep its finger on the pulse of its strategic group, the key is achieving operational excellence and the right product mix. The retailing industry is rather translucent with consumers perceiving many competitors as interchangeable. Strong brands must be developed, whether signifying unique merchandise selection, low prices, convenience, or some other compelling reason to buy. As such, the development of deep knowledge assets is of greater significance than the need to protect intellectual property.

Outside of retail, a firm such as Dell is a similar case. Dell is famous for the efficiency of its supply chain management, stretching from customization for customers to its entire network of suppliers (Rocks 2000). As a PC is ordered, the information/knowledge is moved immediately throughout Dell's system to suppliers of suppliers. And Dell knows its customers so well that it can actually do a pretty good job of forecasting the demand for "customized" units (while also providing marketing incentives to push demand to appropriate styles given production or inventory plans). As with Wal-Mart, Dell makes extensive use of its knowledge resources, sharing them freely throughout its value network. As with Wal-Mart, Dell's competitors pretty much know what it does and, even if able to gain more knowledge through competitive intelligence activities, would have trouble copying the system—partially because Dell has such a huge head start and partially because of structural issues such as established retail systems.

SPF 15: The sun can provide a tremendous benefit to people with the right skin type for a given climate. It is best to use general cover, as a habit, at all times, but some don't need to be as concerned with protection. They can enjoy the sun's benefits without the worry of overexposure.

When you compete in an industry with transparent business models and an 800-pound Gorilla, you need to be aggressive to survive. The primary ingredient for success is the development of deep knowledge assets and collaborative relationships with partners. The Gorilla, with size, brand, and first-mover advantages, has little to worry about in terms of CI Risk, even as it takes some precautions. Those competing with the Gorilla may have greater CI concerns, but they can't afford to fall further behind the Gorilla, and so the KM Risk far outweighs any CI Risk.

This box within the matrix also illustrates a couple of important points. Initially, even companies with the same classification can have different strategic positions. Everything is relative, and although one retailer, for example, might be the 800-pound Gorilla with more concerns about discouraging CI, another might be a challenger and have fewer CI worries (nothing to lose). Both fall into the low CI box of the matrix but would have different positions within that box. Managers need to assess their positions, not only to discern the general knowledge asset management circumstances but relative positions as well. In other words, be as exact as possible even with an inexact tool.

A second consideration is that position in the matrix can change. The 800-pound Gorilla may cease to be the 800-pound Gorilla given a technological dislocation, social/cultural change, or some other event. Indeed, retailing in particular seems to operate on cycles such that those on top in one decade are also-rans thirty years later. Or as pointed out in Clayton Christensen's *Innovator's Dilemma* (1997), the established giants rarely see paradigm-busting technologies coming; it is upstart firms that tend to seize them and eventually overthrow the established leaders. So the initial assessment and accompanying knowledge strategy is not set in stone. It needs to be repeated, especially as conditions change.

SPF 30: Protective Cover, Living in a Glass House

Low KM Risk/High CI Risk.

The glass house is a situation where the risk of discovery is high and advantage from the deep development of knowledge and collaboration is low. The building blocks of the glass house can come from diffuse knowledge across an industry, regulation, and products that are pet rocks. The pet rock is a commodity, dressed to look like something other than a stone so firms can charge more for it. Even if products are different, the embedded knowledge is slight (although not necessarily unimportant). Activities are readily discovered and copied, so developing and sharing deep knowledge assets is not necessarily the best use of the firm's resources. Again, this is not to say that knowledge creation is unimportant. It does suggest that building sophisticated KM systems and creating networks of collaborators is a risky and limited pursuit of competitive advantage given the CI Risks involved. The issue is which knowledge assets to develop to get the biggest bang for the buck and then how to protect them.

This situation is presented in Figure 3.4. KM Risk is low, while CI Risk is high. The result is very limited knowledge asset development as an optimal strategy. Even at this limited level, however, risk is moderately high because so much CI activity is taking place. Organizations operating in this environment will want to have very limited knowledge development but take considerable steps to protect what assets they do choose to cultivate.

Banks exist in a glass house. They operate in a mature and regulated industry. Interest rates are known, and product options are similar. Their actions are visible, and their activities can be easily duplicated. What banks offer are pet rocks for different targeted groups. They differentiate their commodities through positioning and then structure their offerings to satisfy their targets. Positioning then determines which knowledge assets are most important to develop and protect.

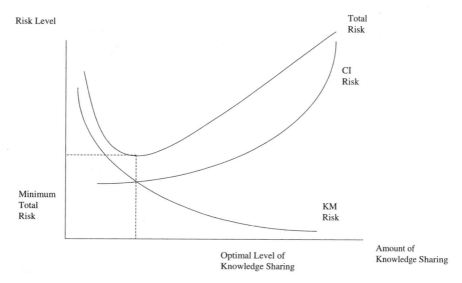

Figure 3.4 SPF 30: Glass House

Commercial banks; investment banks; credit unions; and global, regional, and local retail banks will all have different knowledge asset needs. Banks focusing on the "art of the deal" will rely on human capital. Here, knowledge assets are people who have the experience and creativity to bring such transactions to fruition. Advantage also can come from competitive capital: information on how competitors structure similar deals, due diligence processes, and counterintelligence structures that keep the conditions of the deal secret for as long as possible. Banks that focus on serving the needs of large firms and wealthy clients develop relational capital. Knowledge assets come from personally managing the relationship with the client and leveraging the relationship across product groups. The account manager is the focal point for bringing together product knowledge and customer knowledge. Advantage comes through the development of trust between account manager and client. But all of these examples are limited in terms of extending the knowledge to others in the Value Chain or even to others within the core firm. Knowledge is very localized, so little benefit comes from trying to collect and share. And all the while competitors are trying to ascertain what other organizations are offering in terms of products, operations, financing options, and so on.

Berkshire Hathaway, for example, is a very successful investment organization. As the annual letter from Warren Buffett goes out to investors, however, we see two interesting things happen. Initially, everyone, from investors to competitors to the media, pores over the letter for hints about what Buffett's strategy will be in the coming year. But as much as possible, the reasoning behind the investment strategies is kept hidden, even though it is likely based on some very simple rules. Second, speculation rises anew concerning succession. The success of Berkshire Hathaway is so closely associated with Buffett's perceived personal brilliance that a great deal of concern exists over whether critical knowledge can be captured by the organization, allowing it to go forward without him.

A similar example is found in the recent move of JP Morgan Chase into options (Creswell 2004). The bank struck a deal with

Microsoft to buy underwater stock options from Microsoft employees (at a discount, of course). The exchange gives employees some return on their potentially worthless options while Morgan takes a flier on whether those options might come back into the money at some point in the future. This is a fairly simple scheme but one that Morgan is trying to patent so as to keep this knowledge-based business practice to itself.

SPF 30: The rays of the sun penetrate a glass house. Its temperature can be regulated by venting (strategically letting things out), insulating, and/or using protective glass. What is inside is easily seen. What escapes can be controlled. What keeps the contents healthy comes from the right combination of these processes.

So in the case of financial institutions, development of additional knowledge resources may add little value while exposing the bank to unnecessary CI Risk. While there may be some benefits to sharing innovative valuation techniques or personal client information across the firm, these benefits are often insubstantial and pale beside the possibility of a competitor obtaining the same knowledge. The more that different departments become aware of, the greater the probability that the information could leave the firm's doors. These banks operate in a translucent environment. The need for protection is high.

A similar situation is seen in utilities. There is little new under the sun in terms of power generation, transmission, or delivery, especially since competitors need to cooperate in order for the grid to run effectively. When new knowledge can be applied (trading schemes, for example), it is guarded jealously, with strict controls on what is shared within and without the firm. The authors were present at one conference during which the competitive intelligence officer of prescandal Enron made a presentation concerning the firm's assessment of the future of the industry. On the same dais, a high corporate officer of the Southern Companies took copious notes throughout the speech. Even during a vanilla presentation to laypeople, nothing was left to chance in terms of what was revealed or not revealed. The Enron representative went to great lengths not to reveal anything, but the Southern manager took down every point, just in case.

When KM Risk is low, advantage comes from localized or transparent knowledge. There is not a high need for collaboration or a great risk of being left far behind by a competitor. Competitors are developing their own, similar processes and also trying to keep them close to the chest, but they can only develop so much before they are eventually revealed. When CI Risk is high, protection is essential. The sources for creating a pet rock are hard to come by, easy to imitate once known, and thus need to be safeguarded. The account manager is the key ingredient in relational capital. This person has intricate client knowledge and has earned the client's trust. Any breach can cause the client to lose faith or the account manager to move to another institution, taking the client with her. Dealmakers and their teams have the knowledge in their heads. The firm needs to protect the benefits of these assets internally and keep them from leaving the firm. Some strategic considerations include careful legal delineation of employee and firm intellectual capital. For the dealmakers, the process of valuation and due diligence, if developed while in the firm's employ, may be a firm asset. For the account manager, it is the portfolio of client information. Noncompete agreements, very careful and controlled disclosures to the press, limited access to client files across the firm, and counterintelligence training are all methods for using the correct SPF in a glass house.

SPF 45: Total Block, The Cold War

High KM Risk/High CI Risk.

The Cold War has the highest composite level of risk. This is usually a hypercompetitive industry, either growing (high tech) or mature (pharmaceuticals). The development of all knowledge assets, especially competitive capital, and collaboration are essential for achieving and sustaining advantage. With intense rivalry, the CI Risk is also very high. Firms in industries such as pharmaceuticals, telecommunications, and packaged foods characteristically engage in CI practices, so the need for protection is mandatory for advantage to prevail.

Operational excellence, innovation, branding, and solid alliances are the hallmarks of firms succeeding in this environment. A full array of the firm's knowledge assets is engaged to achieve these key success factors. Once developed, they are susceptible to discovery. At the same time, competitors are creating competitive capital, seeking to capture these valuable knowledge resources. To hold its ground in this arena, the firm needs to be intelligent and capable of protecting its intelligence. And for many organizations currently operating under other SPF conditions, this is the future. Their situations will evolve into SPF 45.

These circumstances are found in Figure 3.5. Both the KM Risk curve and the CI Risk curve are high. Knowledge asset development is fairly advanced (far out along the horizontal axis), a necessary strategy to compete in this type of industry. But because CI is also such a risk, the KM development is not what it would be without

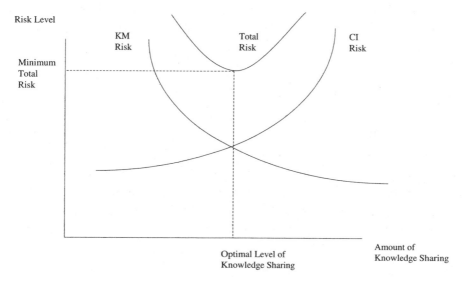

Figure 3.5   SPF 45: Cold War

such competitive attention. But even with the moderate level of KM usage, the risk level is extremely high, much higher than is the case with any other scenario. Knowledge must be developed and used, but every effort must be taken to protect it, and participants must understand the considerable level and nature of the risks they face.

Many of the cases presented in earlier and later chapters operate in the Cold War, as does Procter & Gamble, introduced in this chapter's opening vignette. In the case of Drugs, Inc., mentioned in an earlier chapter, competitors were consistently first to market with new ethical drug offerings. The culprits were scientists sharing their knowledge at professional conferences. How was this discovered? The firm's shadow team operation was investigating a rival firm's FDA approval status on a new product. Deep development of knowledge assets are needed to innovate, manufacture, market, and distribute a blockbuster drug. It costs hundreds of millions of dollars to discover, additional tens of millions to market such discoveries. The stakes are high, and competition is fierce. These firms are engaging in extensive CI practices trying to discover the chicken in each other's pot.

Food Flavors, also mentioned earlier, when launching a new product in a dominated category, ran a war game to determine the best strategy for the launch. A massive amount of competitor information was compiled to simulate its response and capability to compete, down to the product line P&L. A full spectrum of knowledge assets was needed to create and launch the product. Secrecy was also needed. With enough advance warning the competitor could have launched a preemptive strike, making the product launch and competitive contest more expensive.

SPF 45: The sun's rays are powerful, pervasive, and penetrating. They are of considerable benefit to the right recipient, but the strongest measures are needed to harness its power and keep it from burning its target.

When competitive conditions demand the development of knowledge assets in an arena where CI Risk is high, firms have to engage protective and counterintelligence measures. Any unprotected action can result in a burn. At minimum, purposeful access to data mines, corporate awareness training, and strong legal guidelines with partners and employees are in order. On a deeper level, executives in the Cold War have to ask themselves: What would be the impact competitively if this intelligence got out? Who really needs to know this? Should this intelligence be recorded? Sometimes in a Cold War, total block is required. Until the full advantage of a new product launch or new technology can be secured, its release is managed very closely. Interviews with pharmaceutical and television executives revealed that when something has deep competitive significance, only the inner circle is told, and, at times, nothing is written down. In this arena, the firm that doesn't develop deep knowledge assets and/or protective measures will be severely burned.

We believe that a number of important industries and firms are already in the Cold War, and many others are headed in that direction. Although for all managers interested in knowledge and intelligence, this book is particularly directed at executives facing this situation: Knowledge must be developed but must also be carefully guarded. Our discussion of the Cold War will continue, at length, throughout the rest of this book.

Intelligence: Knowing When to Change SPF

Risk assessment is an ongoing task.

The ideal SPF is not fixed. It can change as national, industry, and firm conditions change. The following chapters will address how to determine the different risk levels. It is important to realize that if SPFs do not shift as circumstances change, the firm can land in a competitive disadvantage. Sticking with an old strategy when facing a new situation can cause a firm all sorts of trouble.

Earlier in the book we talked about Western Utilities, an energy company seeking to do business in Mexico. Utilities used to be monopolies. They were regulated by the Federal Energy Regulatory

Commission, had their rates set, and possessed a geographically distinct, guaranteed market. Under these circumstances, they were in a low KM and low CI Risk situation and could operate at SPF 5. At SPF 5, their primary concern was staying on top of changes in regulations and changes in the demographics of their territories. Then everything changed. Deregulation meant that geographic monopolies had to learn how to compete. The market was divided between generation, transmission, and distribution, with different competitive playing fields. SPF 30 became the new and immediate reality as companies had to deal with low KM Risk and high CI Risk. Many players thought advantage would come from selling unbundled services, familiar brand names would keep customers loyal, and change would take time. Instead, change occurred quickly with new players gaining power through acquisitions, construction, and repackaging existing services into new products. Think Enron, its rapid diversification and creation of trading in natural gas futures. While knowledge development was limited, those firms that focused on what competitors were doing in the market were the ones that succeeded (unethical practices notwithstanding).

Western Utilities was operating with only an SPF 8. Not only did it not develop knowledge assets before making its fact-finding foray into Mexico, it hadn't investigated which other competitors were there or whether a competitor had purchased the rights to lay transmission lines to get there. It discovered that a competitor had. It got burned.

As competition picks up, deregulated utilities may move again, even up to SPF 45 if knowledge resources become more important. Alternatively, if reregulated, the industry may move back to a lower SPF. The point is that managers need to keep on top of circumstances, try to accurately identify the levels of KM and CI Risk facing them, and operate with an SPF appropriate to current and expected future circumstances. In the rest of this book, we'll tell you how to do that.

Competition is a risky business. An intelligence approach suggests that decision-makers choose and act upon a knowledge strategy that fits conditions. The right knowledge strategy will help create the right balance between developing and protecting knowledge. One component of this balance is the understanding and flexibility to manage risk relative to environmental demands. An SPF 5 will not protect you in the tropics. An SPF 45 may not be necessary in the national forest. What is essential here is knowing what needs to be known, who should know, when to tell, and when to just get out of the sun.

Executive Moment

In the coming chapters we will introduce considerations for determining your firm's risk levels and SPF. In preparation, here's some food for thought:

- Do you know which knowledge assets are most essential to sustaining advantage in your firm?

In our experience, executives and employees do not always share the same opinion. Not understanding what is important to share and important to keep close to the chest can create a bountiful harvest for competitor intelligence-gathering activities. Disagreements about the firm's core competitive assets are a signal that the firm not only needs to create an internal communications initiative, but that it may not really know the source of what drives its bottom line, thus not knowing what to protect. Ask your employees throughout the Value Chain what they believe the firm's advantage is.

- Are you aware of the level of knowledge asset development in your competitive environment?
- Is there an initiative on the part of employees to talk with upstream and downstream associates about competitor activities? This can be accomplished by activities such as the following.
  - Asking suppliers and channel partners what operational systems (e.g., ERP, SCM, CRM) they prefer working with and why

- ☐ Checking classified ads in newspapers for executive and new hire listings
- ☐ Asking the sales force what they learn from customers about the above questions
- ■ Do you know whether sensitive information is accessible?
  - ☐ While patent and trade secret exposure may be more readily detected, other important knowledge assets may not be
  - ☐ Ask people working in cross-functional teams what the most surprising information they learned was
  - ☐ Inquire whether suppliers or channel partners were asking business questions outside of the normal realm of conversation
  - ☐ Discover whether the firm has legal documentation of information-sharing parameters with alliance and project partners. Then speak to the managers of these projects to discover what really gets shared and why
- ■ What do you think your SPF is? Why?

The next sections will shed light on whether you are appropriately protected or heading for a burn.

Part 1 Wrap-Up:
Knowledge Meets Intelligence

Knowledge is a valuable asset to an organization. Those who espouse knowledge management have been supporting this point of view for years, and the doubters are going to find themselves convinced as we increasingly move toward a knowledge economy. But knowledge is not enough. KM software systems and many practitioners treat knowledge as a library function, and, indeed, identification, codification, and sharing are useful. But such an approach is not enough. Knowledge needs to transform into intelligence. We believe three points are key for systematically building and sustaining a strategic capability, an intelligence approach, in a firm.

Initially, the definition of knowledge assets must be expanded.
Competitive capital is a knowledge asset. Whether outcomes of shadow team activity or a functional department such as marketing, analysis that identifies competitor capabilities, market changes, customer preferences, or industry conditions is an important part of the firm's intellectual capital. It needs to be captured, codified, and catalogued, just as any other form of knowledge asset.

Operational knowledge, embodied in e-business systems utilizing the communication capabilities of the Internet, is also a knowledge asset. Given that ERP, SCM, and CRM systems hold knowledge concerning customers, product sales, production plans, orders to suppliers, service coordination, and other valuable information, firms using these platforms need to recognize the knowledge potential and knowledge risks.

In addition to internal sources, organizations need to understand the value of gathering knowledge outside of their boundaries. Whether a systematic collection or purposeful search, external knowledge can be of great value to many firms. Recognizing that knowledge assets encompass a wider field is the first step toward intelligence.

The value of knowledge is tied to its use.

Knowledge is a strategic asset when it evolves from being static to active, from knowing to doing. In other words, knowledge can become intelligence when it is used to identify competitive challenges or support tactical and strategic decisions. Accomplishing this means that information has to be gathered from inside and outside the firm. This information or knowledge gathering is purposeful, deliberate, and driven by executive questions, strategic edicts, or profiling. Gathered information, whether data or knowledge, published sources or network connections, is integrated, synthesized, and drives analyses that compel the firm to do something.

A practical and effective way for turning knowledge into intelligence is through intelligence teams. Intelligence teams can be patterned on the shadow teams used in competitive intelligence actions. Shadow teams gather and integrate cross-functional HUMINT, existing competitive knowledge, and competitive intelligence into actionable and/or future-focused analyses that identify opportunities and support executive actions. They can develop think-tank capabilities and facilitate organizationwide learning and the creation of new knowledge. Their unfiltered, timely intelligence products can become the bedrock for building layers of competitive advantage.

The key for intelligence is that such teams are purpose-driven, targeted to some specific knowledge purpose. They do more than collect and store knowledge; they do analysis and thereby learn from existing knowledge and generate new knowledge. The collected knowledge is employed in a strategic manner. And if structured correctly, such teams have direct access to decision-makers, ensuring that knowledge is actually used for strategic purposes. Knowledge assets can lead to action at the highest levels and everywhere below.

Knowledge needs to be developed and managed as a strategic asset.

Internal knowledge asset development and external competitive intelligence dynamics pose inherent risks to intellectual capital. Not developing knowledge assets when competitors do puts the firm at a strategic disadvantage (KM Risk). However, as knowledge assets are developed and shared, competitive intelligence activities of other firms make such assets vulnerable to discovery (CI Risk). These risks require the firm to really understand its national and international environments, the competitive dynamics within its industry, and its own capabilities if it is to intelligently choose which knowledge assets to develop and how to protect them.

An SPF defines the firm's risk scenario and helps to identify the challenges in developing a knowledge asset management strategy. It balances the need for internal and external knowledge collaboration across Value Chains and networks, with the need to engage in and protect against competitive intelligence activities. It suggests that not all knowledge assets have the same value in creating and sustaining competitive advantage. By employing the SPF framework, decision-makers can identify the relevant risks they face and then develop knowledge assets in an optimal manner. This optimal manner will minimize the overall risk a firm faces from both KM Risk and CI Risk. And as a dynamic matrix, the SPF approach reminds management that once these risks are balanced, they need to be continuously monitored and shifted as changes in the environment dictate.

In short, the competitive environment demands that firms engage their knowledge assets and intelligence capabilities in strategic decision-making processes. In so doing, the firm must have a sound strategy for managing the risks involved in both developing and using knowledge assets.

Part 2: Strategy for Shifting Knowledge to Intelligence

4

Determining an SPF:
National Considerations

I think there's a change in the weather.

—Ray Davies

As we have seen, knowledge management is not a panacea. No single level of knowledge, in any of its guises, is necessarily optimal for any particular firm in any particular situation. Developing knowledge assets may be important, even critical, to success. Fail to develop your knowledge to the same extent as your competitors, and you may find yourself at a serious disadvantage in the marketplace. You neglect developing knowledge assets at your own peril. But you also run the risk of overleveraging these knowledge assets, spreading them among too many users while maintaining an inadequate protection system. In such a situation, the hard-won knowledge could be easily lost, not only placing a competitor on your level but providing unique competencies to them because of their detailed understanding of your knowledge assets. The key is managing knowledge strategically, creating intelligence by balancing knowledge development against knowledge protection. The intelligent firm chooses a Strategic Protection Factor fitting its unique situation, managing its knowledge accordingly.

In the mid-nineties, New Balance moved production of some of its sneakers to China from other Asian locations (Khan 2002). Competing in the tough athletic shoe industry, which has a surprising amount of knowledge development and competitive intelligence activity, New Balance needed to make decisions about what new product, production, and marketing knowledge to share with its new suppliers. If it did not utilize low-cost partners in countries such as China and failed to share critical technologies and other knowledge with such firms, the U.S. company could find itself at a tremendous competitive disadvantage against serious rivals such as Nike, Adidas Salomon, and Reebok. On the other hand, major competitive intelligence issues confronted New Balance in its new Chinese location, a place where intellectual property and counterfeiting laws tend to be loose, let alone any protections of softer, less well-defined knowledge assets.

The biggest problem New Balance actually encountered came from one of its long-term suppliers, a firm that moved from Taiwan to China when the core company did. The owner of the Chinese firm asked to produce shoes for the local market while still helping to meet New Balance's worldwide demand. New Balance initially gave permission for production of a lower-tech "classic" model, although it later made a strategic decision to stick to the higher-tech, newer models that were more in line with its premium image, eliminating the local product. Armed with the knowledge of how to make New Balance's products, however, the supplier continued unauthorized production on its own. In effect, New Balance found itself competing with its own products (and corporate knowledge) in China and, soon, other markets as a parallel import situation eventually developed, too.

New Balance actually managed its situation reasonably well, doing a good job of balancing the risks and rewards implicit in using knowledge. Initially, the decision to have the supplier make only the low-tech model for the local market, done apparently for market reasons, may have helped to keep some of the core firm's knowledge to itself. Further, the firm made use of both its own existing knowledge (quantity of supplies used to make sneakers versus actual number of sneakers reportedly made) and acquired knowledge (a private investigator was used to ascertain the source of the illicit shoes) to determine that the supplier was using its knowledge inappropriately by producing more than it should have been. And New Balance eventually took further steps to firm up its protection mechanisms, cutting its number of factories in China so as to allow better oversight and control, while also updating its labels to make them harder to copy.

New Balance's experience illustrates the conundrum facing firms seeking to balance the generation and then protection of knowledge and intelligence. In order to move on to intelligence, organizations need to apply strategy to these decisions, assessing risk and reward in several areas. How much knowledge management should be practiced? What knowledge should be collected, what knowledge analyzed, and what knowledge shared? With whom should it be shared? What are the risks of competitive intelligence activities being conducted against the firm? What competitive intelligence or counterintelligence activities does the firm itself need to apply to a given situation? Again, what is the situation and what is the appropriate SPF?

The answers are not simple and will vary widely according to circumstances. A strategic approach, an intelligence approach, to management of all types of knowledge, including competitive, requires an analysis of pertinent factors that influence knowledge applications. The key question, of course, is what those factors might be.

The Risks of Managing Knowledge Assets: Reprise

Remember, organizations face risks of developing and not developing knowledge assets.

In the last chapter, we detailed the risks involved in using knowledge management. Two opposing risks, one decreasing with KM applications and the other increasing, are relevant. *Knowledge Management Risk* (KM Risk) is defined as the risk that a firm will not fully develop its KM potential, the risk of falling behind competitors in the marketplace who make better use of their knowledge assets. As a firm does a more complete job of collecting, codifying, analyzing, and dispersing its knowledge resources (i.e., increases its KM applications), it will decrease this risk.

Alternatively, *Competitive Intelligence Risk* (CI Risk) refers to the risk of surrendering valuable proprietary knowledge to another firm's competitive intelligence efforts. For a number of reasons, including increased sharing throughout the network outside of the core firm, more complete sharing, digitization, and growth in CI activities, increased KM applications expose a firm to ever-expanding CI Risks.

In moving from knowledge to intelligence, one key task for an organization is to assess the risk levels facing it, including the combined, total risk curve (KM Risk and CI Risk added together). We characterized this as determining the Strategic Protection Factor (SPF) because accurate assessment leads to appropriate strategies in terms of sharing and protecting. If done correctly, the firm can operate at an optimal level of knowledge management development, minimizing risk and maximizing competitiveness. We suggested four general SPF conditions (with the understanding that degrees of SPF between the categories can also exist) with accompanying risk situations and strategies.

The key question: How can you determine a firm's own SPF so it can make appropriate strategic decisions concerning knowledge management and protection? How should this assessment take place? What factors are behind the shape and position of the risk curves, those that determine the SPF? To that level of strategic analysis we now turn. The relevant factors can be broken down at the national, industry, and firm levels. This chapter explores what variables managers should review at the national level.

An Eclectic Approach

Each firm faces its own unique circumstances.

As the preceding discussion suggests, determining the SPF is a firm-specific process. We have developed a framework for analysis that will help managers in determining the particular environment facing their organization. We constructed this framework from our understanding of the KM and CI disciplines, existing approaches to managing intellectual property and such "harder" knowledge assets, and Dunning's (1981) Eclectic Theory for national market entry.

The latter has nothing to do with knowledge management or competitive intelligence, and, indeed, the eventual framework we adopted doesn't actually include Dunning's variables or those from later versions of the Eclectic Theory (e.g., Hill, Hwang & Kim 1992). But as the "eclectic" title suggests, the theory really focuses on how some strategic decisions depend on the individual situation of each firm. In Dunning's case, the question is how to enter a market, specifically when to establish a production facility (foreign direct investment, or FDI) rather than exporting or licensing. But the idea is easily and logically expanded to other applications even as the relevant variables change.

Dunning's original structure included three groups of variables: Ownership-Specific Advantages, Location-Specific Advantages, and Internalization Advantages. The former group of variables generally came from size, a multinational presence, experience, and so forth, that could grant competitive advantage and determine whether FDI was helpful or not. Location-specific variables included traditional location decision factors such as infrastructure, government intervention, cultural differences, and so on. And finally, internalization referred to a particular firm's ability to keep its unique advantages to itself, to capture and protect cost advantages, intellectual property, externalities, and so on—with a point similar to what we have been discussing, that the more internalized such advantages are, the more safely the core firm can share them, even with overseas partners.

This framework has found other expressions in the decades since its original formulation. The Hill, Hwang, and Kim (HHK) version just noted, for example, still has three groups of variables but different definitions that help simplify its usage. HHK discuss Global Strategic variables (global concentration of the industry, global synergies to be gained, and global strategic motivations), Environmental variables (country risk, location unfamiliarity, demand uncertainty, and competitive intensity), and Transaction-Specific variables (value of firm-specific knowhow, tacit nature of knowhow).

We have reformatted this approach to our own purposes and propose a three-part framework that includes national-, industry-, and firm-specific variables. These groupings reflect the Eclectic Theory but better fit the subject matter. Indeed, intellectual property and, increasingly, knowledge management, have a long history of study and practice at the national and firm levels, as we shall see. And our own analysis of the importance of industry factors in both knowledge management and competitive intelligence convinced us that this level of examination was also critically important to practicing managers.

As a result, we suggest a framework and analytic tool that is eclectic in approach—each firm will face its own individual set of circumstances and should act accordingly. This framework examines pertinent factors at the national, industry, and firm levels to determine how important knowledge asset development (KM Risk) and competitive intelligence vulnerability (CI Risk) are to individual organizations. By studying the variables we lay out in the following chapters, managers can determine their situation, their SPF standing, and manage knowledge assets to the best benefit of the firm. We turn first to national factors.

National Innovation Systems

Technological development can be influenced by differences between nations.

Noting how differences in national environments can affect businesses' strategies and activities is nothing new, but we sometimes forget to review such factors as we explore new disciplines such as knowledge management and competitive intelligence. And, of course, how to structure this type of analysis is always an intriguing question.

KM scholars and practitioners are just starting to explore the field on a national level, with attempts to assess the intellectual capital stock of nations. We'll discuss the implications of such work later in this chapter. But previous studies concerning innovation in different nations can provide guidance for us in building a catalogue of national factors that should be reviewed when evaluating intelligence strategies. Let's look at some examples before we discuss how these can be combined to provide a framework for assessing KM Risk and CI Risk.

National Innovation Systems (NIS) is a field of research that focuses on the question of why different nations, even if similar in terms of their economic development, can show very different results in terms of innovation and technological output (Mowery 1992; Mowery & Teece 1993; Nelson 1993; Patel & Pavitt 1987). At the national level, countries such as the United States, Japan, and Germany can vary considerably in the amount and quality of innovations. When developing countries are brought into the mix, of course, the differences are even more striking. If the inputs (people, R&D spending) are essentially the same, why does the variation in output exist? The general answer appears to be differences in the environment, including structural factors (such as government spending, regulation, etc.) and softer factors such as "economic culture" (e.g., is a society entrepreneurial or not?).

These conclusions are important to practicing managers for a couple of reasons. Initially, almost all new product development and innovation management scholars, gurus, and consultants focus on finding the single, optimal way in which to identify concepts and turn them into commercial successes. NIS work strongly suggests that the optimal way will differ, depending on circumstances, so there is no single, unique process that is right for all environments. Indeed, what works in Japan may not work as well in the United Kingdom. So it is important for managers to understand the environment within which they operate, tailoring their efforts to the applicable specific antitrust regulations, patent laws, government procurement policies, tax laws, economic culture, and so forth.

Second, NIS results are of interest for reasons of public policy. If lawmakers or regulators want to encourage innovation, in general or of a particular kind (e.g., biotechnology or software), the evidence suggests that they can influence the process. How money is spent, how laws are written and administered, how incentives are structured, and other such variables that can be influenced by government become important parts of a results-oriented national innovation system. Hand-in-hand with this, both for-profit and nonprofit organizations will want to direct their lobbying efforts to areas that have the most potential to positively influence their relevant environments.

The concept of NIS is intuitively appealing, particularly to those with practical experience in developing new products in different national environments, but what are we really talking about here in terms of managerial strategies and activities? Let's talk about a specific example.

Probably the most prominent comparison used in NIS discussions is between the United States and Japan. The two nations are at similar levels of development and per capita national income, and each has had a good deal of success in innovation (notwithstanding the economic ups and downs in both countries). The nature of the innovative output, however, is very different. While the United States tends to have a greater share of pioneering, or "new to the world," innovations, Japan's output tends to produce results regarded as incremental innovations, slight improvements on existing technology. Important exceptions exist, of course, but the data are fairly convincing over the long term.

Why do we see these differences? A number of factors have been proposed, including government procurement/defense spending in the United States as well as antitrust attitudes. But consider a couple of other factors, in particular, that have received quite a bit of attention in the past few years. One is the nature of the two patent systems, both of which protect inventions but differ in both statute and practice. In general, the Japanese system requires a much shorter inventive step in order to receive a patent. One observer characterized it as the difference between patenting a bicycle (under the U.S.

system) and separately patenting all the pieces of a bicycle (handlebars, gears, brakes, etc., under the Japanese system) (Klemperer 1990). Further, the Japanese system would likely allow a new patent to then be filed on a bicycle with a red seat and no other difference from the existing patented technology.

The Japanese patent system also sets up numerous administrative hurdles, allowing competing firms to challenge the validity of patent applications before, during, and after review at the patent office (this has been eased somewhat recently). Howard Spero's classic account of his small firm's experience with filing a patent in Japan details the number of obstacles thrown up by Mitsubishi, making it almost impossible to lawfully use the technology in Japan without cooperating in some manner with the entrenched domestic firm. Spero's company, Fusion Systems, filed a patent in Japan concerning a lighting system. The firm was protected by a similar single patent in the United States, from which no real protection problems arose. In Japan, however, Fusion Systems faced numerous pregrant objections and postgrant objections, administrative procedures initiated by the much larger Mitsubishi. Fusion Systems, with limited resources, had to reply to each in Japanese, often within very tight time frames. Further, when the patent was finally issued, Mitsubishi had "flooded" the core patent with dozens of similar but slightly different patents, preventing Fusion from using its own technology except in the very narrow circumstances described in its original patent (Spero 1990).

The bottom line is that the Japanese patent system is geared toward small steps, protecting pieces of new technologies, but rarely an entire technological domain, as U.S. firms are used to. Sharing of technology is encouraged, leaving firms and individuals with few incentives to take the big chances needed in order produce pioneering innovation. Even if a firm came up with something new-to-the-world, it would be very difficult to gain exclusivity in Japan. Firms like Fusion Systems are almost forced to cooperate with existing powers such as Mitsubishi if they want to bring new technologies to bear in Japan.

This apparent bias against risk-taking and "big" inventions is not surprising given the economic culture of the country. Entrepreneurship has never been viewed as a prominent Japanese trait. Indeed, the idea that the nail sticking out gets hammered down is readily apparent in the innovation statistics both inside and outside major firms. While individual inventors and small firms still have their place in the U.S. data (up to 30 percent of patents received), they are seldom seen in Japan (Helfgott 1990; Kotabe 1992).

Does a patent system or economic culture, all by itself, have this type of effect on an economy and its innovation output? Of course not, but the pieces (patent statute, administration by the Japanese Patent Office, economic culture) fit with the rest of the Japanese economic and social structure to provide a very different environment than what is found in the United States. The NIS of Japan is quite disparate from that of the United States, and the results are seen in the way innovation is pursued by affected companies and in the technological outputs.

And finally, coming back to managing knowledge and managing competitive intelligence, NIS studies suggest that trying to pursue the wrong innovation strategy in the wrong National Innovation System would be extremely difficult. In order to be effective, those setting strategy need to understand the legal structures, as well as governmental predispositions. The strategists need to know how systems are administered and the general state of social and economic attitudes. They need to identify, research, and understand the national factors that affect them. Those charged with managing knowledge assets, both developing them and protecting them, would be well advised to look at similar factors.

National Factors and Intelligence

KM and CI are also affected by differences between nations.

So can this approach be adapted to strategically managing knowledge and competitive intelligence? We believe so, and several pieces of evidence support this view. Initially, we can look at what is currently being done in the field of knowledge management, which is rapidly heading in a national/international direction. Second, we can review a number of contemporary examples that illustrate and reinforce the point.

Over the past couple of years, interest has moved from managing knowledge and assessing intellectual capital at the firm level to trying to evaluate the intellectual capital of nations. One natural outgrowth of such questions is determining the best environment (nation) within which to try to develop such knowledge assets. Alternatively, managers can ask whether their given national environment is conducive to their efforts. Some early evaluations were conducted for Sweden (Invest in Sweden Agency 1999) and Israel (Pasher 1999). As with the field in general, however, Leif Edvinsson kick-started interest in the topic, this time by simply asking how the IC concept could be transferred to nations, allowing us to evaluate the level of knowledge resources in different countries (Edvinsson 2002). Since that time, the OECD (2002) has attempted to assess IC across thirty different countries, and individual evaluations have been conducted for the Arab states (Bontis 2003) and Croatia (IBEC 2002), with more still to follow. In spite of this flurry of work, the actual measures used are still in a state of great flux, and no particular methodology has been established for work in the field.

The work tends to follow the generic IC formula, however, focusing on financial, human, process, market, and renewal/development capital. Financial capital is self-explanatory, whereas human, process, and market capital roughly correspond to human, structural, and relational/collaborative capital (not exactly but close enough for this discussion—interested readers can more deeply explore the constructs within the original articles and studies). Renewal and development capital is essentially a proxy for the future potential of IC.

What is particularly interesting from our perspective, however, are the actual data employed within the constructs. For human capital, for example, Pasher proposes education (advanced degrees, percentage of science and engineering degrees per all degrees and per workforce), equal opportunity (female students, women in the workforce), culture (book publishing, museum visits), and health (life expectancy, physicians, alcohol consumption, youth smoking). Bontis, on the other hand, uses education almost exclusively (literacy rate, number of schools, number of qualified teachers, graduates, new entrants), although he does break down some measures by male/female. In the process capital area, infrastructure measures such as communication and computerization (Pasher and Bontis), management, employment, and immigration (all Pasher) are all employed. Market and renewal are also similar in some ways, different in others—the former emphasizing market success, the latter emphasizing up-and-coming factors such as R&D spending and patents.

Again, the point is not that these measures are well established yet (one can certainly argue with a number of the definitions of what contributes to intellectual capital in a nation and what does not). The point is that academics and practitioners are starting to pay attention to what constitutes knowledge assets at the national level. From there, it is an easy step to an NIS perspective of what factors contribute to intellectual capital formation and what public policies are appropriate to a country seeking to develop its knowledge resources. Does schooling help? Then a nation that invests in education, especially science and engineering, can probably contribute to growing its own intellectual capital, and firms will have an easier time developing their own knowledge resources in such an environment. Do computer skills, PC penetration into homes and businesses, and Internet connections help? Then countries employing policies to encourage such behavior are also helping to develop knowledge assets, and, again, their firms will be better positioned.

Competitive intelligence has often focused on international issues and differences as well. In CI's case, with an approach of gathering any and all competitive information wherever possible, a tendency to identify nations and locations that lend themselves to data collection makes a lot of sense. Looser laws governing data-gathering methods, more laws requiring publicly available filings, and other such factors would clearly affect CI activities.

And just as with KM, attempts have been made to categorize global issues in CI. Elizondo and Glitman (2002), for example, suggest that CI is affected by national differences in social and cultural aspects, infrastructure (secondary data available, government support of firms, telecommunications), business processes and controls, and legal and ethical standards. The concept is very similar: National distinctions can influence how CI can best be practiced, how successful it can be, and whether firms can effectively protect themselves.

And from these perspectives it is only one more short step to the environmental analysis at the core of our discussion. As a firm surveys its circumstances at the national level, it can begin to ask itself whether the conditions are right for the educational structure (legal and cultural) necessary to train knowledge workers who will contribute to a knowledge management strategy. The same firm can assess the regulatory structure and determine if the reporting requirements lend themselves to competitive intelligence actions. The infrastructure can be reviewed with an eye to both KM and CI practices, as can the social/cultural environment. The basic point is that the fields of knowledge management and competitive intelligence are heading in the direction we propose, and existing work provides some suggestions for the factors that firms will want to review as they try to choose appropriate knowledge management and competitive intelligence strategies. When we take this background, combine it with the NIS and Eclectic Theory approaches, and then review what is actually happening in industry, we can begin to develop a framework that practicing managers can actually use in trying to turn knowledge into intelligence.

National Factors: Constructing a Framework for Strategy

What national factors do strategists need to review?

Government

Consider first the role of government in contributing to a firm's KM and CI environments. In terms of KM Risk, the key question is whether conditions are attractive for the creation and use of knowledge assets. In terms of CI Risk, we want to determine whether CI can be practiced in a relatively unhindered manner or if protections exist for proprietary knowledge. If CI is easily done, then KM may need to be scaled back or risk being lost to a competitor.

Governments can encourage the formation of knowledge assets by any number of mechanisms. The most obvious, and the area KM firms need to constantly monitor, are laws and regulations covering knowledge management as well as spending on related matters. From the studies just discussed, we can see that government supports and requirements concerning education, information technology infrastructure, R&D, and even government procurement can enhance the efforts of organizations seeking to develop their knowledge resources. In a more direct manner, government can create a positive environment for firms by encouraging, using, and creating standards for knowledge management. The efforts by OECD countries, for example, to focus attention upon and measure intellectual capital suggest that these governments value and support organizations that want to create and leverage their knowledge (OECD 2002). The United Nations Development Program that commissioned the study seeking to value the IC of the Arab nations also demonstrates a certain level of support (Bontis 2003). The Scandinavian countries, in particular, are known for their work in this area. In Denmark, for example, the Agency for Development of Trade and Industry, in line with national industrial policy, organized a study seeking to develop standards for creating and publishing intellectual capital accounts (Mouritsen, Larsen & Bukh 2002). Sweden also has government-backed initiatives in IC management and has been at the forefront of the efforts to standardize and make strategic use of knowledge assets (Edvinsson 2002). In the United States, prominent efforts, such as those of the Pentagon and, particularly, the Navy, to utilize and publicize knowledge management applications have started to create a more favorable environment for private firms looking to justify such programs (U.S. Navy 2001).

On the other hand, a government that fails to recognize the value and proprietary nature of such assets can be a problem. IMS Health, for example, is a U.S. company that makes money from collecting market information on the health care industry and selling this data to pharmaceutical companies and other interested parties. IMS developed a specific market breakdown for Germany, the "1860 brick structure," that divides the country into 1860 geographical segments. The firm surveys pharmacies within each brick, using the results as inputs for its commercial data product. The brick structure is copyrighted and seemingly preferred by clients, as competitors found it difficult to enter the market without providing the 1860 format. IMS refused to license the system to these competitors. After an unsuccessful court action, the competitors enjoined the European Commission to stop IMS from keeping the proprietary knowledge to itself. The Commission agreed, accusing IMS of "prima facie abuse of a dominant position," requiring it to negotiate licenses within a week or face mediation (Mitchener 2001). Although antitrust is always a difficult field to predict, the simple act of holding proprietary knowledge and keeping it from competitors (even if a monopoly) would not necessarily be considered a problem in the United States and other countries. Legal monopolies are granted all the time for patented, copyrighted, or other proprietary knowledge (e.g., Windows, Viagra). Only if the monopoly power were used for restraint of trade in some other manner would the red flags be raised. But regardless of a feeling for or against IMS in this manner, the point is that a firm needs to be aware of the tendencies of governments regarding the accumulation and use of knowledge assets. If IMS had anticipated the Commission's ruling, it might have managed its proprietary data-gathering system much differently.

Government also serves a critical role in protecting knowledge assets by determining the nature of the CI Risk curve. The statutes pertaining to intellectual property, to trade secrets, to economic espionage, or to anything else to do with proprietary knowledge are critical to a firm's protection strategies. With a strict, straightforward definition of what types of information and assets are proprietary and what types are not, organizations can identify their protectable knowledge assets that are proprietary and take the appropriate steps to ensure that these assets are exclusively retained.

Earlier in the chapter, we discussed how patent systems vary by countries, with seemingly minor differences resulting in quite different outcomes. A strong protection scheme can have a substantial impact on the quality and quantity of innovation in a country. This same perspective applies to softer knowledge assets. To illustrate, consider the U.S. Economic Espionage Act of 1996 (EEA). Trade secret law in the United States has traditionally been rather fuzzy, especially in terms of defining what a protectable trade secret is. The EEA does two things on a national level. Initially, it specifically defines trade secrets as something with actual or potential economic value, including

. . . anything of all forms and types of financial, business, scientific, technical, economic, or engineering information, including patterns, plans, compilations, program devices, formulas, designs, prototypes, methods, techniques, processes, procedures, programs, or codes, whether tangible or intangible, and whether or how stored, compiled or memorialized physically, electronically, graphically, photographically or in writing. . . . [18 United States Code § 1839(3) (Supp. IV 1998]

This is a much clearer and broader definition than what came before, and those in the field of knowledge management should recognize that this wording has the potential to protect just about anything that is defined as proprietary knowledge or intellectual capital. Critically, however, the law has a second component. Not only must the knowledge be valued, but the law requires "the owner thereof has taken reasonable measures to keep such information secret."

These two components create a starkly different statutory environment than what existed previously, especially for firms seeking advantage from knowledge management. If such organizations take the steps to identify and value knowledge (almost the definition of a knowledge management system), and if they make provisions to keep such knowledge to themselves, they are protected from competitors who may want to lift the information. This protection can even include FBI help, if appropriate. Firms in the United States have a very strong protection regime for their knowledge resources, providing less competitive intelligence risk than might be the case elsewhere.

In China, for example, not only are knowledge assets at risk, but property rights of all sorts are still subject to question. Knowledge doesn't have strong protections, and, indeed, there are concerns that the government itself (or at least state-owned firms) may be behind some episodes of appropriation. The introduction to this chapter noted the difficulties faced by New Balance in dealing with its Chinese supplier. Similar or even worse problems have been experienced by firms ranging from Lucent to Cisco, Sun to NEC (Morrison & McGregor 2003; Waters 2001; Wilke 2003). 3DGeo Development, for example, allegedly had its source code for a proprietary software program for identifying high potential oil and gas deposits stolen. A PetroChina employee undergoing training at the U.S. firm was accused of downloading the proprietary information and trying to leave the country with the code on his computer. A password-breaking program and high-capacity detachable storage drive were also found, the latter delivered by PetroChina officials when visiting the employee in the United States (Wilke 2003).

Other key governmental variables might include the number and depth of required regulatory filings (e.g., environmental records; Rice 2000), embassy support in foreign countries (Wheaton 2000), and distinguishing between what is legal/ethical CI and what is illegal/unethical espionage (Ehrlich 2002). The list is long, and experienced planners will likely find themselves adding to it with each analysis.

The intersection of these national laws, regulations, court decisions, and so forth, is also of interest and not necessarily straightforward. Companies operating in numerous countries need to keep track of the different factors affecting their KM and CI efforts, including variables such as where knowledge assets are most productively supported and where protection is strong or weak. Obviously, these sorts of considerations can get complicated. Boston Scientific, for example, was sued in the United States by an Israeli firm, Medinol, claiming the former created an Irish shell company to acquire technology (Tomsho 2001). Medinol was a supplier of Boston Scientific, exclusively providing high-tech stents. Boston Scientific, while negotiating to buy the supplier, allegedly created an Irish firm, BBD, and hired a British engineering firm to copy Medinol's manufacturing system. At the bottom of the convoluted scheme was an apparent strategy to carry out the plan beyond the reach and attention of the U.S. Food and Drug Administration (though Boston Scientific's ownership of BBD was also allegedly kept secret from Irish authorities). So the combination of the locations of the various players, the respective regulatory climates, and the knowledge protection laws resulted in this very confusing scenario.

So the bottom line is that firms looking to manage their knowledge resources strategically need to scan their environments for the governmental factors that support intellectual capital development as well as those that help to protect such acquired knowledge from competitive intelligence incursions. We'll develop a checklist of such factors shortly, but items such as government spending, intellectual property/capital statutes and court rulings, antitrust attitudes, economic espionage laws, regulatory agency powers and actions, international agreements (such as WTO membership), and so on, are important to review and understand. Armed with such information, firms can begin to assess the risk levels they face in terms of knowledge management and competitive intelligence.

Technology/Information Technology/Infrastructure

The current research on national assessments of intellectual capital stresses the underlying information technology and other infrastructure mechanisms that support the development of knowledge assets. Similarly, we'll discuss in later chapters how the Internet, new programming languages, and other such factors have resulted in a dramatic change in how firms and their collaborators share (and lose) knowledge across the Value Chain. Firms trying to gauge their levels of KM Risk and CI Risk need to examine these types of factors in their operating environments.

Factors such as Internet usage, PC market penetration, installation and use of ERP and other such platforms, use of information technology in schools, and other such measures will help strategists to determine their potential for developing intellectual capital. Similarly, as we also discussed earlier, digitization raises some concerns for protecting oneself from competitive intelligence, so these same measures will have some bearing on CI Risk, in addition to variables such as penetration of security software into the market and use of particularly vulnerable communications systems (such as wireless).

In 2000, for example, *BusinessWeek* published a lengthy article on why Asian firms, in general, seemed to lag behind U.S. firms in terms of Internet applications (Belson 2000). In the wake of the tech bust, the conclusions might not be as striking as they were thought to be at the time, but the underlying reasons for the gap remain (even as we recognize that Web applications remain important after the shakeout). The article stresses the lack of available technology in Asia, from Internet penetration (20 percent of employees in Asian companies versus 63 percent in the United States) to unreliable phone lines (let alone broadband). Similarly, banks have been slow to go online in Asia, and many transactions, even between businesses, remain cash or letter-of-credit based. Because of the lack of technological infrastructure, such transactions are not done at the Internet speed required of online networks. Venture capital is lacking, so the startups that often bring new software to B2B applications aren't developing as quickly. And the fabled long supply chains often found in Asian markets remain a fact of life, making full network connections among all Value Chain partners extremely difficult (combine many more partners with a much larger percentage of still unconnected or poorly connected collaborators, and you have a problem).

On the CI side, the infrastructure can also be important. As we'll discuss in later chapters, firms can be much more at risk from CI incursions simply because they have digitized a great deal of their operational information and routinely spread it throughout their e-business networks. And wireless, with attendant security concerns regarding electronic eavesdroppers, has opened up an even bigger can of worms.

In short, the infrastructure, including technology resources, human capital training resources, and even financial development, has the potential to significantly affect whether a firm can develop its knowledge assets to full advantage. As noted, these same factors will affect the application and effectiveness of competitive intelligence. Each should be assessed, as applicable, as organizations seek to judge the risk factors at the national level.

Economic Culture

Finally, beyond straightforward government and infrastructure factors, economic culture must be considered. When we discussed national innovation systems, we brought out the difference an entrepreneurial culture can make in terms of the type of innovation generated. Here, social and cultural factors that have an economic bearing are also important, factors we classify as part of economic culture. Economic culture is important not simply in the marketing sense of understanding customers (although that is a tangential concern, a part of the network's knowledge base), but more in terms of how culture affects business activities. Hofstede's (1983) dimensions, for example, could play a role in KM Risk, with factors such as masculine/feminine orientation or power distance affecting how knowledge is captured, shared, learned, and so on. In the article just discussed on Asian Internet development, for example, the tendency of communication in an organization to be unidirectional (downward) is cited as one of the problems faced by Asian firms. This would be a high rating on Hofstede's power distance index. If workers or lower managers are unused to giving feedback or suggestions back up the line, it will be difficult for them to accept that their personal knowledge is now something of value to the firm, something that should be passed back through channels. Although not from Hofstede, but as a related cultural issue, the article also cites language problems, since most knowledge-sharing software, B2B or otherwise, is in English. Better and easier communication can lead to greater knowledge asset development.

The development of knowledge assets also depends on a number of other economic culture factors, including willingness to share, willingness to work as part of a team, trust, power considerations, and other such variables. As a result, firms seeking to use knowledge assets strategically will need to evaluate these types of variables in applicable countries/cultures. If a culture is individual-based rather than team-based, workers and managers will be less likely to share information, decreasing the potential for knowledge management systems unless heroic steps are taken to get knowledge out of people. Similarly, if employees feel like the firm or its managers are not trustworthy, they will be more inclined to keep their knowledge to themselves. Were a manager to take credit for an employee's useful knowledge or were the organization to lay off individuals after encouraging them to develop knowledge and share it, workers would be far more likely to keep their knowledge to themselves. And where knowledge is associated with power, the problems will be similar. All of these factors can vary substantially by the country and culture involved. So a number of national economic culture issues exist in terms of gathering, codifying, and redistributing knowledge.

Similarly, economic culture can dramatically affect protection issues and CI Risk. In the heady days of the Internet gold rush, Europe and Asia were both markedly slower in pushing supply chains online. Part of the reluctance was quite likely due to weaker governmental and technological protection environments, already discussed, but part was also characterized as a general cultural lack of trust. In the case of Europe, firms seem to recognize the vulnerability of their information when placed online and in the hands of collaborators (Manchester 1999; Marsh 1999). Indeed, Marsh reports on an Arthur D. Little study that core firms are reluctant to share knowledge on inventory levels, for example, for fear that suppliers seeking to cultivate new accounts might deliberately pass it along. Similarly, a Cap Gemini Ernst & Young survey found that most "tier one" suppliers to automakers in Europe had not moved to the online supply chain network Covisint by midyear 2001, even though DaimlerChrysler, Renault, and Nissan (as well as Ford and GM, which both have extensive European operations) were partners in the system. The reason given was a lack of trust between the companies (Burt 2001).

In Asia, similar differences exist, suggesting both greater and lesser protection concerns. Sticking with the auto industry, for example, Toyota reportedly keeps some proprietary machinery in Japan that it will not install in other Toyota factories around the world because of security concerns (Mackintosh & Marsh 2003). So on one hand, an Asian firm feels more secure with the economic culture at home. On the other hand, like Europe, Asian firms have been slow to move to the Internet because of concerns about the security of shared information (Belson 2000). And consider the experiences of Volvo and Nestle in Korea (*Economist* 1999). The Swedish firm took a majority share in a Samsung subsidiary and transferred its "management transparency" system that shared financial information and operations improvement suggestions with and between employees. Given the tendency of employees to routinely share such knowledge when drinking with friends and family (some of whom might work for competitors), the system turned out to be a problem. Nestle had similar difficulties, including a copycat coffee product that appeared less than two weeks after its own innovation hit the market.

Economic culture and its implications are hard to define, let alone measure. It's an admittedly nebulous concept. But the tendency of a nation's people to keep or reveal information can clearly impact the ability of a firm to develop and protect its knowledge resources. As such, as hard as it might be, an organization needs to try to get a handle around how knowledge is handled by managers and employees in the countries within which it operates.

Back to the SPFs

How can we put national variables to practical use?

How does the national level relate back to the Strategic Protection Factors we discussed in the last chapter? As noted, the national environment directly affects KM Risk and CI Risk, the determinants of SPF. A national environment that does not support KM development or that makes it more difficult will cause KM Risk to be low. Alternatively, if KM development and reporting are encouraged, if information technology is in place and available for use, and if the national culture lends itself to sharing and teamwork, KM is more likely to be used and be effective. And in that case, any firm not building its own knowledge assets will fall behind, so KM Risk would be high, tending to increase a particular SPF. Similarly, a national environment that supports CI actions would increase the CI Risk faced by resident firms, also raising the SPF confronting them.

Consider the case of New Balance with which we opened the chapter. In the United States, where KM activities can be conducted under a fairly open and organized government, within an advanced infrastructure, and at least some favorable social/cultural aspects, the firm needs to share some knowledge or risk falling behind the Nikes and Reeboks who do use KM. But they also face some CI Risk because of the same factors. So they operate at a fairly high SPF (~45) and must manage accordingly, distributing some knowledge but also keeping some protected. In China, on the other hand, the conditions are not so favorable for KM, nor is its development as important, but CI Risk may be even higher because of less governmental protections and different social/cultural viewpoints (SPF ~30). In this case, knowledge has even less distribution and is protected just as much (if not more than) in the United States. The risks are high in both nations but of a different sort, and so the knowledge strategy differs by location.

How then does a firm determine the SPF reflective of each nation in which it is operating? Table 4.1 lists factors that help executives make this assessment. They consider each category of thought from the perspective of efforts that support knowledge creation and activities that indicate the need for protective measures. While this list is not exhaustive, it is inclusive to the point of being able to identify the potential for knowledge generation and the need for safeguarding.

By referring back to our earlier SPF scenarios, we can further see the impact of national environment. National environment, all by itself, does not determine the SPF conditions and appropriate strategy, but national variables do tend to increase or decrease KM Risk and CI Risk. So they contribute to an SPF classification and are a determinant when combined with industry- and firm-specific variables.

A country with a government that doesn't spend on developing knowledge assets (e.g., education, R&D), doesn't show much interest in supporting firms that do want to grow their knowledge, or that, through legislation, regulation, or judicial decisions, weakens the KM potential of all resident firms is not KM-friendly. If that country also fails to establish a communications and information technology infrastructure, it can further reduce KM aspirations. And if it includes social factors that preclude communication, understanding, sharing, and other such economic culture variables, it will not be an attractive location to try to develop knowledge assets. Firms operating in such an environment will face low KM Risk, at least in terms of domestic competition. And when combined with similarly low KM Risk inputs at the industry and firm levels, such firms would be classified as SPF 5 (Brilliance) or SPF 30 (Glass House), depending on the relevant CI Risk score, and should operate accordingly.

Alternatively, active support by a government for building knowledge assets, the presence of a state-of-the-art infrastructure, and a positive economic culture will increase the potential level for knowledge asset development and application. Again, combining such a

Table 4.1   National Variables Pertinent to KM Risk and CI Risk

Knowledge Development: National Variables	Effect*	Possible Measures
Government ■ Education resources ■ Laws and regulations relating to diversity ■ Openness to immigration ■ IC reporting (required, supported) ■ Government spending on R&D ■ Tax treatment for private sector R&D spending ■ Antitrust laws ■ Government procurement (of knowledge-supported products) ■ Any other governmental actions that affect the development of knowledge assets ☐ Legislation ☐ Regulation ☐ Court decisions ☐ For example, work for hire provisions—who owns knowledge created by employees?	+ + + + + + + + +/− +/− +/− +/−	Spending on K–12, college, postgraduate, number of graduates at all levels, number of science and engineering graduates. Percentages of underrepresented groups in the workforce. Net immigration. Number of public firms reporting IC in annual reports, government interest in and agencies supporting IC reporting. Government R&D spending levels, subjective assessment of tax treatment. Subjective assessment of governmental attitudes toward cooperation. Government spending levels in key purchasing areas. Subjective assessment of anything else that might be pertinent.
Infrastructure ■ Telecommunications ■ Information technology infrastructure	 + +	Fixed lines per capita, wireless capacity, Internet penetration and usage, broadband installations. Percentage of homes, schools, businesses using PCs; computing power of PCs, servers, etc.; use of enterprise software (ERP, SCM, CRM).

Continued

Table 4.1   National Variables Pertinent to KM Risk and CI Risk—cont'd

Knowledge Development: National Variables	Effect*	Possible Measures
Economic Culture		Hofstede's indices. Subjective assessment may be necessary in terms of how scores affect knowledge development. Subjective assessment of national tendencies in all the other variables.
■ Traditional measures (power distance, individuality, uncertainty avoidance, masculine/feminine)	+/−	
■ Social capital	+	
■ Team orientation	+	
■ Willingness to share	+	
■ Trust	+	
■ Power considerations	−	
■ Any other social/cultural factors that affect business in general and the development of knowledge in particular	+/−	
Any other national factor that might affect knowledge development	+/−	Subjective assessment
Knowledge Protection: National Variables	**Effect***	**Possible Measures**
Government		Subjective assessment of legal statutes, actions of agencies, and court decisions regarding patents, copyrights, trade secrets, as well as economic espionage. Subjective assessment of number and openness of reporting documents. Subjective assessments of remaining variables.
■ Intellectual property protection	−	
□ Economic espionage	−	
□ Openness (required filings)	+	
□ Embassy support	+	
□ Overall legal/ethical attitude toward CI	+	
■ Any other governmental actions that affect the protection of knowledge assets	+/−	
□ Legislation	+/−	
□ Regulation	+/−	
□ Court decisions	+/−	
□ For example, noncompete/ nondisclosure clauses in employment contracts		

Table 4.1   National Variables Pertinent to KM Risk and CI Risk—cont'd

Knowledge Protection: National Variables	Effect*	Possible Measures
Infrastructure ■ Telecommunications ■ Information technology infrastructure ■ Security systems 　□ Firewalls and other systems 　□ Limited access intranets 　□ Security software	 + + − − −	Fixed lines per capita, wireless capacity, Internet penetration and usage, broadband installations. Percentage of homes, schools, businesses using PCs; computing power of PCs, servers, etc.; use of enterprise software (ERP, SCM, CRM). Sales and installations of security systems, subjective assessment of quality.
Economic Culture ■ Traditional measures (power distance, individuality, uncertainty avoidance, masculine/feminine) ■ Social capital ■ Team orientation ■ Willingness to share ■ Trust ■ Power considerations	 +/− − + + − +	Hofstede's measures with subjective appraisal of impact. Subjective assessments of other factors. Note that the same factor can have opposite effects on development and protection.
Any other national factor that might affect knowledge protection	+/−	Subjective assessment

* +/− refers to the relationship of the variable with the relevant risk. A (+) indicates a positive relationship, so as the variable increases, so does the corresponding risk. A (−) indicates an inverse relationship, with the risk decreasing as the variable increases.

national environment with similarly positive variables at the industry and firm level would result in high KM Risk, with firms not taking advantage of such circumstances finding themselves at a considerable disadvantage to other firms that do. Such organizations would be considered SPF 15 (800-pound Gorilla) or SPF 45 (Cold War) and, again, should choose an intelligence strategy appropriate to that situation.

On the CI side, governments that don't require firms to publish a lot of internal information or knowledge, that have strong intellectual property or capital protection schemes, and/or that vigorously pursue espionage activities can significantly lower the risk of competitive intelligence incursions by competitors. Similarly, without an open communications or information technology infrastructure, the CI threat is lessened. And if the economic culture is such that trust is low, that sharing outside the firm isn't common, or that knowledge leakage just isn't considered ethical, then conditions are also less favorable to CI. Such a combination of scores on these variables, added to poor circumstances at the industry and firm levels, would lead to low CI Risk. Firms operating in this type of environment would have a classification of SPF 5 (Brilliance) or SPF 15 (800-pound Gorilla), depending on the relevant KM Risk score, with the associated recommended intelligence strategies.

On the other hand, the opposite conditions, including open governmental filings and weak intellectual property or capital protection, highly digitized infrastructure, and too open an economic culture, would lead to the opposite conclusion. Firms in such an environment, if combined with the right industry and firm circumstances, would face high CI Risk. These organizations would then face SPF 30 (Glass House) or SPF 45 (Cold War) conditions.

In terms of specific SPF classifications, definitive statements are difficult because conclusions will always depend on the total circumstances of the individual firm (it is an *eclectic* framework!), but a few general points can be made:

SPF 5: Just in Case, Brilliance as Hit or Miss

In this scenario, KM Risk and CI Risks are low. Knowledge assets are developed on an individual basis, with little support or interference from the government. Government support for knowledge development is limited, with little supporting legislation or regulation, little relevant spending, or other relevant governance. Protection regimes, however, are strong enough to discourage widespread pilfering of intellectual property or capital. The communications and IT infrastructures are likely weak, not allowing easy or reliable sharing, although what exists is protectable. Precisely because the technology doesn't allow wide distribution or sharing, competitive intelligence attacks are unlikely. The economic culture does not support sharing, learning, trust, or other such factors either, further diminishing knowledge potential. At the same time, however, CI attacks are unlikely to gain much, whether because the knowledge is individual or because trust and sharing don't exist. This can be a fragmented entrepreneurial culture where the individuals prefer to open small businesses rather than work for corporate entities. Larger firms operate in a tacit environment where the means of operation are known and success is driven by leaders, vision, and happenstance. This is a landscape of fragmented markets, small business owners, little advantage from knowledge asset development, and minimal CI activity.

SPF 15: Play It Safe, 800-Pound Gorilla and Symbiosis

In this situation, KM Risk is high and CI Risk is low to moderate. From a national perspective, this is a very conducive environment for the creation and protection of knowledge assets. Government statutes and regulations, spending, education support, and other such factors encourage the creation of knowledge and protect it through strong intellectual property/capital protection standards. In addition, there are incentives for innovation, a supportive technology and educational infrastructure, an entrepreneurial spirit, and a culture of trust and sharing evidenced in the sharing of knowledge assets across network partners. Power distance between layers of management is low, communication systems are well developed, technology is pervasive to the culture, and efforts have been expended in the creation of asset protection in software systems and corporate protocols. When these conditions exist, we expect to see industries with dominant firms, hard-to-copy knowledge advantages, and lots of other organizations surviving by avoiding direct confrontations with Gorillas.

SPF 30: Protective Cove, Living in a Glass House

This landscape has a low to moderate KM Risk and a high CI Risk. Laws, regulations, and court decisions don't really encourage the development of knowledge, nor do other factors such as government spending, education, and so forth. The technological infrastructure isn't conducive to the development of knowledge assets and network partnerships. Power distance is likely to be high, and the culture in general does not encourage teamwork or sharing. At the same time, competitive intelligence activity is encouraged by a lack of protection for knowledge assets, unsecured infrastructure, and/or poor relationships with employees that can result in disloyalty. This is the type of nation that can be supportive of basic needs but not one where proprietary technologies are shared with partners.

SPF 45: Total Block, The Cold War

This environment is challenging in that both KM Risk and CI Risk are high. In this nation, need to develop knowledge assets is high, whereas protection mechanisms to safeguard such assets are wanting. Government policy can be very encouraging of innovative activity, demonstrated by sponsored incentives, favorable tax policy, and a supportive infrastructure. The educational system supports the development of knowledge, and there's a culture of sharing. On the other hand, statutes protecting intellectual capital may not be as positive. Open regulatory filings, little regard for intellectual property as demonstrated by difficulty in prosecuting offenders, and nonsupportive court rulings all indicate open game on knowledge assets. Information is shared across networks but is not secure. Economic culture can be diverse, with enough trust, sharing, and other factors present to allow knowledge development but also perhaps too much trust and sharing outside the core organization (and, again, the potential for employee grievances to result in protection problems).

Summary

In taking a strategic approach to managing knowledge, decision-makers need to review their operating environment. On the one hand, if the prospects for developing knowledge resources are attractive, firms could be at a competitive disadvantage if they fail to pursue an aggressive knowledge management strategy while other firms push on. As noted, this is Knowledge Management Risk.

At the national level, the point is to review the conditions that may affect the attractiveness of expanding a firm's use of knowledge assets. These conditions can influence the identification, measurement, collection, codification, and/or redistribution of the assets. They may be a factor only inside the firm or throughout its value network. And as stressed repeatedly, as these conditions make knowledge management a more attractive strategy, the potential risk level goes up. A firm will operate at a decreasing point on its relevant risk curve as it expands its own KM activities.

Alternatively, these same conditions, and others, can affect Competitive Intelligence Risk. Firms need to review the environment within which they operate in order to determine the risk of losing proprietary knowledge to CI incursions by competitors. The germane conditions will determine the risk faced by firms as they conduct their own knowledge management activities. As CI becomes easier to practice or has fewer strictures placed on its users, the potential risk level increases. A firm will operate at an increasing point on its relevant risk curve as it expands its own KM activities.

This chapter has suggested several of the national-level variables that could face any given firm. In terms of government, the policies toward and expenditure on education, financial reporting regulations (and encouraging the reporting of "soft" assets whether required or not), government procurement, antitrust, intellectual property, and trade secrets can have a considerable impact on whether KM or CI Risks are high or low. Similarly, the level of technological development; penetration of PCs, Internet usage, and telecoms; B2B networking software; and other such matters can also influence one or both of the key risks. Finally, the economic culture, however measured and defined, can also have an impact. These concepts were more formally and specifically developed in the checklist, but the important point for now is that very real and very important factors exist at the national level that should influence how managers choose to develop their knowledge management programs. Prudent strategies will take account of these factors as the programs are constructed and executed.

Executive Moment

In thinking about how to strategically manage knowledge assets, one needs to understand the environment within which the company operates. How do you determine your SPF? Look at the conditions. A big piece of this environment includes the nation(s) where the firm has business operations or relationships. Ask yourself the following questions.

- Am I aware of all the laws, regulations, court rulings, and so on, that might affect how I develop and protect knowledge?
- Do I understand the potential impact of all these factors?
- Do I know these things about all relevant countries?

The number of variables at the governmental level that can affect knowledge management or competitive intelligence are considerable. And their impact may be complex. But ignoring them is no answer. Strategists need to develop a framework to review possible governmental factors and then manage knowledge assets accordingly.

- How does the state of technological infrastructure stack up in the countries in which we operate?

- How do technological developments affect our knowledge management and competitive intelligence activities?
- What do we understand about the "economic culture" of the countries in which we operate?
- Do these sorts of people-management factors affect our KM and CI activities?

Government is an important part of a national operating environment, but it is not the only critical category, especially with regard to KM and CI. Information technology, social and cultural variables, and related factors are also important, and, again, strategists need to account for them. Review the situation, determine the conditions and how they affect you, and then manage knowledge according to the appropriate SPF.

Review the checklist we've included to start identifying the factors that might affect your business. Then expand your perspective beyond the national level. Ask what other types of environmental variables might affect your knowledge assets. We next consider those at the industry level.

5

Determining an SPF:
Industry Considerations

The sun never shines on the poor.

—Richard Thompson

In 2000, Amgen was involved in a patent suit regarding its anemia drug Epogen. The audience at the trial was full of lawyers representing other biotech and pharmaceutical firms. Although the technical information revealed at patent infringement trials can sometimes be out-of-date, this proceeding concerned a protein used in production by Trankaryotic Therapies (Amgen's opposite in the trial) and was of great interest to competitors. Beyond the technical details, patent proceedings can also reveal legal strategies, management strategies and styles, and potential applications/target markets, so other biotech firms had good reasons to pay attention (Bennett & Mantz 2000).

In 2002, GlaxoSmithKline (GSK) sued Geneva Pharmaceuticals, a subsidiary of Novartis, claiming that the firm had inappropriately incorporated proprietary production methods into its process for making Augmentin. The drug had recently lost patent protection, but GSK suggested that Geneva had appropriated a strain of bacteria used in producing a generic version of the drug and that the bacterium was, in fact, a trade secret. A former GSK employee had stolen the bacterium, and it had somehow wound up in the hands of Geneva, as well as firms in Israel and India (Dyer 2002).

Pharmaceuticals and biotechnology are fields that feed on knowledge as their lifeblood, and the amount of activity involved in creating and protecting knowledge is matched only by levels of ongoing competitive intelligence. Chemo Iberica is a Spanish pharmaceutical manufacturer that attracted the attention of a number of major pharmaceutical firms when it introduced copycats of patented products into the Spanish market. During the early nineties, Spain still only granted process patents (this has since changed), and Chemo Iberica claimed that it had engineered new processes that did not violate existing patents. The patent holders were skeptical. Companies such as Bayer, Glaxo Wellcome (at that time), Merck, and Pfizer hired private investigators to dig up evidence that the Spanish firm had appropriated and was using their process technologies, and they later sued for patent infringement, along with then-SmithKline Beecham and Roussel Uclaf. Chemo Iberica, meanwhile, hired Kroll, a well-known security firm, to help it keep the other pharma firms' investigators out. Everything from dumpster diving to proselytized former employees, bugs to intercepted faxes, bribed government officials to fake companies became part of the episode, "sullying the reputation of the sleuthing industry" (Burns & Pilling 1999).

The obvious question is whether the value of knowledge and the level of competitive intelligence activity vary by industry, and the obvious answer is: Of course, they do. This chapter explores the questions managers need to ask concerning their industry as they assess KM Risk and CI Risk, as well as how industry factors influence the SPF and accompanying strategy. Are there factors in the industry that dispose firms toward using knowledge management, including competitive knowledge, such that organizations will be at a competitive disadvantage if they fail to pursue KM programs of their own? In terms of our previous discussion, are firms subject to more KM Risk given the way their industry is structured and operates? Alternatively, do industry variables exist making a firm more subject to competitive intelligence incursions? Answering these questions can help a firm to understand the level of the risks facing it, choose an optimal knowledge strategy, and take steps to support such a strategy given the risk levels.

Interaction with National Factors

Is this a national or industry variable? Does it matter?

Industry characteristics that may influence KM and CI strategies can go hand-in-hand with the national factors we discussed in the previous chapter. The pharmaceutical industry, for example, is heavily dependent on both patent law and the regulatory structure in place, much more so than other industries that may not be subject to an FDA or similar agency. Similarly, Boeing was accused, in 2003, of pilfering thousands of documents from Lockheed Martin relating to a large government contract. The violation was enough of a problem in terms of the far-reaching Economic Espionage Act, but Boeing also found it had violated an obscure law pertaining specifically to defense contractors (Squeo & Pasztor 2003). Those in the defense industry have particular responsibilities in terms of their acquisition and use of competitive information, making competitive knowledge an asset to be used with care.

Similarly, governmental standards, on several levels, exist concerning environmental compliance. But they do not affect all industries equally; some are subject to more stringent reporting than others. In the plastics industry, for example, a CI team was able, solely from public environmental records, to construct a site plan and process diagram, including specific machinery down to the screw size on extruders. A list of additives shedding light on material components was also obtained. As a result, the team was able to develop a highly accurate estimate of capital costs and prior knowledge of a change in target market by the competitor (Rice 2000). This type of open public record is just not available in all industries.

Technology infrastructure and economic culture at the national level can also affect industries differently. In Japan, for example, long supply chains are common in many industries. These distribution channels aren't really needed today, if they ever were, but remain a part of the Japanese business structure. As we will discuss shortly, the structure of a firm's Value Chain, including the supply chain, can have an enormous impact on its potential to use knowledge, as well as its ability to protect such proprietary knowledge. But the length and width of these supply chains can vary not only by industry but also by nation.

The point is that the categories of nation, industry, and firm, while neatly divided for this book, are not necessarily clearly defined categories. Some overlap is obvious. But whether a situation such as Boeing's belongs in the national variable group (government statute and interpretation) or the industry variable group (only applies to defense contractors) is immaterial to the main argument. What is important is that such considerations enter into the strategic planning process somewhere, that planners explicitly include all potentially relevant factors. Where the factors or variables are included is not the key matter. That they are included, wherever decision-makers might be comfortable including them, is.

Industries as a Unit of Study

Knowledge is used differently in different industries.

Chapter 3 examined specific industries—those with 800-pound Gorillas or Glass Houses, for example. To a large extent the idea that KM and CI Risk vary sharply by industry is an obvious concept, but how can we define those differences to allow practicing managers to analyze their own industries and situations? We'll talk about a basic framework shortly, but let's initially consider some examples of how industries vary in their use of knowledge and in the CI activities used to acquire knowledge assets.

In the airline industry, we had characterized the position of Southwest as low KM Risk, low CI Risk, and, therefore, suggested low SPF (Brilliance). This is generally true for the industry, given that it is a service with most of the operation right out in the open for all to see. Although some knowledge assets do exist and some CI activity does occur, the point is simply that both are less prominent than in other industries.

But the valuable and unique knowledge in this industry is generally seen in marketing efforts more than in other areas. Yes, financial results are important and reviewed by competitors, including costs (e.g., labor agreements), as are operational details (type of aircraft flown on specific routes). But the key knowledge is found in questions such as what marketing alliances are being constructed, what marketing tactics (e.g., promotions) are being employed, and how customers are responding. As a result, CI programs typically focus on monitoring competitor activities, Web sites, advertising, promotions, and so on. In trying to gauge the success of a competitive promotion, for example, one airline simply had employees stand at gates and count passengers boarding a competing airline. Deeper but still related information, such as market share and customer satisfaction, is also sought (Mysore & Lobo 2000).

In retail, on the other hand, with everything from Wal-Mart to corner stores as participants, the valuable knowledge and the CI techniques are quite different. We'll discuss modern information systems and their impact shortly, and readers should also note that marketing activities are monitored at retailers just like they are at airlines (right down to counting customers entering stores, if necessary, to gather information). But anyone who has ever had any contact with retailing knows that inventory is a critical factor in success or failure in the industry. One CI analyst suggests that inventory can be the key to discerning the standing of retailers, even if financial reports from the industry can be particularly untrustworthy (Yake 2001). Inventory buildup, shrinkage, abrupt changes in either, charges against inventory, and other such tipoffs in publicly available documents can provide important information to competitors, and, of course, close observation of the actual stores and inventory levels can also provide a wealth of information.

Finally, utilities are a good example of how an industry is changing as its external conditions have changed. At a time when they faced no competition, utilities tended to focus on political issues. Indeed, compared to other industries surveyed by The Futures Group, they were still much more concerned about regulatory environment as the most important external influence on their business (77 to 18 percent). Alternatively, other industry respondents, especially the largest, were much more concerned about competitive actions (55 to 20 percent) (Wing 1999). But utilities are starting to shift their focus more to customers and competitors, monitoring public documents such as annual reports and FERC filings for information about competitive activities. Some have also begun to develop internal reporting networks, including salespeople, and customer networks as devices for collecting information.

So industries do vary in their concerns. What type of knowledge is particularly important for a particular industry? How well do industry participants develop and deploy their knowledge assets? How serious a concern is competitive intelligence? What types of information are targeted by industry CI efforts? To answer such questions, one needs to be organized, and we suggest the following structure as a start.

Knowledge Industries

How important is knowledge in your industry?

Probably the key industry factor that planners need to consider when looking at their knowledge management strategy is the importance of knowledge to their particular industry. This is critical in terms of developing knowledge assets (KM Risk will be high if the tendency in the industry is to stress knowledge and an individual firm fails to do so) and protecting knowledge assets (if knowledge is critical for competitive advantage, the efforts of competitors to abscond with it may also be substantial, resulting in high CI Risk).

As we discussed in the last chapter, national issues have started to receive attention from KM scholars. Industry conditions have not seen a similar level of development, although the topic has been broached. One instance is McEvily and Chakravarthy's (2002) consideration of the source of knowledge-based competitive advantage. They proposed the factors complexity, tacitness, and specificity. Complexity refers to the difficulty of comprehending the knowledge. Tacitness deals with how hard the knowledge is to articulate as well as how personalized it is (similar to the standard definition of tacit knowledge used in intellectual capital discussions). Specificity has to do with whether knowledge is more useful at a particular firm.

While these types of factors are advanced by McEvily and Chakravarthy as firm-specific, they are obviously influenced by the type of knowledge useful in that firm's industry. And although carefully defined in academic terms, the factors are somewhat nebulous in everyday conversation and are not of obvious use to a working manager needing to assess knowledge potential and protection schemes. But they can be an extremely useful guide as we try to get our hands around what factors are important to consider, particularly at the industry level. As we look at an industry and the importance of knowledge in that industry, issues such as the complexity of the knowledge, the ability to capture it (tacitness), and transferability (specificity) start to address the key factors. While difficult to define, managers who grasp their descriptive power for the type of knowledge in their industries can begin an assessment of the industry variables that will influence intelligence choices.

So this conceptual approach can be a good start, but what are the more practical matters that would interest managers? Consider first the knowledge management side. One place to start is with the degree to which knowledge is tied up with firm valuations. The entire field of KM essentially started as an attempt by accountants and top managers to try to define and measure the intangible assets of corporations. Indeed, Tobin's Q predated even these efforts as economists tried to get their hands around the difference between market valuation and book value (of hard assets). While the measurement techniques and definitions have gotten better and certainly more specific, simply going back to the valuation "remainder" with which the field started can be a quick and dirty method to judge the importance of intangibles in an industry. When Microsoft, Oracle, and SAP all possess market valuations ranging into the hundreds of billions of dollars while holding limited hard assets, we know that the software industry highly values softer assets, including resident knowledge. This approach needs some interpretation, of course, as not all soft or intangible assets are intellectual capital (e.g., brands or image), but, again, it provides a good start for assessing the importance of knowledge in an industry. So to a certain extent, a manager can use common sense. Harder evidence (all relative to other industries) such as heavy investment in R&D, high numbers of patents or other intellectual property, levels of high-tech exports, and other such variables could be used to support such analysis. Industries relying on innovation or knowledge-added services would obviously value knowledge and have high-risk levels in terms of KM.

As mentioned, however, this is also an area where the KM Risk assessment and the CI Risk assessment can be done hand-in-hand. Industries heavily dependent on knowledge will often spur competitive intelligence efforts. Alternatively, indications of heavy CI activity imply that acquiring a competitor's knowledge assets is a priority. If prized so highly, this knowledge must be of some importance in the industry. So when we read about heavy activity in pharmaceuticals (as detailed earlier) or in information technology, we know that the firms behind the CI operations consider knowledge acquisition to be a competitive priority. In the latter case, IT companies noted in the press for acquiring or trying to protect knowledge assets read like a Who's Who of Silicon Valley and other high-tech locations, including the infamous Oracle/Microsoft dumpster diving case, Lucent, Sun, Intel, SAP, Seibel, and numerous others (Kerstetter et al. 2000; Wilke 2003).

The prevalence of CI in Silicon Valley illustrates a related point, that the presence of industry clusters may be an indicator of knowledge development potential and/or aggressive competitive intelligence activity. Industry clusters, concentrations of firms in the same business that grow up in a given area, are not necessarily a new idea but received increased attention as part of Porter's (1990) strategy work over the past couple of decades. Universities specializing in a research area important to an industry, a suitable workforce, close access to raw materials or key suppliers, and other such factors cause firms to locate together, still competing but also taking advantage of access to key competitive factors. In such situations, however, both knowledge management and competitive intelligence are likely to be high priorities, implying relatively high risk levels for both. Silicon Valley remains the obvious example, with firms seeking to better exploit their own knowledge assets while constantly fighting off competitive attempts to lift those assets. When Oracle hires away almost an entire engineering team from Informix, Seibel absconds with a number of SAP's U.S. managers, and some firms (Infinata) purposely locate out of the Valley in order to retain staff, we're seeing the cluster phenomenon at work and its effect on KM and CI (Kerstetter et al. 2000). Similarly, in geographical areas such as Philadelphia and Boston, where pharmaceutical firms are prominent, the risks of not developing KM capabilities and/or of succumbing to CI are also amplified

Another indicator of highly prized knowledge assets, as well as CI interest, is regulatory or court cases involving proprietary knowledge. Essentially, the assumption is that where there's smoke, there's fire. When enough interest exists to risk violating the law to obtain or pass along information, that information is likely to be especially valuable to firms in that industry. In the United States, everything from patent actions to prosecutions under the Economic Espionage Act (EEA) can be evidence of valuable knowledge. In the case of the EEA, for example, we have cases in which information is important enough to risk prosecution by acquiring it through questionable methods. Of the cases to date, we find everything from pharmaceuticals to label-making (Carr, Erickson & Rothberg 2004), although we do see trends. SIC's 35, 36, and 73 (machinery and computer equipment, electronic equipment, and business services—chiefly software, respectively), for example, make up a substantial number of the cases prosecuted through late 2003.

Similarly, interest in knowledge can be indicated by membership in professional organizations that relate to such matters. KM doesn't really have such institutions yet (though conference attendance might be a good proxy). CI, however, does. Competitive intelligence is represented by organizations such as the Society of Competitive Intelligence Professionals (SCIP), among others. We collected membership data from SCIP for a number of years in the mid-1990s. Sorting by SIC code from 1996, for example, we found pronounced differences between industries, with particularly heavy activity in communications (48), agricultural production/crops (1), rubber and plastics (30), leather (31), and depository institutions (60). Those with low SCIP memberships included transit (41), retail—building materials and home furnishings (52, 57), motion pictures (78), and social services (83). As before, heavy CI activity can be an indicator not only of competitive intelligence itself but of the perceived value of knowledge assets.

Finally, strategists need to be aware that industry conditions can also change. New entrants, technological disruptions, and similar occurrences can result in different risk situations. Indeed, CI has recognized that an ability to spot important technological changes coming can be invaluable to strategic planning (Hill & Dishman 2001).

So, all in all, strategists need to think about their particular industry and assess the value of knowledge to competitive advantage. Presumably, many experienced managers can do this intuitively, but if hard data are desired, they are available in common measures of intellectual property and capital such as intangible assets, patent filings, clustering, and similar such information. Also available is information on competitive intelligence activity in an industry, including EEA violations, SCIP membership, and similar measures.

Value Chain Coordination

How important are outside partners in your industry?

We noted in an earlier chapter that a broader definition of knowledge and knowledge management itself is appropriate in the age of the Internet and end-to-end enterprise management systems. Indeed, real-time information about what is going on in an organization's operational systems has the potential to be the most valuable knowledge asset possessed by a firm, and we'll discuss the details in a later section. Planners would be well advised to consider the degree of network coordination and knowledge sharing in their industry, both upstream and downstream, and how relatively tight or loose ties between collaborators help determine the nature of competition.

In retail, for example, Wal-Mart is well known for its highly efficient inventory and logistics systems that link up its individual stores with major suppliers, and we've already discussed the firm in some detail. 7-Eleven has also established a strong reputation for its electronic links and use of knowledge to improve its operations (*Economist* 2001). The Japanese firm's proprietary system can help discern customer preferences, allowing individual stores to cater better to their clientele's needs and even spot day-to-day trends in demand. As a result, quality, pricing, and new products are all better managed, and supply chain efficiency is legendary, with processing times in minutes and deliveries within hours of ordering.

So if one is to compete in today's retailing environment, unless efficiency and pricing are not a concern, some thought must be given to how knowledge is managed throughout the supply chain. A firm might develop such a competence on its own, as is the case with Inditex/Zara, which uses highly developed, geographically close inventory systems to rapidly transfer sales knowledge to production facilities (Vitzthum 2001). Or an organization might partner with someone else who has expertise in such knowledge-sharing systems in order to become more competitive. JC Penney, as mentioned in an earlier chapter, has reinvented itself as a leader in merchandise turnover and inventory management by partnering with one of its suppliers, Taiwan's TAL Apparel (Kahn 2003).

TAL makes and delivers Penney's own-label shirts. TAL's managers convinced Penney brass to let it make individual forecasts for all of the retailer's U.S. stores, determine inventory levels at each unit, and handle delivery to the individual locations. The result has been a sharp drop in inventory, from nine months' worth of goods held at times before the system was installed to virtually no warehouse inventory and half as much at the stores themselves. In order to accomplish this improvement, Penney had to tie the supplier into its POS systems, allowing all the sales data to be beamed directly to TAL in Taiwan. Without this close cooperation and sharing of to-the-minute operational knowledge, this type of activity couldn't occur nor these efficiencies be attained. And, again, a big part of the environment driving retailers to seek out such systems and such collaborations is the tremendous gains in efficiency achieved within the industry by competitors such as Wal-Mart, 7-Eleven, Zara, Amazon.com, and others.

Indeed, another interesting and prevalent trend in retailing is the emergence of category management (Desrochers, Gundlach & Foer 2003). Retailers have taken to giving management of an entire category of goods (e.g., laundry detergent) over to a favored supplier, allowing that supplier to determine things like merchandising, pricing, promotions, and so on, for itself and for its competitors (e.g., Procter & Gamble makes decisions for all detergent products in a given grocery store). The retailer turns over its detailed POS information and management control, while the supplier uses its embedded knowledge of the category (including more experienced, more educated, and more specialized managers/analysts than would typically be found in the stores) to help sales for everybody. Given the retailers' obvious preferences to offer consumers choice within the category, any overt attempts to favor the lead supplier's products over others would likely be dismissed, but concerns do exist over these suppliers' biases for their own goods. Aside from such issues, the logic of the system is again that information and knowledge sharing benefit all partners, even expanding the category for all competitors. And again, the practice is a growing trend within the industry that may very well spur many retailers to adopt such systems if they are to be competitive.

So in moving to an intelligence approach, part of the industry analysis needs to focus on how much knowledge sharing goes on between value network partners. Do public exchanges exist, such as Covisint in the auto industry? How advanced are they, and how universal is their membership? Are private network structures used, with proprietary information shifted between trusted partners? Regardless of the system, are they simply exchanges of data, or are they sources of knowledge or even intelligence? Does knowledge analysis occur? How is the information or knowledge applied? The more that knowledge sharing of this type is a factor in an industry, the greater the KM Risk, as any individual firm choosing to keep its information and knowledge to itself will run the risk of competitive disadvantage. Similarly, the greater the collaboration, the greater the CI Risk, not only because of the obvious importance of the knowledge (and competitors' consequent desire to acquire it) but because it passes through so many more heads, both inside and outside the core firm.

Competitive Arena

What drives competitive dynamics in your industry?

Beyond the importance of knowledge in Value Chain coordination, other industry factors can enter into the mix. Here, we consider a few key indicators for determining industry dynamics and the level of rivalry (i.e., intensity of competition). In general, the importance of knowledge increases with rivalry, since well-managed knowledge assets can spell the difference in a hypercompetitive environment. We can also expect the level of competitive intelligence activity to increase. Firms will pay more attention to what competitors are doing when the stakes are highest and changes in industry conditions imply that margins and share will be harder to achieve and maintain.

Industry structure or concentration, for example, can be an important element of the competitive environment, as the example of 800-pound Gorillas in Chapter 3 suggests. A highly concentrated industry or an industry with a single dominant firm has very different competitive conditions than a fragmented industry. Firms in consolidated industries will watch each other more closely than those in industries without clear leaders. And consolidation issues such as merger and acquisition activity can obviously impact this equation. Darveau (2001), for example, argued that Rolls-Royce's acquisition of Vickers in 1999 was predictable by employing standard CI practices. Within industries, concentration in the Value Chain can also be a factor. An industry with an 800-pound Gorilla can be surrounded by a more fragmented group of partners. The fragmented supplier industry might face a substantially different risk situation than its symbiotic customer, although that relationship would also be a risk issue.

The stage of the industry's life cycle is also a factor. As an industry progresses from birth to maturity, information becomes more diffuse, both to competitors and consumers. During the introductory and growth stages, knowledge concerning innovation, cost reduction, marketing plans, and so on, can be vital to firms in the young industry. As the life cycle curve flattens into maturity, consolidation takes place, though rivalry often decreases, since competition can become less bloodthirsty. Knowledge can still be important, even if not as dramatic in scope, as firms seek to differentiate themselves in the mature market. Competitive intelligence activity could be high or low in different stages of the life cycle, with the emphasis on new product development, marketing plans, operations, and so on, during the early stages. During the later stages, knowledge concerning brand extensions, network relationships (suppliers, distribution partners), and sales promotions could be of great interest to competitors.

Another set of factors that influence competitive rivalry in an industry is the power of buyers and suppliers, and the threat of substitutes and new entrants—for example, Porter's Five Forces Model (Porter 1979). Even if current competitors don't demand the fullest use of knowledge or effective CI systems, possible entry by more threatening potential competitors can substantially increase the importance of both KM and CI in an industry. And obviously, if new competitors are a possibility, firms will need to scan their environments constantly, collecting information on the threat of entry and the strengths and weaknesses of the top suspects.

Overall, while the preceding discussion certainly isn't exhaustive, it brings to light some of the competitive issues that can affect the KM Risk and CI Risk levels of the firm's industry. In general, rivalry will increase the importance of both types of risk, although the degree would remain an open question.

Back to the SPFs

Think back to the pharmaceutical industry featured in our opening vignette. The industry is heavily dependent on knowledge, with innovation the source of profits for most firms. This fact can be verified by looking at such objective measures as patents, investment in R&D, ratio of tangible to intangible assets on balance sheets, and so forth. And Value Chain coordination has been increasing in the industry, including acquisition, as both development (allying with biotech firms in the search for new drugs) and delivery (prescription management systems) have become more incorporated into the industry structure. Pharmaceutical firms also widely share R&D techniques and production processes across locations within companies. Knowledge is a key asset in terms of competitive advantage, and industry participants manage it carefully. KM Risk is high. And the importance of the knowledge, the lack of a dominant firm (the largest pharmaceutical firm holds only about 14 percent of the market, and perhaps a dozen have 5 to 14 percent market share), the transferability of this kind of knowledge, and its wide distribution throughout firms and partners also make CI Risk very high. Pharmaceutical firms, by and large, face the Cold War as they evaluate their SPFs and plan strategy. National and firm factors will also contribute to this, but industry is an overriding factor for most of these firms. Their SPF should include reasonably wide development of their knowledge assets but also establishing tight controls and counterintelligence systems to protect their resources.

Generally, industry factors can affect knowledge asset development in a number of ways. Some of the variables we suggest reviewing are included in Table 5.1. Industries not subject to stringent government reporting requirements or disclosures, particularly affected by the lack of a national technology infrastructure or particularly impacted by a national economic culture, will have lower KM Risk. In addition, if the terms of competition of an industry don't depend on transferable knowledge or if knowledge assets are generally unimportant, KM Risk will be similarly lowered. And if Value Chain coordination and knowledge sharing are of minimal importance or if intensity of competition is low, similar results will accrue. All in all, scoring a checklist with such factors will lead to a conclusion that knowledge assets development is difficult or unimportant in a given industry. If so, the firm faces relatively low KM Risk if it fails to pursue knowledge assets aggressively. The result, as before, would be classification as SPF 5 (Brilliance) or SPF 30 (Glass House), depending on the CI Risk result.

Alternatively, positive government laws, regulations, and court decisions; a great technology infrastructure; or an economic culture that affects a particular industry will increase KM Risk. Heavy dependence on knowledge assets or on competitive weapons that are knowledge-related, close Value Chain coordination, and heavy intensity of competition will all result in higher KM Risk. Combined with national and firm factors, this could place the firm with an overall high KM Risk level. Consequently, any such firm would be

Table 5.1   Industry Variables Pertinent to KM Risk and CI Risk

Knowledge Development: Industry Variables	Effect*	Possible Measures
Interaction with National Variables	+/−	Subjective assessment. Do any of the factors discussed in the previous chapter (and in the previous checklist) particularly affect your industry in developing knowledge assets?
Knowledge Use ■ What are the bases of competition? ■ Which firm activities are most important?	+/− +/−	Subjective assessment of what is important for competing in this industry, what kind of knowledge is required.
Knowledge Industries ■ Nature of knowledge (complexity, tacitness, specificity) ■ Value of knowledge in an industry ■ Clusters	− + +	Subjective assessment of how difficult knowledge is to comprehend, how difficult to share, and how closely associated with a specific firm. Objective measures of valuation include market/book value, heavy R&D spending, patent rates, high-tech products/exports. Subjective assessment of whether geographic industry clusters exist.
Value Chain Coordination	+	Subjective assessment of how closely industry firms are tied into Value Chain partners (suppliers, vendors, other collaborators) and how much knowledge is shared.
Competitive Arena, Level of Rivalry ■ Industry structure/ concentration ■ Life cycle stage ■ Threat of new competitors	 +/− +/− +/−	Subjective assessment of ferocity of competition. Objective measures such as Hefferdahl Index, market share percentages, growth rate in total industry sales can help.
Any other industry specific factors that affect knowledge development	+/−	Subjective assessment

Continued

Table 5.1 Industry Variables Pertinent to KM Risk and CI Risk—cont'd

Knowledge Protection: Industry Variables	Effect*	Possible Measures
Interaction with National Variables	+/−	Subjective assessment. Do any of the factors discussed in the previous chapter (and in the previous checklist) particularly affect your industry in protecting knowledge assets?
Knowledge Use ■ What are the bases of competition? ■ Which firm activities are most important?	+/− +/−	Subjective assessment of what is important for competing in this industry, what kind of knowledge is required, and how hard it may be to protect.
Knowledge Industries ■ Nature of knowledge (complexity, tacitness, specificity) ■ Value of knowledge in an industry ■ Clusters	− + +	Subjective assessment of how difficult knowledge is to comprehend, how difficult to share, and how closely associated with a specific firm (all make it less valuable to a competitor). Objective measures of valuation include market/book value, heavy R&D spending, patent rates, high-tech products/exports. Industry interest in knowledge might be indicated by high SCIP membership rates, high number of EEA violations in the industry. Subjective assessment of whether geographic industry clusters exist.
Value Chain Coordination	+	Subjective assessment of how closely industry firms are tied into Value Chain partners (suppliers, vendors, other collaborators) and how much knowledge is shared.
Competitive Arena, Level of Rivalry ■ Industry structure/concentration ■ Life cycle stage ■ Threat of new competitors	 +/− +/− +/−	Subjective assessment of ferocity of competition. Objective measures such as Hefferdahl Index, market share percentages, growth rate in total industry sales can help.

Table 5.1   Industry Variables Pertinent to KM Risk and CI Risk—cont'd

Knowledge Protection: Industry Variables	Effect*	Possible Measures
Any other industry specific factors that affect knowledge development	+/−	Subjective assessment

* +/− refers to the relationship of the variable with the relevant risk. A (+) indicates a positive relationship, so as the variable increases, so does the corresponding risk. A (−) indicates an inverse relationship, with the risk decreasing as the variable increases.

considered to be operating under conditions of SPF 15 (800-pound Gorilla) or SPF 45 (Cold War), depending on the CI Risk result.

Regarding that CI Risk, negative government factors (e.g., little forced disclosure, strong protection laws), a closed or limited technology infrastructure, or a closed economic culture that specifically impacts an industry will lower CI Risk. Similarly, few knowledge assets or bases for competition that don't benefit much from knowledge will also lower CI potential, as will weak Value Chain coordination or a low level of rivalry. Consistently low assessments on all these ratings would result in an overall low CI Risk evaluation when combined with equivalent low national and firm evaluations. The resulting classification would be SPF 5 (Brilliance) or SPF 15 (800-pound Gorilla) when combined with the KM Risk result.

On the other hand, positive government factors, strong technology infrastructure, or an open economic culture that affects a particular industry will raise CI Risk, making CI actions more likely. If knowledge is critical to the industry or the means of competition, if Value Chain coordination (and sharing of knowledge with partners) and rivalry are high, then CI Risk will again increase. Combined with similar assessments at the national and firm level, the overall CI Risk would also be considered high, and the resulting classification would be either SPF 30 (Glass House) or SPF 45 (Cold War).

As in the last chapter, some prospective SPF scenarios come to mind.

SPF 5: Brilliance

The Brilliance industry is one where knowledge management and competitive intelligence risks are low to moderate. This is an industry with transparent processes (airlines) or star systems (artists), and no great reliance on networks. Structure can be fragmented (nail salons) or tight (airlines), but there are no clusters. Resources are not focused on developing a full palate of knowledge assets or on protecting them as operations are open for all to see. Instead, resources focus on the marketing function. The life cycle stage can be either startup or mature. Rivalry varies depending on concentration and growth stage. More mature concentrated industries will have greater rivalry than fragmented or introductory industries, but overall risk of both types remains low to moderate. The threat of new entrants and substitutes in either case is low.

SPF 15: 800-Pound Gorilla

The 800-pound Gorilla is a scenario where knowledge management risk is high and competitive intelligence risk is low to moderate. Knowledge is important to success in the industry, but its potential applications vary by who the player is. The development and leveraging of knowledge assets across the value network can also be important to industry success. Processes have some transparency, yet their inner workings are held close to the chest and protected. Power rests with the firms, the Gorillas, that are essential to the survival of symbiotic firms and untouchable by smaller competitors. Industry life cycles are more mature and the structure of the industry can have tiers, the dominant Gorilla and the perhaps more fragmented symbiotic firms. The life cycle stage tends to be growth or maturity.

SPF 30: Glass House

The Glass House, where CI Risk is high and KM Risk moderate to low, is a transparent, perhaps regulated industry where certain types of knowledge assets are more important than others. Patents may be sought to protect processes, as is the case with JP Morgan Chase, or client relationships protected through noncompete agreements and controlled sharing of client knowledge across the Value Chain, divisions, and alliances. There can be clusters. What matters competitively are positioning and the ability to create real or perceived differentiation. Networks are less important, and if capabilities or Value Chain functions are needed, they are usually acquired rather than created organically. This is a fast cycle, hyper-competitive industry, consolidating, with intense rivalry. There may be many segments in different stages of concentration, but they all face slow growth or maturing markets with knowledgeable and discriminating consumers who have numerous choices and low switching costs.

SPF 45: Cold War

Cold War means that both risks are high. Knowledge needs to be developed and protected, as it is critical to success and rivalry is con-tentious. Although some levels of regulation and reporting require-ments exist, this is not a particularly transparent industry. Instead, it is one where networks are created yet secrecy expected and legally delineated. There may be clusters where rivalry turns as much on enticing competitor personnel as it does on gaining market position. This industry can be in growth or maturity. All knowledge assets are extremely important, needing development and protection. Patents, trade secrets, disclosure agreements, noncompete agreements, and reliance on economic espionage enforcement are often of critical importance. Because the industry is fraught with rivalry, protection against competitive intelligence incursions is crucial.

Summary

Strategists seeking to assess how to best manage their knowledge assets will find industrial factors an important component of the process. Although firm-specific analysis will always deal with strengths and weaknesses *vis à vis* competitors, a general sense of what is happening in an industry, the terms of competition, and prominent trends will be critical to determining how risky it is to develop or not develop an intelligence capability.

On the knowledge management side, if intellectual capital is important to firms competing in a given industry, then one had better develop such resources. Falling behind in such a key competitive weapon, if it is used in the industry, is tantamount to commercial suicide. Managers will presumably be able to intuitively grasp the importance of knowledge in their particular field, but such objective measures as high market capitalizations without accompanying hard assets, high levels of investment in R&D, high levels of science and engineering employment, intellectual property filings (e.g., patents), or high-tech exports may be relevant to the analysis. Significant competitive intelligence activity would also be indicative of both the importance of knowledge development and the threat of CI itself. So factors such as EEA (or similar) prosecutions, SCIP membership by industry, and so forth, would be pertinent measures.

Another critical consideration is how tightly the value networks in industries are tied together. When operational and other knowledge is freely shared and applied across organizational boundaries, both types of risk will again increase. If other firms in the industry are gaining competitive advantage from close relationships and information or knowledge sharing with suppliers, customers, and other collaborators, an organization can be at tremendous risk if it chooses to go its own way. KM Risk will be high. Similarly, when so much sharing goes on within an industry, the risks of having such knowledge fall into the wrong hands will also be amplified, so CI Risk will also be high.

Executive Moment

In evaluating your industry, consider how knowledge assets and competitive intelligence might figure into your planning processes. Ask yourself questions such as the following.

- Are there any governmental or other national factors that particularly affect knowledge development or competitive intelligence in my industry?
- How important is knowledge in my industry?
  - ☐ Are intangible assets an important source of competitive advantage?
  - ☐ Do the top firms use knowledge strategically and tactically?
  - ☐ Is the knowledge of use to others, useful enough to make competitive intelligence an effective option?
- How important are knowledge-sharing networks in my industry?
  - ☐ Do firms benefit from tight coordination of the Value Chain?
  - ☐ Is this coordination accomplished by vertical integration or partnering?
  - ☐ Does wide sharing of knowledge put firms in my industry at risk from competitive intelligence?
- What are the competitive dynamics in my industry?
  - ☐ How concentrated is the industry? Is there a dominant firm? Are there several major players? Is it highly fragmented? How are partner markets structured?
  - ☐ Where is the industry in its life cycle?
  - ☐ Are any new players likely to enter the field (suppliers, vendors, substitutes, or new entrants)?
- Do any other industry-specific characteristics exist that will affect how we (and our competition) use knowledge?

As one scans and analyzes an industry, typical concerns such as rivalry, concentration, or consolidation can be germane to employing intelligence. Managers need to be aware of the common rules of the game in their industry, as well as the opportunities to break the rules for competitive advantage. So analyzing one's own firm and the competition to see how knowledge is used, both within and without the core firm in a Value Chain, is an important step in planning a knowledge strategy. And identifying how competitive intelligence is or can be used is just as important. As before, a starter set of possible questions can be found in the accompanying checklist.

Industry variables will face all firms in a given industry, and all will be subject to what is going on around them. But the factors may affect them differently. Indeed, firm-specific variables will play a big part in how the national and industry factors play out. So the third level of factors is critical to a complete analysis, both in combination with the other levels and in and of itself. We consider the firm and its unique characteristics in the next chapter.

6

Determining an SPF: Organizational Considerations

I think it's going to rain.

—Randy Newman

As strategists attempt to determine how much to develop and protect their firms' knowledge assets, they need to pay attention to a number of variables at the national and industrial levels that define their unique level of risk. As with any such environmental assessment, however, the circumstances facing an organization include not only those that are fairly generic for any participant in that business but also those that are truly unique to the individual firm. Any level of strategic planning will call for a good, honest assessment of the strengths and weaknesses of the firm in question when measured against its competitors. Moving from knowledge to intelligence is no exception. Indeed, an eclectic approach demands it.

Intel, the renowned semiconductor manufacturer, conducts a program called "Copy Exactly" in its processing facilities around the world (Clark 2002). Technicians referred to as "seeds" are charged with duplicating existing facilities down to the last operational detail when new plants are opened. Supplies, machinery, worker techniques, and even such mundane factors as wall paint are copied in every location. The point is to transfer best practice knowledge, of whatever type it may be, around the multiplant corporation.

The result is, as you might expect, highly consistent, highly efficient output. Moreover, if problems do occur, expertise can quickly be applied to provide an answer. Similarly, knowledge can be transferred from one location to another to improve processes, even if no obvious issues exist. In one case, defect anomalies between two identical tools were traced to cleaning procedures (wiping in a circular manner as opposed to back and forth) after workers using the tools were switched between the plants. Similarly, another process irregularity between two plants was attributed to a better quality of oxygen used in one of the plants. By identifying differences between locations and then transferring the knowledge from the better performing unit, Intel has been able to formalize and embrace a best-practices knowledge management system.

But not all firms would be able to successfully manage such a system. Intel starts ahead of the game, of course, simply because it has the financial resources to conduct the program. Its size is also important in terms of the number of identical manufacturing lines it runs, something that is fairly rare, even among large firms. Auto firms, for example, will often have only a single facility or even a single assembly line dedicated to a particular brand or model. Other microprocessor manufacturers, much smaller than Intel with its 85 percent market share of PC chips, obviously don't have such a capability. Intel's manufacturing quality and efficiency levels are already high enough that it can afford to sweat small details such as these as it seeks ever better performance. The firm is also a unique mixture of command structure and employee input that is flexible enough to take in employee suggestions but forceful enough to install and discourage experimentation with best practices. Other unique factors exist, but the basic point is that Intel's circumstances are such that it can and does pursue knowledge management at a highly developed level, even if it doesn't necessarily refer to the program in that manner. And it does so in an environment where the threat of competitive copying is very real. AMD runs a similar program called "Copy Intelligently" that almost certainly borrows from Intel. But Intel has undoubtedly weighed the risks, benefits, and costs of conducting knowledge management to this degree and pushes ahead anyway. The firm also undoubtedly has some counterintelligence processes in place to try to keep its knowledge advantages to itself.

So what factors do firms need to review if they are to evaluate their own eclectic circumstances regarding knowledge management and competitive intelligence? A number of variables we already know from the existing literature concerning each field, but a few are less obvious. Let's examine several in turn.

Interaction with National and Industry Factors

Examine your firm here or examine it there, but do examine it.

As was the case between industry and national factors, firm factors will have some relation to the areas we have already discussed. At the national level, for example, firms with experience operating within a particular regulatory environment may have developed unique talents in dealing with that environment—for example, handling FDA requirements. Similarly, experience with protecting trade secrets under a given national law may allow a firm to pursue the development of knowledge assets to a greater degree without consequent worries about competitive infiltration.

And on the industry level, the main consideration is how the firm stacks up against industry practice. If the industry tends toward a lot of integration along the supply chain—including knowledge sharing, for instance—the firm needs to evaluate its supply chain integration and its ability to effectively and comfortably pass knowledge along to collaborators. It should be noted, however, that in this regard, firms still need to strategize and draw their own conclusions from what they find in the environment. One source of marketing advantage has always been to perform according to the industry paradigm better than anyone else. But another source is to bust the paradigm. How do you sell PCs better? Go away from the established distribution system, as Dell did. How do you do a better job with air travel? Change the offering with different operating procedures, locations, and pricing, as Southwest did. This approach surfaces in intelligence as well. The Covisint structure built to support the auto industry by sharing information between the big manufacturers and their suppliers has always had the curious absence of Toyota among its participants. The Japanese firm seemingly chooses to go its own way in terms of its value network and the information it shares throughout it. Similarly, Wal-Mart always stayed out of proposed retail exchanges, claiming advantages and relationships in hand that it had no intention of sharing (Ansberry 2000). Indeed, the huge retailer recently pulled out of market research agreements with AC Nielsen and IRI. The two research organizations aggregate POS information from the retail industry, processing and selling it to manufacturers and others. Wal-Mart "concluded that manufacturers need data from Wal-Mart more than it needs sales data from its competitors" (Barnett, Dalton & Thompson 2001: 26). Industry structure and other such variables are important factors in making strategy and certainly influence how one evaluates firm-level variables. But there should be no immediate rush to judgment that the optimal strategy for all circumstances is to conform to the industry standard when it comes to knowledge management or competitive intelligence. As with all factors, it really depends on the environment, including the characteristics of the firm itself.

Resources

What do you have or not have versus the competition?

One obvious set of variables that will affect a firm's ability to develop and protect knowledge assets is available resources. Intellectual capital studies, from their earliest appearances until today, have often focused on the organization itself. Indeed, interest in IC on the national level is only now emerging, and, as noted, industry issues have rarely been explored. Although some of these factors, such as R&D intensity, are industry-specific as well, they will vary by firm within an industry. One study, for example, suggested that size, profitability, and R&D intensity are all indicators of the likelihood of an individual firm to use and report knowledge management efforts (Beaulieu, Williams & Wright 2002).

Similarly, the innovation literature is chock full of studies as to the type of firm and the type of practices employed, examining how such variables affect success in new product development. Everything from available capital to size (plus and minus, as we'll discuss shortly), diversity to entrepreneurial spirit, ability to form alliances to possession of product champions who will shepherd new products throughout the development process have been examined in some detail. Note that some of these are very concrete and measurable. Others are more qualitative, the type of soft variables difficult to identify and measure but that may make a big difference to an effort to develop and protect knowledge assets. And all these factors, of course, will influence the KM and CI Risk levels facing a firm.

The KM literature itself often deals with similar soft or cultural factors that seem critical to successful programs. Trust and power, for example, are important generic management topics that are absolutely essential to KM efforts (Bontis 1999). Sharing knowledge, both within and without organizations, requires trust between partners, as the individual or organization surrendering its tacit knowledge to the system gives up some personal power. This individual or organization trusts that the knowledge will be properly used, trusts that the source of the knowledge will not be ill-used (e.g., terminated) after making a valuable contribution, and trusts that the gesture will be rewarded or reciprocated in some way. Further, formal power brokers (managers) need to be receptive to the usefulness of knowledge coming from informal power brokers (e.g., line workers).

Blackmer/Dover Resources, for example, manufactures heavy-duty pumps (Aeppel 2003). One line worker at the factory is uniquely talented at cutting metal shafts for pumps, a task that requires a high degree of accuracy. He is also "hours faster" at setting up his machine tool when changing over for different types of shafts. But he refuses to share any of his accumulated knowledge on how to make accurate cuts or do quick setups because "management could use [them] to speed things up and keep me at a flat-out pace all day long." He also fears being moved between different jobs if he shares his knowledge on how to do his own. Other workers fear downsizing or job losses if knowledge helps increase productivity or can be transferred to plants in other locations. So because of a lack of trust in management, workers will sometimes keep their personal knowledge to themselves, refusing to share because of the power they then retain.

The flip side of the coin, at the same plant, is an assembly worker who is often used as a troubleshooter because of his in-depth knowledge of how to make things work better at the facility. After outside consultants changed the assembly process from cells (with a single worker executing all activities) to a line (with several workers each performing limited tasks), deliveries slowed, costs increased, and worker dissatisfaction jumped. Workers were then given input into improving the process and, while the assembly line was kept, numerous changes were made, including how to move the pumps around the area. The assembly worker in question, who participated in the changes and willingly shared knowledge, noted that "the most frustrating part of sharing your ideas is when nobody listens." So a trust component also exists in terms of whether the knowledge is used properly and effectively when it is surrendered. And being recognized as a source of knowledge is, of course, a different but equally valid route to power.

While the preceding examples refer to tactical issues, the same dynamics hold for the generation of intelligence regarding strategic issues. Whether using shadow or intelligence teams, or serving as a knowledge expert, people have to trust that their contribution will be used in context, that key decision-makers will benefit from unfiltered analysis, and that they will not be shot if they are the bearer of news management wasn't expecting to hear. Further, trust building is seen as a two-way street. Those who contribute knowledge have an expectation of being the beneficiaries of knowledge. Without the sharing of knowledge, the intelligence process gets short-circuited. Trust then is an essential component for fueling the intelligence engine.

Social capital is a related concept that is similarly important to a firm's self-assessment of its KM capabilities. Social capital has developed into a topic of some depth in the academic literature, but the idea in a nutshell is that relationships develop over time, between individuals, between organizations, and that these relationships can become valuable. Those with a lot of useful relationships possess a lot of social capital. So if the relations between managers and workers are frayed, a distinct lack of social capital exists, and installing an effective knowledge management program will probably prove difficult. Similarly, if relations are prickly between a core firm and potential collaborators, a system to promote knowledge sharing between organizations will be slow to pay dividends. On the other hand, with high levels of social capital, KM processes function much more effectively.

Cemex is a huge Mexican firm that competes very successfully in the international cement industry (*Economist* 2001a). The firm has embraced the Internet and established *de facto* knowledge-sharing programs throughout its global locations, largely because of a foundation established over the past twenty years. Current CEO Lorenzo Zambrano established information systems when he was first promoted to the position in the mid-eighties. Although well before the Web became a reality, Cemex began installing automation, sensors, and data transmission systems throughout its operations. With electronic digital interface (EDI) communications, pertinent internal data was constantly sent to headquarters for monitoring and analysis. With the advent of the Internet, the company has turned more and more to Web-based technologies aiming for "all its employees having access to their own files, the company's data and outside information through a single, personalized portal." The firm's network of small distributors in developing countries (as opposed to large distributors serving competitors) will be similarly plugged in.

Cemex has, for example, installed computers and global-positioning systems in all of its trucks. Matched up with cement plants and customer locations, the system is able to determine efficient schedules that best match available output, truck locations, and customer destinations. The system not only plans schedules but routinely allows redirection during the course of the day. By reducing expected delivery timeframes from three hours to twenty minutes, the system has leveraged Cemex's resources, allowing assets such as the transportation fleet to substantially increase the number of trips per truck per day.

But Cemex not only does operational knowledge sharing. The firm has also long had a system, referred to as "the Cemex Way," that governs both operations and attitudes. While a top-down structure in terms of how things are to be done, the Cemex Way also stresses that the "open information and easy communication" structure be two-way. So managers are expected to be open to ideas from below, and knowledge from throughout the organization is expected to be shared with employees. Indeed, some managers voiced concern that the system might be too transparent, particularly once the system was extended across the Internet to partners outside Cemex itself.

Cemex is a success in e-business and knowledge management because the firm had the resources in place to install a first-rate KM system. Size, financial resources, an information technology base, and so forth, are all available to the firm. And openness, trust, sharing, and social capital (within and without) are all apparent in what the company does. If we had evaluated Cemex's prospects for KM at the beginning or middle of the nineties, the hard resources (information systems) and soft resources (receptiveness to knowledge sharing) would both be in place. Further, the firm had experience with knowledge systems, even if they were not referred to as such.

All of these factors can also apply on the CI side. Hard resources can be critical to establishing and perpetuating a competitive intelligence effort. Again, size, financial resources, and information technology systems can all be advantages in conducting or protecting against CI operations. Microsoft's shadow team against Linux (Gomes 1999), for example, is only possible because of its size, financial resources, and market dominance. To illustrate the point, simply consider the opposite situation. Could Linux's loose confederation ever mount a similar effort against Microsoft? And the latter's resident expertise in operating systems is also an important resource, as it interprets the competitive knowledge it obtains.

Soft resources can be equally important. Would a salesperson be willing to share knowledge she uses concerning a competitive product's weaknesses if her compensation or evaluations are diminished when colleagues improve their performance by using such knowledge? Would a researcher volunteer technical information obtained concerning a competitive product development effort if his supervisor fails to share credit or simply doesn't pay attention? And what types of employees are more likely to leave a firm and share knowledge with competitors—those with trust and social capital or those without? Soft resources can dramatically affect CI, both the gathering and the protection. Indeed, social capital is essential in the intelligence process. The ability to synthesize and integrate knowledge into analyses that produce actionable intelligence is reliant on the capabilities of those conducting analyses as well as their willingness to work with each other in finding, exploring, and using knowledge. Social capital between employee and manager, and manager and executive is crucial in ensuring that analytical reports make it to strategic decision-makers in a timely and unaltered fashion.

Execution

And so what do you do with those resources?

So the company needs to assess its resources. But just as important are its capabilities in deploying available resources and actually executing an intelligence program, including both the development and protecting knowledge. A general sense of the competence of key individuals is the important part of the evaluation. This can be broken down into some more concrete variables, such as experience.

Cemex, for instance, already had a great deal of experience with both its operational information systems and its knowledge transfer up and down the organization. When the Internet arrived, offering everything from e-mail to GPS capabilities to enterprise systems, installing and executing Web-based knowledge management systems was an attainable objective given what had come before.

What types of experience are relevant? Clearly, anything to do with information systems would be helpful. A certain demonstrated technical prowess would be extremely useful with the nuts and bolts of the system. On the other hand, human interaction capabilities, including experience with openness and knowledge transfer on interpersonal or departmental levels, is helpful with the softer side of installations. The main point is that experience helps (indeed, it helps to build resources), and firms looking to better establish an intelligence capability would be well advised not to do it all at once. Gradual steps make more sense, and developing techniques on one level that can later be extended to a broader level makes a lot of strategic sense.

Specific competencies that can help with developing intelligence have been identified and examined in the intellectual capital literature. Communities of practice (COPs), for example, and storytelling are techniques that have been demonstrably successful in helping to construct a KM competency. COP (Lave & Wenger 1991; Wenger 1998) concerns "common tasks, methods, goals or approaches among a group of people" (Thomas, Kellogg & Erickson 2001). Successfully implementing a COP on a small scale within a firm can help to implement COPs and a KM program on a full scale. COPs can also be established throughout a value network, with members sharing techniques in lean manufacturing, quality methods, environmental efforts, gathering competitive information, dealing with a major client or supplier, and so on.

Similarly, storytelling can help managers and employees to express and share knowledge that might be difficult to convey (Boje 1991). Indeed, storytelling can sometimes bring out information the subjects didn't even know they possessed. Photocopier technicians, for example, were shown to pass on a great deal of technical knowledge throughout a corporate network through storytelling means (Orr 1996). As with COPs, demonstrated experience and prowess with such tools can position a firm for further steps in establishing a full-blown KM system and intelligence capability.

While sharing knowledge through COPs and storytelling can develop knowledge assets and fuel analytical products, it can also provide an environment ripe for strategically sharing too much knowledge indiscriminately. So full-fledged KM systems can actually leave the firm more open to CI infiltrations. On the CI side, however, effective protection can be bolstered by experience with counterintelligence as well. We'll discuss matters such as compliance programs later in the book, but keeping one's knowledge to oneself typically involves formal procedures (information technology security systems, personnel procedures including how documents are handled and answering outside inquiries, etc.). The more outside collaborators, managers, and employees are schooled in such systems and use such systems, the more effective they should be. As with any system, experience can help to ensure that it works better.

Competitors

Are you the 800-pound Gorilla, is it the other guy, or are there a bunch of Gorillas?

A firm's relative standing versus competitors is something that has to be taken into account when evaluating intelligence strengths and weaknesses. A good amount of competitive evaluation will probably take place during the industry assessment (as in the previous chapter). Industry concentration is important, but then you have to ask yourself whether you are the industry leader, a strong threat to the leader, a follower, or a niche competitor. Are you Intel or Microsoft with market dominance and over three quarters of the market, or are you a market leader like Pfizer or Toyota with a market share nearer 15 to 20 percent? Or do you compete with one of these guys? Or are you Apple, with a consistent but nonthreatening 5 percent of the market? Who are you and who are your competitors? It's not just how your industry is structured but what your place in it is.

We've already talked about Microsoft's resources *vis à vis* Linux, but there are also implications to be drawn simply from the fact that Microsoft has Linux as a competitor and Linux providers have Microsoft as a competitor. Microsoft is presumably free to pursue development of its knowledge assets even though the Linux threat is limited, at least in KM applications, simply because it doesn't have the means to exploit knowledge in the same manner. On the other hand, Oracle can and does compete directly with Microsoft, in other markets, by developing and protecting knowledge assets—because it needs to, given its competitor, and because it can. Similarly, we discussed Procter & Gamble and Unilever in an earlier chapter. Both have particular reasons to develop their KM expertise simply because of the presence of the other. But finally, in a market with no dominant presence everyone might face little incentive to invest heavily in developing knowledge assets.

So KM Risk is influenced by the nature of a firm's competition. But so is CI Risk. As we have repeatedly noted in this book, substantial risk also exists from putting a KM system out there that is vulnerable to competitive intelligence incursions. From a CI Risk perspective, firms need to assess themselves in terms of the likelihood of CI activities from competitors and their own competencies in protecting knowledge from those competitors.

In the first instance, judging the level of CI activity among competitors, a subjective assessment can certainly be part of the process. Planners should have enough awareness of their competitors to know whether they have aggressive competitive intelligence units. And previous industry-level assessments should also help, as heavy CI emphasis in an industry will obviously be present in individual competitive firms. But some of the same tools can also be applied to individual competitors in order to get a more objective take on the situation.

Firms that are constantly in the press with stories concerning their CI actions, that have allegations made against them (as in the EEA case files, once again), or that have substantial SCIP or similar memberships will need watching. As noted previously, tech firms are notorious for CI, and names like Oracle and Microsoft pop up frequently as both aggressor and target. Firms competing against them should be forewarned.

Competitor analysis of this sort also cries out, of course, for counterintelligence efforts on behalf of the core firm itself. Competitive capital can be developed with an understanding of individual competitors and their actions regarding CI. And all the typical CI activities and techniques already covered in this book can be employed to the end of discerning what competitors are doing in the same arena.

So one aspect of assessing CI Risk at the firm level is examining the environment and determining the threats present from specific competitors. The other aspect is found in examining the core firm's own protection mechanisms—essentially how prepared the organization is to keep its proprietary knowledge to itself given the competitive threats. This again includes an analysis of physical barriers (building security, digital security) as well as softer barriers (employee training, noncompete/nondisclosure agreements, file/document usage procedures, etc.) and counterintelligence processes. And, again, we'll cover a number of these issues in a later chapter on implementation, but the firm should have a good sense of its own abilities to anticipate and prevent CI incursions. Obviously, the less experienced and less prepared an organization is in terms of protection, the greater the CI Risk it faces in keeping its knowledge assets proprietary.

Network Considerations

Who else is helping develop and protect your knowledge?

Implicit throughout this discussion is an understanding that all of these factors include an analysis not only of the core firm itself but also all collaborators in its knowledge network. Chains are only as strong as their weakest link, so all of the above variables, from available resources to experience to competitor threats should be evaluated for the entire value network, not just the central firm. So questions such as whether a key supplier has the resources to install a complementary KM system, whether a key vendor has experience with KM processes, and whether a key R&D partner has knowledge protection structures in place and working effectively are central to the firm-level risk assessment. When Rhinotek, for example, was trying to uncover information about Hewlett-Packard's new chip-based toner cartridges, it went after Value Chain partners of HP more than the core firm itself (Tam 2002).

Indeed, while a weak link is important to identify—either to be strengthened or to be denied knowledge access—it is not the only reason to bring network considerations into the analysis. Important resources, experience, or other factors that might help knowledge processes can be brought to the table by network partners. Core firms that find themselves lacking certain competencies might be able to supplement their own capabilities by taking on the right partner. We mentioned earlier that size might be an advantage or disadvantage in terms of developing knowledge systems. Large firms certainly have more resources and, often, experience to apply to knowledge processes. But such organizations may also be overly bureaucratic and locked into existing ways of doing business. Small firms are often more entrepreneurial, and they can more willingly and more quickly adapt to change. So partnerships between entrepreneurial, innovative small firms and larger firms with operational processes already in place have always been common, but knowledge sharing between large and small firms has become an even more pronounced trend in recent years (Marsh 2003). The larger firms seek "to gain insights into fast-moving areas of technology," whereas the smaller firms have at their disposal a larger partner with experience in development and commercialization. Because of the sensitive nature of the knowledge involved, issues of trust and openness are important in making this cross-fertilization work.

As another example, consider Wal-Mart's use of knowledge in its businesses. The retailer's practices illustrate once again the factors we have advanced in this chapter, particularly as they relate to network partners (*Economist* 2001b). Wal-Mart, of course, has long been recognized as a leader in the use of technology as a means to greater efficiency in its everyday operations. Its operational systems shift knowledge throughout the company and directly to network partners, particularly suppliers.

In terms of resources, the firm wasn't always the largest retailer in the world, but it now certainly has the capital and experience that allow it to pursue knowledge sharing at the highest level. While slow to the Internet, it is now recognized as a leader in Web-based enterprise systems. One of the reasons is available resources (when it did move forcefully to the Web, it could do it right and at whatever pace it desired) and its prior experience with information systems. Wal-Mart used EDI systems, with satellite dishes at individual stores attaching them to major suppliers, for years before the Internet became a major business tool. The Web simply allowed it to expand its existing systems on a different platform and to bring all of its partners into the network, even those for whom EDI may have been prohibitively expensive. Wal-Mart, while also legendary for its headquarters micromanagement of things like utilities, has experience with openness and knowledge transfer between different organizational levels. Department managers are free to run their own stores within the overall unit, putting the system's sales and inventory information to their own use. And individual employees of any level can influence pricing by providing information about lower competitive prices.

In its strategy for sharing knowledge, however, Wal-Mart's approach to intelligence is particularly enlightening. Suppliers just starting with the firm often have bad experiences, feeling pressured to squeeze prices and fit into the Wal-Mart template for collaborators. Longtime suppliers, however, are "given full and free access to real-time data," allowing them to operate more efficiently themselves. Wal-Mart shares "information that other retailers jealously guard" and "treats suppliers as an extension of its company." But this approach only extends so far. Only trusted suppliers such as Procter & Gamble get such treatment; they must be vetted and shown to be a trusted member of the network. Wal-Mart is well aware of the value of its proprietary knowledge and so limits its distribution while aggressively pursuing potential security breaches.

When Amazon tried to hire away a significant piece of Wal-Mart's information technology staff, for example, the giant retailer took the Internet startup to court, eventually gaining Amazon's agreement not to poach more employees (Nelson & Anders 1999). And in 2001, as noted earlier, Wal-Mart pulled out of a data-sharing agreement with market research firms AC Nielsen and IRI (Barnett, Dalton & Thompson 2001). And recall that Wal-Mart's suppliers already have access to the data, so there is no need to distribute the information outside the network.

Back to the SPFs

Finally, let's relate firm-level factors explicitly back to the SPF categories and strategies. The greater the potential a firm has in terms of resources and execution, the greater the risk if it fails to develop knowledge resources. This could be exacerbated by a particularly able competitor or mitigated by a weak one. And available collaborators with resources, expertise, and so forth, to add to the core firm's network (versus competitors' network partners) can also add to the risk that knowledge will not be fully developed. Again, KM Risk is a combination of the potential and the actual in terms of knowledge development. Changing either can increase or decrease KM Risk. CI Risk is determined by a firm's resources and experience in protecting its knowledge resources, the dangers posed by specific competitors, and the strengths or weaknesses found in the protection mechanisms of collaborators.

If we go back to our opening scenario, we can think about Intel in this respect. As noted there, Intel has considerable advantages in terms of size, financial resources, experience with knowledge systems, and demonstrated expertise. The firm also has a competent network surrounding it, both upstream and downstream, helping in applications of knowledge assets (though Intel is also known as being fairly insular and a sometimes difficult partner; Edwards 2004). Its direct competitors in terms of PC microprocessors are small, but different types of semiconductors are made by scores of companies, some quite large and undoubtedly capable of matching Intel's commitment to KM. Intel's KM Risk is substantial, in part because its potential and that of competitors is so great. Its CI Risk is also high. The company has the resources and experience to help protect its intellectual property and other knowledge assets, but it has also distributed its knowledge widely. Even with strong collaborators, it runs certain risks because its knowledge is so valuable and is desired by competitors. And again, some of those can be formidable. National and industry factors are certainly at work in Intel's situation, but firm variables help to place the firm squarely in a Cold War scenario given the high KM and CI Risks. The firm does a good job of managing the development and protection of its knowledge accordingly, with aggressive application of knowledge assets but also limitations and protections.

In evaluating risk levels, firm factors that would tend to affect knowledge asset development are suggested in Table 6.1. Those that would limit KM Risk would include hard resources such as small size, limited financial assets, and low profitability, as well as soft resources such as lack of entrepreneurship, social capital, and trust, unequal power, and other such variables. Inexperience with knowledge management would also be a limiting factor, as could be the nature of the competition (e.g., a highly fragmented group). Finally, the firm's network relationships and the knowledge capabilities of its partners would also work against knowledge development. Low scores on these aspects of the checklist, in conjunction with similar low ratings on the national and industry lists, would result in low KM Risk, as a firm would risk little if it did not aggressively develop knowledge assets. Depending on the CI Risk, such firms would then be considered to be SPF 5 (Brilliance) or SPF 30 (Glass House).

Table 6.1 Firm Variables Pertinent to KM Risk and CI Risk

Knowledge Development: Firm Variables	Effect*	Possible Measures
Interaction with national and industry variables.	+/−	Subjective assessment. Do any of the factors discussed in the previous chapters (and in the previous checklists) particularly affect your firm in developing knowledge assets?
Resources ■ Size/financial resources ■ Profitability ■ R&D capability ■ Industry knowledge ■ Entrepreneurial spirit ■ Diversity ■ Social capital ■ Trust ■ Power relationships	 +/− + + + + + + + −	Objective measures of factors such as size, profitability, R&D spending, perhaps diversity. Subjective assessment of factors such as industry knowledge, entrepreneurship, diversity, social capital, trust, power.
Execution ■ Experience with information technology ■ Experience with "soft" aspects, human relationships ■ Experience with KM techniques (e.g., COP's, storytelling)	 + + +	Subjective assessment, though might be based on identified, assessable activities in past.
Competitors ■ Resources ■ Experience ■ Industry concentration ■ Rivalry ■ Potential new competitors	 + + +/− + +	Just about all of the variables in the resources and execution sections above, but now applied to the competition. Also borrows from a number of measures in the Industry checklist, but now from the individual firm's perspective, not the entire industry.
Network Considerations ■ Development of firm's value chain ■ Strengths and weaknesses of specific network partners	 + +/−	Subjective assessment of firm's Value Chain operations versus key competitors. Subjective assessment of competencies of Value Chain partners versus collaborators of key competitors.

Table 6.1   Firm Variables Pertinent to KM Risk and CI Risk—cont'd

Knowledge Development: Firm Variables	Effect*	Possible Measures
Any other firm-specific factors that affect the ability of the firm to develop knowledge assets.	+/−	Subjective assessment
Interaction with national and industry variables.	+/−	Subjective assessment. Do any of the factors discussed in the previous chapters (and in the previous checklists) particularly affect your firm in protecting knowledge assets?

Knowledge Protection: Firm Variables	Effect*	Possible Measures
Resources ■ Size/financial resources ■ Profitability ■ R&D capability ■ Industry knowledge ■ Entrepreneurial spirit ■ Diversity ■ Social capital ■ Trust ■ Power relationships	 − − +/− − +/− +/− +/− +/− +	Objective measures of factors such as size, profitability, R&D spending, perhaps diversity. Subjective assessment of factors such as industry knowledge, entrepreneurship, diversity, social capital, trust, power.
Execution ■ Experience with information technology ■ Experience with "soft" aspects, human relationships ■ Experience with CI techniques and initiatives ■ Experience with protection systems and procedures	 + + + +	Subjective assessment, though might be based on identified, assessable activities in past.
Competitors ■ Resources ■ Execution ■ Industry concentration ■ Rivalry ■ Potential new competitors	 + + +/− + +	Just about all of the variables in the resources and execution sections above, but now applied to the competition. Also borrows from a number of measures in the Industry checklist, but now from the individual firm's perspective, not the entire industry.

Continued

Table 6.1 Firm Variables Pertinent to KM Risk and CI Risk—cont'd

Knowledge Protection: Firm Variables	Effect*	Possible Measures
Network Considerations ■ Development of firm's value chain ■ Strengths and weaknesses of specific network partners, especially in terms of protection mechanisms	+ +/−	Subjective assessment of firm's Value Chain operations versus key competitors. Subjective assessment of competencies of Value Chain partners versus collaborators of key competitors.
Any other firm-specific factors that affect the ability of the firm to develop knowledge assets.	+/−	Subjective assessment

* +/− refers to the relationship of the variable with the relevant risk. A (+) indicates a positive relationship, so as the variable increases, so does the corresponding risk. A (−) indicates an inverse relationship, with the risk decreasing as the variable increases.

Alternatively, with substantial resources of all types available, both tangible and intangible, with a breadth of experience in managing knowledge, with aggressive competition that must be matched in terms of knowledge assets, and/or with a promising network structure, KM Risk levels would start to rise. Again, combined with national and industry assessments, KM Risk could be quite high. Firms in these situations would be classified as SPF 15 (800-pound Gorilla) or SPF 45 (Cold War) according to the associated CI Risk result.

On the CI side, hard resources such as size and financing or soft resources such as industry knowledge would tend to raise the ability of the firm to protect itself from CI. Other resource variables would likely vary in impact depending on circumstances. R&D knowledge, for example, would be a plus in terms of helping counterintelligence but a minus because outsiders might be more interested in what secrets a firm holds. And note that power is a positive—if power distance is low, disgruntled employees may be less likely to reveal or defect, reducing CI Risk. Other factors are similar. More experience with counterintelligence helps a firm, as would competition without substantial CI programs or experience. A strong network, with competent partners, would also help. Put it all together, and a strong ability to protect itself from CI incursions reduces CI Risk for the firm. With similar scores on national and industry scales, overall CI Risk would be low, and the firm's classification would be SPF 5 (Brilliance) or SPF 15 (800-pound Gorilla), depending on the KM Risk result.

The opposite factors, of course, would increase CI Risk. A lack of resources, a lack of counterintelligence or protection experience, competitors with dangerous CI capabilities, network partners with weak controls, and other such variables would make the firm more vulnerable. Again, combined with national and industry weaknesses, CI Risk would be high, and the firm would find itself in an SPF 30 (Glass House) or SPF 45 (Cold War) situation. Let's look at the factors in terms of some general tendencies within the SPF groups.

SPF 5: Brilliance

In a Brilliance scenario, KM Risk and CI Risk are low to moderate. This is a firm where individual expertise or knowhow is a key driver. This type of knowledge is hard to develop and share, so few resources are spent on such efforts. Firms will tend to have a star system or a strong culture based on trust or relationships, and their products and services will be unique or transparent, rendering competitor infiltration unimportant. In the star system, success can be independent of competitor positioning. Organizations may be small and/or inexperienced with both knowledge development and protection. Network partners provide opportunities (such as product distribution or maintenance) but have minor roles in generating or disclosing knowledge. As a result, firms have little incentive to further develop knowledge nor do they have to be concerned with competitive infiltrations.

SPF 15: 800-Pound Gorilla

The 800-pound Gorilla firm is more concerned with developing its knowledge assets and less concerned with CI Risk. If it is the leader in the field, it has the size, resources, social capital, and experience necessary to develop and safeguard its knowledge. Smaller players may be more limited in size and resources but are often quite experienced in their niche areas, and they obviously have to think about the knowledge systems facing them (those of the Gorilla). And smaller firms developing a symbiosis with the Gorilla will have access to its resources and experience through their network relationships. Competitors keep an eye on each other but are more concerned about staking their own positions, and, of course, there are questions about the available resources (small firm) and/or interest (Gorilla) in the other firm's knowledge anyway.

SPF 30: Glass House

Glass House indicates that the firm operates in a fishbowl, as KM Risk is low and CI Risk is high. Well-resourced firms have the advantage of developing select knowledge assets and implementing multiple layers of protection. In addition, all firms are probably engaged in CI activities, so everyone has experience and everyone faces competitors with CI programs. Internally, trust and social capital go only so far because sharing knowledge assets across the Value Chain is not encouraged, nor is the development of network partners. Those with network partners limit relationships to specific functions and have exclusive agreements. What matters most to firms needing protective cover is positioning, not being outdone by competitors, and trying to protect knowledge assets long enough to accomplish both.

SPF 45: Cold War

A Cold War firm has highly developed knowledge assets and collaboration across its Value Chain. The firm not only generates competitive capital itself but is also likely to be subject to substantial competitor CI activities. Size, resources, experience, trust, and social capital probably exist in the firm and its network. This opens the firm to CI activities from competitors of all sizes. If so, many of these firms will also be able to use their size, resources, and experience to defend themselves. These firms need to partner but will also need to scrutinize partners, as they do their own employees, in terms of trustworthiness.

Summary

Wal-Mart undoubtedly understands that it has the corporate strengths to benefit from knowledge management of all sorts, establishing competitive advantages over competitors who are less well versed. It knows it has the resources to do it better and is seeking to be even bigger and do it even better. The firm is now exploring the possibilities of using radio-frequency identification tags (RFID) on palettes and, perhaps, individual units of merchandise to even better leverage its knowledge capabilities. Wal-Mart, as much as any company, really illustrates understanding KM Risk as it identifies the opportunities open to it (its fullest potential) and seeks to grasp those opportunities. It also manages CI Risk by guarding its proprietary knowledge even though it freely shares it with trusted network partners.

All firms need to take this approach, conducting a self-assessment of their own capabilities regarding knowledge management. What resources does the firm possess that might help (or hinder) it in installing or extending a KM system? What skills does the firm possess that suggest it can execute such a system to fullest advantage? A general, subjective assessment is a good start, but a number of more objective measures are also available.

At the same time, the organization needs to be aware of whether it can protect these valuable proprietary assets. Managers identify and understand the competitive intelligence efforts aimed at them by other firms. Further, those planning the KM system need to evaluate protection systems, both technical- and personnel-based, that will keep key knowledge from CI operatives. In terms of both KM and CI Risk, the strategic firm will work to understand its own individual situation, installing systems to take advantage of knowledge resources while minimizing the risks.

Executive Moment

So in determining relevant KM and CI Risks, the resulting SPF, and appropriate strategy, self-analysis is critical. The firm's specific competencies, as well as those of its unique set of competitors, contribute to determine its knowledge strategy as it moves forward. In looking at your own firm, it is important to ask these questions.

- Are we good at managing knowledge?
  - □ Do we have the appropriate hard resources as well as the necessary soft capabilities?
  - □ Can we execute the plans we have for our knowledge assets?
  - □ How does all this match up versus our competitors' knowledge initiatives?
- Are we good at protecting our knowledge assets?
  - □ Again, are the appropriate resources and capabilities in place?
  - □ Again, can we execute?
  - □ How good are our competitors at competitive intelligence? Do they pose major threats?
- What about collaborators?
  - □ Is our network helpful in managing knowledge?
  - □ Is our network secure, does it protect our knowledge well?
  - □ How good are our competitors' networks at managing and protecting knowledge?

Obviously, brutally honest self-analysis is imperative to this process. Overlooking weaknesses because someone or a given partner is a "good guy" isn't helpful and doesn't help the weak link to improve. Once risks are determined and appropriate strategies identified, such problems can be solved, but honest analysis must take place if that is to occur.

As before, we offer a suggested checklist to help start the process. In completing the process, all managers must understand how critical the network/collaborator perspective is in all this strategic planning. Because of recent advances in technology, knowledge flows between business partners at an exponentially increasing rate. Indeed, we noted early on in this book that KM has had certain definitions about what constitutes knowledge assets, but we believe that the list needs to be dramatically expanded, especially given the new e-networks that are driving growth in the next economy. In the next section, we begin to develop how these realities affect knowledge management, competitive intelligence, and the process of developing intelligence.

Part 2 Wrap-Up:
Strategy for Shifting Knowledge to Intelligence

Each organization's situation regarding intelligence is unique. Any number of variables can affect its ability to identify and apply its knowledge assets, and a further collection of factors will influence how vulnerable those assets are to infiltration. The trick is capturing the relevant variables for your firm and figuring out how they impact your knowledge situation. Get it right, with the correct strategies to handle KM Risk and CI Risk, and you've gone a long way toward attaining intelligence as an organizational practice and potential competitive advantage.

But the process is eclectic. Although we provide some generic checklists to begin the journey, every firm will need to think carefully about its peculiar set of circumstances. Not all variables apply to every situation, and new variables are undoubtedly going to occur to strategists working through this type of analysis. We offer guidelines but not individual answers. If you understand at least some of the reasons why, you're developing a capacity for an intelligence approach. But that being said, what guidelines are there for evaluating KM Risk, CI Risk, and determining an appropriate SPF?

Initially, nations differ, and it matters.
The field of knowledge management has awakened to differences at the national level, something that diverse disciplines relating to international business have stressed for years. Indeed, cousins to KM such as innovation and intellectual property have long noted differences in national policies and how they impact development and protection. Based on what we already know from such fields, what is presently drawing the attention of KM and CI practitioners, and what we observe in industry, we recommend executives continuously review what is happening in the countries in which they operate.

For example, what's the government up to? Legislatures pass laws, agencies establish regulations, and courts interpret these actions. To illustrate, how the government is spending money on defense or education can affect knowledge development. How regulators treat the reporting of intangible assets or how courts define antitrust law in terms of vertical coordination can also affect knowledge growth. Similarly, factors such as trade secret law, the openness of regulatory filings, and court decisions concerning noncompete agreements impact protection.

Beyond governments, technological infrastructure matters. Can information or knowledge be transferred easily between points, whether by copper wire, broadband, or wireless? What is the level of Internet penetration? Is the infrastructure open to outside attacks? A final issue is whether the culture of particular countries affects your knowledge development and protection activities. Does the culture share enough? Does it share too much? Do people work well in teams? Are hierarchical, formal reporting structures common? Any or all of these factors and numerous others like them can make a big difference in whether you can get your organization to better collect, share, analyze, and act upon knowledge. They can also drastically affect your ability to protect whatever knowledge assets you do develop.

Second, industries differ, and this also matters.
We all know that not all industries are the same and often have different requirements for success. Different cost structures, different types of assets, different marketing requirements, different human resource requirements, and other such factors exist and are a part of understanding how the industry you're in affects how you do business. Different industries also vary in terms of the potential for knowledge development and the dangers of knowledge loss. Whether R&D success or other knowledge generation is important in an industry, whether a tightly integrated supply chain or distribution channel is required, whether your industry contains an 800-pound Gorilla or 500 mom-and-pops can all affect knowledge growth. The same factors, or similar ones, can also affect the vulnerability of a knowledge system.

Third, your firm differs, and that also matters.

Relative strengths and weaknesses of an organization have always been important in strategic planning, and determining an intelligence strategy is no exception. Does your firm have the hard assets and soft assets necessary to install a system to create and grow knowledge? Does social capital exist within and without your company? Do you have experience with common KM tools, knowledge analysis, or typical CI techniques? How about your competitors regarding these factors? How about your collaborators? Every organization thinking about implementing an intelligence approach has to do a full and honest appraisal of its standing on all relevant points of comparison versus its most important competitors.

As a contemporary example, consider what is happening with Radio Frequency Identification (RFID) tags. The technology holds the potential to revolutionize information and knowledge sharing in certain applications as minute pieces of inventory can be identified and managed at an increasingly low cost. But the impact of this technology will vary. At the national level, the U.S. Congress has expressed privacy concerns related to consumers that may limit certain applications. Alternatively, China intends to draft standards for the tags so as to establish itself as an important player in the burgeoning technological field and to allow its firms to more quickly incorporate the tags into their operations. At the industry level, those industries in which inventory management or supply chain efficiency is particularly important will likely be quicker adopters of the tags. Retail, for example, is often mentioned as one of the earliest applications. And in retail, Wal-Mart looks to be one of the drivers of the technology, already alerting a number of its major suppliers to be ready to employ RFID within the next couple of years (the firm was also reportedly one influence on China's move to embrace the tags). So firms that compete with Wal-Mart need to be aware of this change and think about making a similar move (Germany's Metro, for example, has also taken early steps to install RFID). And firms that cooperate with Wal-Mart also need to think about their readiness for this change. RFID is only a small piece, even if fully installed, of a larger information and knowledge sharing system, but it illustrates how many factors at different levels can affect whether a firm decides to adopt and extend even one part of a knowledge creation, use, and analysis system. All of these factors would also need to be reviewed in determining the knowledge vulnerabilities of RFID.

The amount of risk a firm faces must be evaluated when making decisions concerning intelligence. KM Risk decreases as knowledge asset use expands, whereas CI Risk increases as knowledge asset use expands. The intelligent firm must balance these risks by choosing an optimal strategy minimizing total risk. But that point can't be determined unless decision-makers know what variables affect their organization's risk levels. Numerous, complex variables matter. We can't enumerate all the factors that affect any specific firm (again, it's eclectic and unique to that individual firm), but the three-level structure and suggested points of interest can provide guidance to intelligence-oriented strategists.

Part 3: Knowledge to Intelligence Across the Enterprise

7

Intelligence Across the Enterprise

If Siemens only knew what Siemens knows.

—*Economist* 2001a

Although it is a budding management discipline, knowledge management's supporters have always been somewhat reticent about claiming a grand scale for their practice. Examples of human, structural, or relational capital typically involve some concrete but limited application (how to run a machine, how to organize a work group, dealing with a certain customer, etc.). Understandably, grand claims about the importance of the discipline to the overall competitiveness or survival of the firm probably don't resonate with doubters about the validity of the field. Still, we believe KM, as a discipline, is too modest—especially since we have redefined it to include competitive knowledge and an intelligence perspective. When extended in this manner, the broader field that we have been discussing is (1) much more entwined with absolutely everything that goes on within a firm and (2) quite likely a critical matter in the survival of an organization as we move into the next economy.

We previously mentioned Intel's Copy Exactly program, designed to transfer manufacturing and process knowledge across different plant locations (Clark 2002). This is traditional KM stuff, but Intel does many other kinds of knowledge sharing. Indeed, the firm employs two Chief Information Officers (CIOs), a typical Intel management approach but fairly unique concerning information/

knowledge management. And it also works quite well, given the way the duties of the dual CIOs are structured (Foremski 2003).

Doug Busch runs Intel's internal IT applications, including the enterprise system (and other operations-related matters) and R&D systems. Sandra Morris heads up external IT systems such as e-business on the supply side (supply chain management) and customer side (marketing, sales, ordering, etc.). Their work has included both massive shifts in systems and changes in philosophy. Ms. Morris, for example, seeks advances in information quality and follows KM principles. Intel has moved from "silos" of information to a companywide IT system based on an SAP enterprise platform. It has moved its customers from telephone and fax ordering to the Web (85 percent of orders in 2002, resulting in $500 million worth of savings). And the operations systems, of which programs like Copy Exactly are a part, monitor chip manufacturing processes that include over 300 steps and can take three months.

Intel has information and knowledge flying around the company, from customers directly to manufacturing, from scientists to suppliers. While much of this wouldn't be included in what we typically term "intellectual capital," it is vital to the firm, is of great value as a knowledge asset, and would be of considerable interest to competitors. Intel "holds the view that [IT functions] are key to its competitive abilities and therefore core to the company." As a result, it devotes resources to such systems, values the information or knowledge provided by it, and uses protection. Mr. Busch notes that manufacturing is similar to the other systems but kept separate because of concerns about viruses and worms. The firm not only protects its perimeter from incursions (competitive or otherwise) but employs "tiers of security at different levels." Again, while customer orders, supply requests, and production plans may not be considered traditional KM territory, such knowledge would be of great interest to competitors, encompassing high potential competitive knowledge/capital.

In this chapter, we'll talk about modern e-business systems and how and why the information they manage should be considered a part of the firm's knowledge assets. From such a perspective, an organization's interest in an intelligence approach—maximizing all of its knowledge assets while also protecting them—becomes that much more important (and its situation that much more complex). We'll extend the analysis in this and the succeeding chapters with examples of just how much information/knowledge is out there, upstream and downstream from the core firm, and why the security concerns are so great.

E-Business

The Internet changes everything.

The tech boom of the late 1990s promised a lot of things that never panned out. Although some major success stories exist among the survivors (eBay, Amazon), numerous startups with potential burned through their capital and bottomed out. Consequently, in the proceeding tech bust, a lot of Internet concepts, good and bad, were discredited. And deservedly so. Many didn't have sound business models, unique or defensible competitive advantages, fulfillment capabilities, or other requirements of a successful business. But part of the promise of the Internet still lives, has changed the way many firms do business, and has the potential to revolutionize business practices even further. And it all has to do with using technology to transfer information or knowledge—connecting people in different functions and locations in their quest to solve problems and create new knowledge. During the tech boom, the business press often ran articles about the next big thing, from business-to-consumer (B2C) to peer-to-peer (P2P) to business-to-business (B2B) strategies. Again, many fell to nothing, but B2B, at least in some ways, persisted. Part of its success is undoubtedly that it is designed to sell to business and so had to be rational to have appeal (and thus was not the pipe dream of most consumer-oriented dotcoms). But not all. B2B approaches were not magically successful either, and not all came to fruition.

Exchanges, for example, were a fad for a while (Ansberry 2000). The concept was that of an auction, with firms putting supply needs out for bid and then receiving proposals online from potential business partners. The process was supposed to lower purchasing costs by injecting more competition into the supply chain.

For the most part, such exchanges failed, primarily for very familiar reasons: knowledge transfer and protection (Harris 2001; Little 2000). It turned out that sending contracts out for bid could result in an initial savings but that the transaction costs of constantly renegotiating deals and getting suppliers up to speed with specifications, delivery procedures, and so on, invariably cost the core firms more in the long run. And on the CI side, putting contracts out to bid on the Web potentially made too much useful information available to competitors. Organizations that avoided the exchanges, continuing strategies of close relationships with suppliers and knowledge sharing, often came out on top, especially in terms of efficiency. Wal-Mart, for example, shunned a retail exchange site specifically because it had no wish to share its supply chain and supply chain secrets with anyone else (Ansberry 2000). And the most efficient automaker, Toyota, was always noticeable in its absence from the automobile buying site Covisint (which still exists but now operates chiefly with qualified, known suppliers).

What has persisted in the wake of the tech bust are e-business systems that move knowledge within firms and among exchange partners. Interestingly, the basics of these types of systems already existed, but they gathered in power as they were moved to the Internet. Enterprise Resource Planning (ERP) systems have been around for decades, but the Internet provided an opportunity to move operations data around within the firm (and, eventually, to collaborators) immediately and cheaply, opening new vistas. Supply Chain Management (SCM) and Customer Relationship Management (CRM) systems also extended existing capabilities by using the Internet as their communication medium.

What all of these types of systems tend to do is enhance communication and knowledge sharing. ERP provides a mechanism for taking information, generated by orders or forecasts, and transferring it between departments, such as operations and purchasing, and between collaborators. SCM performs a similar task, emphasizing sharing operations requirements with suppliers so as to ensure seamless production, assembly, and service delivery. CRM operates at the other end of a business, collecting, processing, and applying knowledge about customers (allowing customized products, promotional offers, etc.). The details of each are less important than the fact that today's firm can install Web-based systems that instantly send information and knowledge from one end of the organization (customer contact) to the other (suppliers). And because this information includes such things as customer identification and preferences, product design and features, prices, delivery schedules, and so on, it is useful knowledge from an intelligence perspective. And it would also be useful to a competitor.

The key to the Internet and how it is changing business, even after the dotcom bust, is found in how it has put knowledge sharing into hyperdrive. This is easiest to see if one considers that the types of firms benefiting most from the trend are those that adapted what they were already doing to the new information technology tool. Wal-Mart, for example, has long had close connections with suppliers. Its well-known information technology infrastructure allowed individual stores to transmit sales information directly to companies such as Procter & Gamble, obtaining near-immediate replenishment. The system ran on an electronic data interface (satellite dishes atop individual stores and supplier facilities). The Internet, however, allowed Wal-Mart to employ a communication medium that was less expensive and provided easier integration among all the information technology systems across the firm. As a result, all suppliers, not just those with deep pockets, could be brought into the system. Further, the inventory systems could be combined with sales and marketing systems, operations systems, and so on. Wal-Mart continued to do what it had always done well; it was just able to take it to another level with the Internet.

Similarly, SAP made its name as a provider of end-to-end ERP systems during the eighties and nineties. The projects tended to require expensive software customization and lengthy installation periods. As the tech boom commenced, a number of Internet-based B2B providers popped up, providing the ERP, SCM, and CRM systems we've been discussing, while many observers thought SAP to be late to the party. In fact, SAP was taking its time to move its existing knowledge concerning end-to-end systems to the Internet. As the smoke cleared from the tech bust, a number of the Internet startups remained (Seibel, PeopleSoft, JD Edwards) and were still strong competitors. But SAP, along with Oracle, was again one of the two dominant firms in the field. The company did not so much change what it did as adapt to the new communication medium, helping other companies to do the same thing with its new Internet e-business solutions.

The bottom line is that the Internet has had its biggest impact on business by allowing firms to better communicate among different functional areas, across different geographic locations, and with outside collaborators. Information and knowledge are easily shared, and the cost is such that just about anyone can do it. Further, new programming languages such as XML have allowed easy compatibility, and different systems can now communicate with one another—again, within the firm or across company borders. The technology is not a panacea. Just as with KM or CI systems, if the knowledge is not used, the technology doesn't help much. The shared knowledge has to be managed. But the potential exists to move information and knowledge sharing to another level. By broadening our definition of what valuable knowledge assets are and by taking an intelligence approach to their use, we can take this potential even further.

E-Business at Work

What type of knowledge are we talking about here?

From an intelligence point of view, it's important to understand that several trends are occurring that only increase the urgency to rethink traditional approaches to managing knowledge assets. The information/knowledge that is flying around ERP/SCM/CRM systems is not usually included in KM discussions or plans, but these digital tools can hold important knowledge concerning the firm's strengths and weaknesses as well as those of competitors. The vast amounts of knowledge generated through such systems can be analyzed for further insights and fed through intelligence systems to aid strategy formulation. And, of course, they should be protected. The digitization of business networks, via the Internet, is in the process of revolutionizing how information/knowledge flows through the firm and its collaborators. Siemens has gained a reputation over the past few years as something of a KM pioneer, installing and using a Web-based knowledge system dubbed ShareNet (Ewing 2001). ShareNet is the epitome of the cutting-edge KM program, with the Internet used as a tool to collect, store, and share knowledge previously held tacitly by Siemens's 450,000+ employees. Incentives are in place to encourage knowledge sharing and knowledge use (bonuses for managers or prizes for employees, for example, for contributing knowledge of value or using ShareNet knowledge for a profitable purpose), even up to the business unit CEO and CFO level. The company can point to anecdotal successes such as a Malaysian broadband bid that benefited from knowledge of a similar submission in Denmark, and a telecom systems bid to hospitals in Switzerland that succeeded despite a 30 percent price premium because technical data from the Netherlands could be used to establish reliability justifying the higher price. The American Productivity and Quality Center voted ShareNet "best practice" two years running, and companies such as Intel, Philips, and Volkswagen used the system as a benchmark when establishing their own KM systems.

ShareNet, of course, is standard KM practice, albeit at a high level. But Siemens is also in the midst of moving itself into the e-business fastlane, establishing programs for online purchasing, customer contacts, and general "Value Chain" coordination, ensuring that everything from the customer order to the furthest supplier is handled in an integrated, centralized fashion (*Economist* 2001a). While removing some independence from business units, the e-business platforms are expected to cut costs by 3 to 5 percent in the long run, allow different existing systems to better communicate with one another, and provide the conglomerate with a more unified, easily navigable face toward customers. While ShareNet is considered part of the Siemens e-business practice, the other pieces are not necessarily considered part of Siemens's knowledge assets. We believe, of course, that such knowledge is critical to the success of Siemens or any other firm and that any organization can gain from better managing and protecting these assets.

We'll be covering some illustrative, in-depth examples of how firms are using their e-business platforms to strengthen and extend their network relationships, but first let's talk about some basics. In ERP systems, organizations typically shuttle demand requirements, input requirements, human resource schedules and requirements, cost information, inventory levels, and other such information/knowledge. In SCM systems, firms exchange similar information/knowledge, but where an ERP platform may extend to include suppliers, SCM is dedicated to such relationships. Thus, again, all of the core firm's demand, input, and HR requirements are shared, along with those of suppliers (and their suppliers and their suppliers . . .), as well as their cost structures, product information (e.g., features offered), logistics capabilities, and any number of other pieces of knowledge that are important to competitive advantage. And as key as a lot of this knowledge can be to the success of the organization, it can be even more valuable to a competitor.

Finally, CRM structures could include such things as customer lists, sales histories, contract terms, customer likes/dislikes, selling approaches, and pricing information. Again, this is key information for a firm, and it is often used in what is called business intelligence efforts—mining the customer data for patterns, trends, and links, allowing strategic insights in some of the ways that we have discussed throughout this book. And, again, this knowledge can be absolutely invaluable to competitors.

Li & Fung is a prominent example of both the power of these systems and the connection to knowledge. "The world's biggest supply sourcing company" (Lee-Young & Barnett 2001) doesn't own any hard manufacturing assets but trades on "optimizing supply chains for other companies" (*Economist* 2001b). The Hong Kong firm provides sourcing services for major retailers such as The Limited, Kohl's, and Abercrombie & Fitch, as well as for manufacturers such as Levi Strauss, Guess, and Reebok. Li & Fung's operations are such that it can determine the best place to obtain supplies and perform manufacturing given global constraints including price, quality, legal issues, and other such factors. In one example, a coat for the U.S. market is optimally sourced by gathering artificial fur from Thailand, cotton from China, shell and fleece from Taiwan, stainless steel for the zipper from Japan, and snaps from Germany. After gathering, the coat is actually stitched together in Thailand, perhaps because China's textile quota has already been filled. Or final assembly might be done in Guatemala, since it is close to the U.S. market and quick turnaround is important in this case. Li & Fung specializes in finding the appropriate partners and putting the whole operation together.

Knowledge is the basis of Li & Fung's entire business and was so before the age of the Internet. While previously done by means of telephone and fax, the firm now links customers and potential suppliers through the Web. The Internet has expanded its capacities. It can now deliver retail orders in weeks in an industry that used to require months for ordering and delivery, but the business model was already in place. Managing knowledge of where to source to best advantage has always been the firm's *raison d'être;* the Internet has only added to its advantages. Li & Fung's talent is taking a request from a client and determining the best mix of suppliers to get it accomplished "with a machete in one hand, a laptop in the other" according to Victor Fung. Or as William Fung puts it, "There are no secrets in the actual manufacturing. . . . We would rather build on something proprietary, like what information it takes to make that shirt faster or more efficiently." Li & Fung manages supply chains for clients (de facto SCM), and its own ERP system incorporates elements of CRM, given how it deals with client needs and wants. It is the epitome of the modern organization that uses knowledge to establish competitive advantage. Indeed, the firm has discerned that operational knowledge, of the e-network variety, is the key to its competitive advantage. Operational knowledge (SCM, ERP, CRM) can become intelligence, and intelligence is competitive advantage. Input changes, production plans, customer knowledge, and numerous other pieces of information or knowledge can be gleaned from these types of systems. Put together by a well-trained intelligence team, they can become critical intelligence for a competitor.

E-Business, Knowledge Management, and Competitive Intelligence

What are the implications for an SPF approach?

Adding operational knowledge systems such as ERP, SCM, and CRM to the mix of what we consider KM has a number of implications and makes a number of other concerns more explicit. Initially, and most obviously, this is additional knowledge not often included in discussions of KM. Operational information is often viewed as just that: information that doesn't rise to the level of knowledge, let alone intelligence. As the example of Li & Fung, among others, suggests, this is a mistake. Operational information, managed well, can become knowledge and even intelligence, yielding strategic insights and competitive advantage.

But other, less obvious considerations also emerge. Initially, consider the development of knowledge assets. As just noted, the range of knowledge available to an organization has been expanded exponentially. So when we talk of better using knowledge through collection and sharing, through analysis, or by applying it to strategic purposes, a lot of pertinent knowledge is available. Further, it is often digital and easily passed around, whether a formal, computerized KM system is actually used or not. Every employee likely has access to a much greater percentage of the firm's knowledge asset stock, increasing their own intellectual capital potential. And much of this stock is shared outside the firm, enhancing the knowledge through further leverage and increasing the knowledge capabilities of collaborators. The possibilities of knowledge, and of intelligence, have been substantially enhanced by e-business trends. To return to SPFs, KM Risk can be much higher today, simply because the ideal or potential level of KM development is that much greater.

It's on the CI side, however, where the implications of e-business are really apparent. For all the same reasons—much more knowledge, in digital form, available to many more individuals, inside and outside the firm—CI Risk is much greater. Competitors seeking to lift knowledge have many more targets. Each target will have, or at least have access to, a greater percentage of the firm's total knowledge base. So each incursion has the potential to be much more serious. Digital knowledge is much more easily lifted (and less likely to be noticed missing). And the knowledge is held not just by a KM team but is dispersed throughout the organization and, indeed, throughout the network of collaborators. Once the knowledge passes into so many hands, both inside and outside the core firm, ensuring that it is properly protected becomes a substantial challenge.

Another obvious complication is the fact that these e-business networks can be, and often are, global. So the conditions for use of knowledge and protection of knowledge will differ markedly depending on where a company does business, where its collaborators do business, and where its competitors do business. As discussed in previous chapters, KM Risk and CI Risk are affected by national factors, and so they may be quite different, depending on the number of locations. But the firm's knowledge assets, in terms of its digital systems, are not limited by borders. Unless a plan is in place to condition availability by location, both knowledge development and knowledge protection can again be an issue.

And finally, as we'll be discussing in the upcoming chapters, these knowledge systems can change over time. ERP, SCM, and CRM essentially contain operating information. While that can be useful knowledge or even intelligence, especially if managed strategically, their basis will still be operating information. But as firms get comfortable sharing this type of information or knowledge, and as they build a structure for doing it, other types of information or knowledge (even intelligence) will inevitably start to flow through the network. Firms can and do share their intellectual capital throughout their e-networks, and the smart ones do so only by design. As comfort levels grow with bytes flowing throughout extended organizations, however, the content of those bytes can increase without necessarily being part of the knowledge plan. Again, this can threaten proper knowledge development and increase CI Risk substantially.

Otis Elevators, the United Technologies subsidiary, is an illustrative example (Linsford 2003; Rocks 2001). The firm has always kept close relationships with customers, as service, maintenance, and repair revenues are just as important to its business as the manufacture of the original elevators. Indeed, single technicians can spend their entire careers servicing one client. The firm also took over emergency services for some customers some time ago, installing direct lines from the car-based telephones. More recently, the firm has moved customer services to the Web, with online ordering and online maintenance—the latter allowing remote monitoring to help identify the problem and the severity before technicians are dispatched. The Web systems also link with suppliers and across the company, supplying typical CRM, SCM, and ERP information transfers.

But Otis does much more. The R&D function is very important to the company, providing a point of differentiation with its competition. New safety systems, more efficient cable systems, scheduling programs, and other such innovations come from a parent (UT) spending $2.5 billion on R&D and a core company that works directly with customers on the types of new features that will benefit them. So besides operating information, Otis tends to deal with customers in the area of technological knowledge. The firm also has shared knowledge across the conglomerate. UT CEO George David came out of Otis and has established mechanisms to share business practices throughout the rest of the parent company. Otis, for example, was one of the first U.S. manufacturers to adopt lean manufacturing, and its experience is now shared across UT, including through a lean school. Otis's background with international manufacturing, sales, and service also provided a base of experience that could be shared with the rest of the firm.

The point is that the company has all sorts of information and knowledge-sharing systems, from ERP to a learning facility. As relationships throughout UT and with its external collaborators or customers flourish, and as e-business systems are rationalized, the firm will share more and more different types of information and knowledge across units, organizations, and countries. In the case of Otis and UT, this will apparently be done in a deliberate and strategic manner. Other firms need to take the same approach by considering how knowledge, including all types, is developed, shared, and protected everywhere in the extended network. All systems, all information and knowledge, and all entities need to be included in the planning.

The Value Chain

A tool to organize one's thinking.

Microenvironmental analysis—trying to evaluate the strengths and weaknesses of a firm compared to its competitors—has often presented a similar problem. Given everything a firm does, including its entire e-network of collaborators, how does one make sure all facets have been considered? Several tools exist, from Ansoff's (1988) Grid of Competencies to Lehmann and Winer's (1991) "Checklist of Assets and Skills." But we recommend Porter's Value Chain, shown in Figure 7.1.

The Value Chain (Porter 1985) is a framework that demonstrates how a product moves from the raw material stage to the final user. It helps the firm understand the different parts of its operation, its cost positions, and where value is created. The template identifies

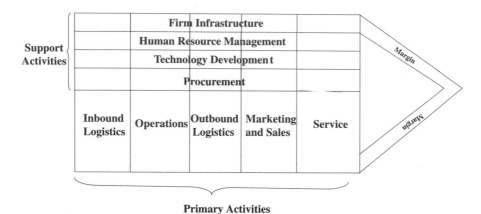

Figure 7.1 The Value Chain
(From Porter 1985)

two sets of firm activities. Primary activities are involved with production, sale, and service after sale. They include inbound logistics, operations, outbound logistics, marketing and sales, and service. Support activities provide assistance for the primary activities and include the firm's infrastructure, human resource management, technological development, and procurement.

The key to the Value Chain, and its particular usefulness for our purposes, is the emphasis on the competencies that are created through the interaction of support and primary functions. We would argue that competitive advantage is more likely to be sustainable when grounded in support function competencies, since they are hard to duplicate or substitute and they add value to the firm and its constituency. Sources of advantage have their roots in the interplay between support and primary activities as they jointly create lean operations, increase responsiveness to customer needs, and build strong relationships with network partners. Digitization has enabled Value Chain activities to operate at lower costs and greater efficiency in the core operation (ERP) and upstream (SCM). Downstream, channel activities are streamlined, and knowledge about end users (CRM) facilitates customizing offerings and providing feedback to the supply chain or to outsourcing partners. In addition, interactions between primary and support activities can create strong incentives for knowledge sharing. Salespeople can digitally share real-time client information with designers of new products and services, or with purchasing managers. Information from a great SCM can keep the firm running effectively by minimizing inventory costs and avoiding the possibility of having technology make stock obsolete. Finally, while a Value Chain exists for an organization, organizations themselves are part of industrywide Value Chains. This interconnectivity suggests that the better the firms in an industry manage their Value Chain together, the healthier the industry will be.

The Value Chain can help decision-makers organize their thinking about their primary and support activities, and those of their collaborators. By doing so, they can begin to locate where their key knowledge assets reside and start to manage them in an intelligence manner. A common analysis practice is to not only construct a Value Chain for the firm but also a comparative Value Chain for competitors, identifying and amplifying strengths and weaknesses. This intelligence perspective helps the firm identify where it has potential competitive advantages and disadvantages, especially in terms of knowledge.

In the upcoming chapters, we'll use the Value Chain as a platform for discussing how knowledge assets are being used upstream and downstream from core firms. These illustrative examples are intended to present the range of issues concerning those pursuing an intelligence approach. With a better awareness of all these issues, managers can more purposefully engage and protect knowledge assets.

Back to the SPFs

Returning to the example of Intel, the firm's application of two CIOs to its situation makes a lot of strategic sense. The firm has ERP, SCM, and CRM systems and shares other knowledge inside and outside its borders as well. From manufacturing processes to R&D, supply partners to customers, Intel zips information and knowledge throughout its e-network, using the Web to share these assets more widely and to better effect. Given the division of labor between an inside and an outside CIO, the organization has also realized the importance of protecting its knowledge assets—keeping some to itself while allowing many to spread far and wide.

Intel's SPF situation appears to be Cold War, with the sharing of knowledge being of critical importance (high KM Risk), as is the protection of knowledge (high CI Risk). And the firm vividly illustrates the wisdom of an intelligence approach as it strategically manages its knowledge. As just noted, Intel has a good handle on its e-network systems, applying such operational knowledge assets upstream, downstream, and across its facilities. In a similar manner, it shares other, more recognizable KM assets via the Internet. And it takes steps to protect its most valuable knowledge assets as well.

When operational information systems are possible in a nation, widely used in an industry, and/or within the capabilities of an individual firm, KM Risk escalates. When these structures further lend themselves to wider sharing of other types of knowledge as well, the KM Risk grows even greater, as the firm failing to apply them will find itself at a serious deficit relative to its own knowledge potential and the level of knowledge development of its competitors. Firms in this type of environment will find themselves operating in high-KM-Risk SPFs such as SPF 15 (800-pound Gorilla) or SPF 45 (Cold War). Those in nations not presenting a strong environment for systems development, in industries in which sharing knowledge in such a manner is impossible or not important to competitive advantage, or without requisite firm capabilities will face the opposite situation. And again, if other KM assets don't transfer well to e-network systems, the risk will be even lower. These low-KM-Risk organizations will face SPF 5 (Brilliance) or SPF 30 (Glass House), depending on the attached CI Risk.

In a nation with conditions allowing or promoting wide sharing but minimal protection, a highly competitive industry, or a firm with poor protection mechanisms or experience, CI Risk will be especially high when Web-based operational systems are common. So a firm leaving itself wide open to competitive incursions while employing ERP and other such tools will find itself in high-CI-Risk scenarios such as SPF 30 (Glass House) or SPF 45 (Cold War). Alternatively, with strong legal and other national protections for knowledge assets, industries without a lot of CI activity, or firms with strong protection skills or nonthreatening competitors, organizations will face low-CI-Risk situations such as SPF 5 (Brilliance) or SPF 15 (800-pound Gorilla).

Essentially, the operational systems we've been discussing amplify everything we discussed in previous sections. The conditions for any particular SPF are enhanced by a communication network that allows greater distribution of all sorts of knowledge but with less control (and, therefore, more difficulty in protecting these assets). Again returning to Intel, the firm would be an SPF 45 regardless, but the installation of Internet-systems over the past decade have only ingrained that situation. The firm's knowledge assets are more easily spread more widely (and to better purpose), there are additional fonts of information that have now become knowledge assets, and everything is much more at risk. The situation hasn't changed so much as the stakes have been raised. One more time, the digital, global, wider sharing of more complete knowledge only accents everything we've been discussing.

Summary

To summarize: The Internet has allowed firms to take operations-oriented information technology systems and expand them at warp speed. While previously difficult to synchronize, these systems can now speak to one another through common languages such as XML. While previously too expensive to be adopted by all collaborators, these systems can now use the cost-effective Web to link every last supplier or vendor. So operating information in ever increasing volumes can fly throughout the extended enterprise, the e-network, by means of ERP, SCM, CRM, and other such systems.

This information, managed according to KM principles, can become valuable organizational knowledge. Operational insights, customer preferences, cost information, forecasts, supply chain capabilities, and other such factors can all be important parts of competitive advantage and can yield competitive capital as well. Further, this knowledge can become intelligence and should be managed in an intelligence manner. Intelligence teams can be formed to search out and gather the most relevant knowledge, analysis can yield further advantage, and if directed to decision-makers, can further swell competitive advantage. But from the standpoint of strategic knowledge management, protection of this information/knowledge can also be important. So again, intelligence can and should be the approach, with some thought given to protecting this information/knowledge.

And with protection in mind, it's critical to note that this trend makes an intelligence approach imperative. Digital knowledge spread far and wide in more complete chunks inside and outside the organization is difficult to keep to oneself. And other trends, such as the fact that outsourcing often moves to foreign markets or includes firms in more competitive industries than that of the core organization, further amplify the issue. Finally, firms such as UT are using the e-network structure already in place to share nonoperational—what we would consider more traditional KM-type—knowledge. With information/knowledge sharing online, firms need to take an intelligence approach to managing these suddenly overflowing knowledge assets and then protecting the critical ones. But how do decision-makers organize their thinking so that they accurately identify all the organization's knowledge assets, isolate the critical ones, and establish appropriate protection systems?

Executive Moment

In thinking about your situation, ask yourself the following questions.

- How is our organization using Internet-based operational systems?
  - □ Do we employ ERP, SCM, and/or CRM systems?
  - □ If not, should we?
- Do our competitors?

These types of systems are to be the future of business. While the dotcom bust proved there is nothing magic about the Internet, the ability to use a new technology to enhance the movement and exchange of valuable knowledge has had a tremendous impact on a number of firms. And it promises to have an even greater impact in the future. Firms not choosing to install ERP, SCM, and/or CRM systems while competitors do may find themselves at a tremendous disadvantage.

- Do we treat operational information of this sort as knowledge, or even intelligence? If not, should we?
  - □ Do we understand the value that some of this information has?
  - □ Do we harvest that information/knowledge by employing analysis, intelligence teams, and a process to get it to key decision-makers?
- Do our competitors?

The obvious applications of ERP and related systems are to operations and a sense of what is going on right here, right now. But matters related to supplier capabilities, operational processes, and customers can easily pass into the realm of knowledge and intelligence. Firms failing to take advantage of this potential can again be at an enormous disadvantage, particularly if competitors do take advantage.

- Do we understand the vulnerabilities of employing these systems? The fact that they:
  - □ Are digital

- ☐ Place knowledge in many more heads
- ☐ Give those heads access to a much more complete dump of the organization's knowledge assets
- ☐ Are inside and outside the core firm (i.e., in the hands of numerous collaborators)
- ☐ Including across organizational and national borders
- ■ Do our competitors?

For all these reasons, knowledge is much more vulnerable to competitive incursions. Firms need to recognize the risk and do something about it. The more the systems are employed, and especially if they include knowledge beyond the operational systems, the more an organization needs to guard against competitors' infiltration. If you're still not convinced, consider the examples and scenarios we present in the following chapters.

Intelligence Across the Value Chain: Upstream

This is the modern world.

—Paul Weller

The most recognized applications of intelligence tend to occur upstream in the Value Chain because close, knowledge-sharing relationships have characterized supply chains for quite some time. In this chapter, we'll discuss the types of knowledge that are shared at both the same level of the enterprise and upstream from it (i.e., throughout the supply chain). As noted in the last chapter, a lot of information has always flowed in this direction because suppliers and other collaborators, by definition, need to synchronize their efforts with core firms. But the tools provided by the Internet have enhanced communications and the resulting information flows. As we shall see, knowledge has also started flowing throughout upstream relationships, and we'll discuss some specific examples. Firms that learn to use these flows effectively can eventually develop intelligence, and they should, if they are to protect valuable knowledge assets.

Dell Computer has long been renowned for its direct-to-the-customer business model that added manufacturing efficiency during the 1990s. This manufacturing efficiency included suppliers and other collaborators, and moved to the Internet early, well before e-business was widespread. So behind Dell's cost advantages in the marketplace are a short distribution structure, highly efficient manufacturing processes, and low inventories. Behind the scenes, these advantages flow from information and knowledge sharing. Indeed, inventory is "a substitute for information: you buy them because you are not sure of the reliability of your supplier or the demand from your customer" (*Economist* 2000).

Dell has created a business model that minimizes inventory by handling information and knowledge well (Cohen & Agrawal 2000; Daniel 2002; Grande 2001; Park & Burrows 2001; Park & Burrows 2003). The firm uses Web-based (and, still, telephone) systems to take in orders from customers, offering "customization," but it is also able to influence that customization by steering customers to configurations that are less expensive or more readily available because of on-hand or easily procured parts. From the first step, the system matches up knowledge about customer desires and the status of the supply chain. The orders immediately flow throughout Dell's e-network, alerting first-tier suppliers, second-tier suppliers, and so on down the line. So Texas Instruments, which supplies digital signal processors to Solectron (Dell's motherboard producer), knows what is required of it as soon as the customer clicks the mouse. The suppliers are also directly tied into Dell's assembly floors, monitoring the status of units and delivering parts, as needed, every couple of hours. Dell has been able to drive its inventory down to a few days' supply, even measuring it in hours while competitors are still talking about weeks. And again, the key to this type of performance is information and knowledge. One ex-HP executive commented, "Michael Dell's laptop gives him more information each day than we got in a quarter's time" (Park & Burrows 2001). While HP has undoubtedly improved since then, the point is still well taken.

Much of this detail isn't new to a lot of people, but the implications for an intelligence approach are. In light of the discussion from the last chapter, consider not just the information flying throughout Dell's e-network but also the knowledge or even intelligence. On the one hand, Dell has improved its manufacturing by discovering and sharing knowledge, reducing the "touches" required to build a PC from 130 to 60. Many of these process improvements are patented. In similar ways, the firm is open to other suggestions from personnel throughout the company, with the company president taking in, for example, a suggestion on saving paper costs from a line team. Critically, the firm shares this knowledge across locations and throughout its supply chain. But Dell can do so because its supply chain is very tight (around 200 firms with 30 supplying almost three-quarters of Dell's volume) compared to a standard of about 1000 in the industry. Dell develops a close, collaborative relationship with suppliers, allowing it to share sensitive information and knowledge because it trusts those partners and can keep close controls on such a relatively small group.

The point, of course, is that supply chain management (SCM) or supplier relationship management (SRM, the newer buzzword for the technology/strategy) systems, while based on technology, are essentially information-sharing systems. This information, in and of itself, can be very important to a firm (as in the case of Dell) and would be of great interest to competitors. As the relationships grow closer and the links along the chain tighten, other knowledge may also be shared, and the entire network can be strengthened by an intelligence approach that enhances the knowledge through purposeful search, analyzes the knowledge, delivers it to decision-makers, and so on. A supplier, for example, may note increasing orders of a particular component. It may ask the core firm for help in finding ways to decrease the cost of that component while also exploring ways to incorporate it into more products. Further, firms with extended supply chains need to recognize that shared operational information and knowledge are at risk from competitive incursions when spread so widely.

The Value Chain: Upstream

Integrated, communication-rich supply chains are a growing source of competitive advantage.

To recap from the last chapter, e-business systems such as ERP, SCM, and CRM are in the process of revolutionizing how firms deal with their networks of collaborators, allowing widespread sharing of information and even knowledge at a low cost and with minimal technological complications. This chapter revolves around the ERP and, especially, the SCM/SRM pieces of the networks, focusing on suppliers, inbound logistics, and operational partners, as well as such secondary upstream activities as research and development and procurement.

To recap from recent history, the initial attempts to apply the Internet to the early pieces of the Value Chain revolved around exchanges, allowing buyers and sellers of industrial inputs to meet in an auction setting. Although the exchanges were made technologically appealing by means of the Web, and they had their advantages in terms of soliciting the lowest price on inputs, the basic fact of life in industrial supply chains is that price is only one component of relationships between suppliers and procurers. Quality, reliability, and other variables have long been important considerations of industrial buyers (along with price, of course), and the types of relationships engendered by auctions did not lend themselves to much beyond price. Even though online exchanges limited their bids to qualified suppliers, they still fell short of the relationships that buyers increasingly recognized as important parts of a supply chain.

Indeed, supply chain wizards tended to avoid the online exchanges, amplifying the fact that something besides price information and price auctions was important to this process. The best supply chain applications, it turned out, were proprietary—though it also turned out the Internet was a pretty good tool for installing and managing proprietary exchanges, too. The really critical thing to realize, however, is that it's not the technology that matters here but the nature of the relationships and how they are enhanced by the technology. E-business, e-networks are growing, even after the tech bust, but the reasons have more to do with information and knowledge sharing than with technology. Thus, our interest.

While the initial passion for open exchanges focused on reducing costs, both for the inputs themselves and for process administration, the more recent and more successful implementations of supply chain systems have focused on knowledge exchange. Indeed, the circumstances are such that they almost have to. If supply chain applications have only to do with driving down input prices and increasing the efficiency of inbound logistics, the suppliers see no obvious benefits for themselves beyond holding on to an increasingly demanding customer. When the relationship is about sharing knowledge, so as to benefit both partners (and, by the way, drive down costs through better communication and better use of knowledge), then we see reasons for all network members to come together and cooperate (Bragg & Kumar 2003).

This perspective is one of the drivers behind SRM (Thomas 2003). Instead of squeezing suppliers for the best price, core firms tend to look at how network partners can work collaboratively to share knowledge and eliminate duplication or waste. With this approach—with all network partners potentially benefiting from shared knowledge and better performance—participation and cooperation tend to increase. Schlumberger, for example, found its suppliers cooperative because its e-procurement system standardized ordering, sending everything by the Internet rather than by alternative means such as phone or fax—saving time and money. And British Airways' Spend Management program reduced the number of suppliers from 14,000 to 3,000, but those remaining found themselves in a much closer relationship with the airline. The standardized templates and knowledge of whom to go to for what improved the efficiency of supply chain partners (and British Airways). Recognizing the benefits of the closer relationship, British Airways even worked with suppliers appearing to offer inputs below cost (rather than just taking advantage of the situation and moving on). George Lawrie of Forrester Research suggests that the key is reducing suppliers' uncertainty by providing a less opaque system, by providing access to more knowledge.

Boeing, for instance, has a supply chain including forty separate processes and twenty different purchasing systems (Talacko 2003). The firm outsourced its coordination process to a company called Hubspan, a "trading partner integration" specialist. Given Boeing's legacy of disparate systems, inherited from a number of acquisitions, it needed a firm with experience in integrating different supply systems by means of the Internet. Hubspan was able to offer this integration, giving Boeing a Web-based supply chain system that coordinated its information flows in one place. So when Boeing needs cooperation with designing a new jet, with delivering the appropriate inputs for assembly in Seattle, or with knowledge about maintenance issues, it has a networked information technology system that allows the sort of close relationships that allow it to deal with such issues.

These close relationships directly affect both KM Risk and CI Risk for organizations. The potential network of collaborators allows a firm to gain access to more knowledge assets, often in disciplines or concerning industries in which they were previously lacking. The diversity of the assets is also enhanced, providing perspectives outside the structure of the single core firm. E-networks, both because of the technology-enhanced communication and because of the closer relationships they entail, can greatly expand the range of knowledge assets available to firms and the number of useful targets for sharing those assets. Managed intelligently, with attention to filling knowledge gaps, analyzing the knowledge for strategic purposes, and ensuring delivery to decision-makers, this knowledge can substantially aid the competitiveness of the core firm and its network. Failure to take advantage of the possibilities while competitors do, however, will sharply increase KM Risk.

But CI Risk also comes into the equation. Although these closer relationships are often predicated on sharply reducing the number of participants in supply chains, the fact of the matter is that much more valuable knowledge is placed in the hands of numerous partners outside the firm. Partners can be in different countries and different industries, with varying levels of knowledge protection and CI activity. Partners will also have different strengths and weaknesses in terms of protection. So the easy communication and increased cooperation has the potential to change the protection environment, exposing the core firm and the entire network to more threatening competitive intelligence actions.

As noted repeatedly, the type of information and knowledge typically flowing through e-networks is valuable. But as core firms grow comfortable with their e-network systems and their closest collaborators, they will be inclined to spread other knowledge. Those taking an intelligence approach, especially, will find it to their benefit to seek out, analyze, share, and act upon knowledge from throughout their Value Chains. If a collaborator has particular skills in quality management, for example, it makes sense to develop and share that firm's knowledge throughout the network. Strategic management of knowledge assets can help a core firm construct an e-network that effectively lets each member perform the activities and contribute the knowledge that it does best (i.e., Hamel & Prahalad's (1994) core competencies with knowledge assets attached). The potential for knowledge asset development is tremendous—but so is the competitive intelligence risk.

KM Risk and Reward: Upstream

Supply chains offer rich opportunities for knowledge sharing.

The outsourcing trend of the past few years is a good illustration of the idea. Although sending backoffice and programming tasks to India is only the latest and perhaps most visible example of the trend, it has been happening throughout the Value Chain and both domestically and internationally for a number of years. Part of the trend is sparked by management theory (again, Hamel and Prahalad laid the theoretical foundation some years ago), part by logistics execution. But an important underlying cause is the Internet and its ability to allow knowledge sharing across firms and countries (Sawhney 2003).

Indeed, Sawhney argues that a key contribution of the Internet is that it allows "decoupling." Decoupling is essentially the core competency approach with the addition of expertise being found anywhere—and connected by modern communication and synchronization technology. The importance of this is that things take place where they make the most sense. GE, for example, has a subsidiary, GE Capital International Services, in India, providing staff activities such as accounting, business analysis, and software development. On the other hand, downstream activities benefiting from what goes on at GECIS are located closer to the customers. The way the Internet and related technologies allow communication and long-distance synchronization is the key. We also saw this in the dispersed manufacturing and services network of Li & Fung discussed in the last chapter.

Another example is found in small suppliers outsourcing their manufacturing to overseas locations (Aeppel 2004). As their customers have demanded the lower prices that foreign production promises, they have had to find collaborators in other countries. As in the previous case, the knowledge sharing allows them to find partners and then coordinate operations. To illustrate, Younger & Sons Manufacturing uses a Chinese engineering concern with manufacturing connections to find collaborators. Younger, and firms like it, are then able to manage the e-networks by using the Internet to monitor production, delivery, and other such matters—particularly important to small firms for whom every order is critical and deserving of personal attention.

What other types of knowledge are being shared in the upstream portion of firms' Value Chains? Besides just operational information or related knowledge, firms are increasingly working with their closest network mates and handing over more knowledge, sometimes even that contributing directly to competitive advantage. Consider several illustrations.

John Deere, as is the case with many U.S.-based manufacturing firms, is constantly looking over its production environment with the aim of driving down costs (Ericksen 2000). And, as is the case with many other manufacturers, the firm is also looking to suppliers to drop its costs. Deere has developed a competency in lean manufacturing that the organization is willing to share with long-term suppliers. Deere's industrial engineers will come into a supplier's plant, conduct a *kaizen* event, and implement the efficient solutions that come from such analysis. They apply Deere's core manufacturing knowledge to the supplier's situation, invariably sharing some of the core secrets. And as an incentive to suppliers, when cost savings result in terms of interventions, Deere splits the savings with the supplier (50 percent of the savings off the cost of the good, 50 percent to the supplier). The result is a stronger partnership, going beyond a typical seller/customer relationship, based on the sharing of critical process-improvement knowledge.

Similarly, but focusing on a different operational concern, Kennametal is an engineering and manufacturing firm whose chief product is machine tools. The firm installed a centralized procurement system and also practices and shares some lean manufacturing principles (Konicki 2002; Sanborn 2002). But what's really interesting about Kennametal is that the firm has developed some expertise in environmentally friendly manufacturing techniques (Steele 2002). And in order to leverage this competency, the company seeks better environmental results from its supply chain, so Kennametal is willing to pass the valuable knowledge back to its network partners. As the entire Value Chain of Kennametal's products becomes less wasteful, its competitive advantage in environmental awareness is enhanced. And again, as the overall relationship gets closer and the network functions more as a single entity, we see examples of firms who leverage their critical knowledge assets by sharing them with collaborators.

Similar stories concerning the upstream part of the Value Chain are readily apparent, ranging from cooperative research and development (Intel and Xerox, for example, developing a new chip for office products; Clark 2003) to inbound logistics. In the latter case, outsourcing is in the process of moving from third-party logistics (3PL) to fourth-party logistics (4PL). While 3PL focused on physical movement and coordination (and so a Fedex or UPS needed to become a part of an ERP or SCM system), 4PL promises "the management of everything in the product cycle from design and development to manufacture, transaction processing, and after sales support . . ." (Manchester 2003). We'll talk more about logistics in the next chapter.

The key point here is to recognize that e-networks bring collaborators closer together, in this case upstream partners in the Value Chain. By their very nature, these collaborations share operational knowledge to good effect. But as the relationships become ever tighter and the partners more committed to (and trusting of) one another, even more information or knowledge is now changing hands. And again, from a knowledge sharing point of view, this growth is to good effect. The knowledge assets of the entire network are being identified and employed. With an intelligence process in place to manage this wealth of knowledge assets, the potential is tremendous. Firms finding, analyzing, and acting upon best practices throughout extended e-networks can raise their knowledge potential and practice to levels that competitors will find difficult to imitate and answer. As with KM in general, the prescription would seem to be more, more, more, with the network's knowledge assets spread far and wide. But, of course, that other side is still out there. What of the competitive intelligence considerations?

CI Risk and Reward: Upstream

Supply chains also offer increased vulnerability.

We've already discussed, at some length, the typical CI techniques used against organizations, as well as the special threats that come from e-networks that spread substantial, digitized knowledge far and wide. But let's talk a bit about how upstream and co-level activities along the Value Chain illustrate the potential vulnerabilities of firms seeking to apply their knowledge assets.

At its simplest level, managers need to understand that all the same vulnerabilities exist, but now they are found in dozens or even hundreds of partner organizations with tens or hundreds of thousands of employees. And, of course, the security schemes present in the core firm may or may not be as carefully planned and executed elsewhere in the e-networks. Secure networks, appropriate employee training, and counterintelligence may exist at the center, but the ability of the core organization to extend the protection scheme throughout its Value Chain is a key question. If difficult, that core firm will likely face much higher CI Risk.

For starters, just consider some of the things that we know go on in today's knowledge and CI-oriented business world. Documented examples exist of activities such as camera phones in manufacturing facilities (Ward 2003), stolen or missing laptops (Wingfield 2000), employee pilfering (Solomon & Thurm 2000), or eavesdropping/wandering eyes on airplanes (de Lisser 1999). The most well-informed firm may be prepared for such actions, but what about its suppliers? What about the suppliers of its suppliers? What about independent contractors working with third-tier suppliers? Are they briefed on what information or knowledge is critical and what appropriate protection procedures are?

Of the Economic Espionage Act cases prosecuted to date (www.cybercrime.gov), for example, one involved MasterCard's proprietary information (and an offer to secretly tape future meetings) forwarded to Visa. Visa turned over the case to the FBI, which determined the culprit to be a contract food service employee. Another case involved trade secrets of DirecTV, specifically the access card allowing the system to work. This information was traced to a student who had been working for a copy service used by DirecTV's lawyer.

Aside from pure espionage, consider the case of Newbury Comics, a small music retailer in Massachusetts (Singer 1999). The firm turned in weekly sales data (by artist, label, and location) to a national market research firm, as do 85 percent of U.S. music retailers. After analysis, the researcher sells the compiled information back to record labels (upstream), retailers (co-level), and elsewhere. The owner of Newbury found out that a major competitor (the rack jobber handling the music departments at nearby discounters) was receiving not just the compilation reports but location-specific reports on what was selling at the Newbury stores as well as other spots. Independent stores like Newbury consider their competitive advantage over mass market retailers to be their knowledge of who the "hot" acts are before the general public and other stores realize it. If a competitor has access to that knowledge almost as soon as a Newbury does, the smaller firm loses whatever slight advantage it held over the larger firms that can underprice it. And although the researcher claims that the same information can also be passed along by third parties like the label representatives ("store x just reordered thirty units of so-and-so; don't you think you should, too?"), computer interfaces help to make this type of knowledge exchange almost instantaneous and more verifiable.

The same thing can happen in the other direction (small firms using intelligence against larger ones). Rhinotek is a manufacturer of toner cartridges that fit HP printers, essentially generic versions of HP cartridges (Tam 2002). In an attempt to tamp down such competition, HP began to develop a printer requiring smart cartridges with an embedded chip. Development of a copycat chip by a company such as Rhinotek would presumably take months, even years, especially since some of the technology was protected by patents. Rhinotek, however, has a network of "informants" throughout the industry. Some of these are downstream (e.g., retailers), but many are also upstream, particularly in product development. Indeed, Rhinotek received a tip six months before a chip-carrying cartridge was to be introduced. The firm sent its CI network into overdrive, gathering knowledge about the new product, even obtaining a prototype of the new chip (again, from the informant network). The firm's "war room" analyzed the collected competitive knowledge, even cooperating with other knockoff firms, and was able to launch a competitive version of its own within six months of HP's introduction (without, apparently, violating any patents).

So the illustrative point of all of this discussion is that e-networks exist, they have a place in passing operational information among collaborators, and the close connections that result often lead to the exchange of more high-level knowledge as well. Because of the nature of the beast, these systems also make a firm more vulnerable to competitive infiltration. The many different heads and systems holding so much more knowledge, perhaps overseas, in digital form, inside and outside the firm all contribute to increased susceptibility. As compelling as the case is for sharing information and knowledge far and wide throughout the network, a firm has to be aware of the risks it faces and act accordingly.

Back to the SPFs

Returning to the example of Dell, the firm vividly illustrates how close coordination and knowledge sharing with collaborators can help to establish sustainable competitive advantage. The firm has cutting-edge technology in its supply chain management system, allowing instantaneous communication between itself and suppliers out to the nth level. It shares critical operational information and higher levels of knowledge throughout its e-network, gathering, sharing, and employing knowledge in ways a firm without such capabilities could not. And once again, the technology is less the key than the enabling mechanism. The resulting close relationships spur the collaboration and knowledge sharing to even higher levels.

But wide dispersal of knowledge leads to other problems. Dell's supply chain reaches through numerous levels, involving numerous firms and multitudes of people. The more knowledge is shared, the greater the share of Dell's knowledge assets that can be held or at least accessed by an incredible number of individuals. As such, the targets for CI are multiplied, the impact of an infiltration can be much more severe, and the core firm may have much less control over the precautions taken. The presence of many collaborators overseas and the digital form of the knowledge only further complicate the scenario.

If integrated, knowledge-rich supply chains and other upstream collaborations are of little competitive benefit to a firm, the KM Risk will be low. If it chooses not to install SCM or ERP systems and widely disseminate the related information, it will not likely suffer because competitors will see little value either. Sharing higher levels of information or knowledge won't be a priority either. Whether the knowledge is hard to share or just immaterial to competition for that firm, the low KM Risk suggests that leveraging knowledge assets will be a low priority. Such firms will face an SPF 5 (Brilliance) or SPF 30 (Glass House) situation.

On the other hand, if ERP, SCM, or even SRM systems are a priority, if closer relationships are necessary and require even higher levels of knowledge sharing, then KM Risk will be high. A competitor developing its supply chain and other upstream relationships to an ever deeper level will discover a diversity and depth of knowledge that an organization will find hard to match if it does not follow a similar path. The technological systems, supply chain efficiencies, and closer relationships must be in place if a firm is to compete at the highest levels in some situations. Otherwise it will fall behind competitors who do engage in such practices. When sharing knowledge across wide vistas is critical to success, high KM Risk will result, with firms looking at SPF 15 (800-pound Gorilla) or SPF 45 (Cold War) scenarios.

In terms of CI Risk, closely held knowledge and a limited relationship with supply chain and other partners will reduce an organization's vulnerability. If e-networking systems are not installed, a firm has less to worry about. As noted earlier, fewer organizations and people involved, less knowledge shared, more controls in place because the knowledge doesn't go beyond the core organization, less knowledge sharing across borders, and less digitization of information and knowledge all decrease CI Risk levels. Those firms keeping operational information and other knowledge close at hand, not necessarily in the hands of all collaborators, will have less vulnerability. As a result, they will be facing SPF 5 (Brilliance) or SPF 15 (800-pound Gorilla) environments.

Alternatively, firms sharing their operational information and other knowledge freely throughout their supply chains will be looking at high CI Risk. More knowledge, in more heads, outside the control of the core firm, digital, and perhaps overseas, will dramatically increase the vulnerability of that organization (and its entire e-network). Installation of e-networks and closer relationships with supply chain and other collaborators will expose the firm and place it in an SPF 30 (Glass House) or SPF 45 (Cold War) situation.

Or, to sum up, SPF 5 (Brilliance) scenarios will be characterized by organizations that have little reason, because of national-, industry-, or firm-level circumstances, to fully employ knowledge assets through SCM or ERP systems. They also have little to worry about in terms of losing their knowledge assets to competitors. SPF 15 (800-pound Gorilla) organizations will find that establishing e-networks is important to them but that the same range of circumstances make competitive incursion concerns minimal. SPF 30 (Glass House) situations will again present little reason to install e-networks, but such relationships, even if at low levels, will need to be carefully monitored because CI issues are so pronounced. And SPF 45 (Cold War) firms will need to create and use SCM and ERP systems, as well as develop ever closer knowledge-sharing collaborations, while at the same time recognizing the pronounced threats posed by aggressive competitor intelligence efforts.

Summary

As executives using an intelligence approach ponder their knowledge strategies, they need to recognize what is happening with information technology, the Internet, and business practices. Web-based ERP and SCM systems allow instantaneous and substantive communication between a core firm and its upstream partners. Operational information such as product forecasts or actual sales, inventory levels, input needs, and so on, flows throughout such e-networks. As the systems have evolved, many of the core firms move to closer relationships with fewer collaborators. Another result is that many of the core firms start to share even more information and knowledge with their partners.

From an upstream perspective, this knowledge can include product development plans; manufacturing and service delivery insights concerning efficiency, quality, and environmental impacts; purchasing considerations; and more. E-networks provide firms opportunities to spread valuable information and knowledge to collaborators, not just because of the technology involved but because of the tight relationships that develop.

For firms in nations with conditions supporting the development and use of such systems, in industries moving toward e-networks as a means of competition, and/or with the individual means to install and benefit from these structures, the KM Risk will be substantial. As such, failing to take advantage of the knowledge asset development, sharing, and analysis possibilities in front of them can result in a tremendous missed opportunity. Similarly, for firms finding little national protection for such knowledge assets, a high degree of industry intelligence activities or leakage of knowledge, and/or with weak firm-level protection capabilities, the CI Risk will be substantial. In such cases, firms overdeveloping and oversharing their knowledge assets through e-networks will leave themselves vulnerable to competitive intelligence infiltrations.

Executive Moment

As you review your own situation, think about how your firm collaborates with upstream and coequal partners. Ask yourself these questions.

- How tightly integrated are our operations and supply chain?
- Do we use Internet-based synchronization tools to their fullest potential?
- How close are our relationships with our upstream partners?

Whatever your information technology and relationship situation, you should also think about how information and knowledge are used within the structure. Think about the following questions.

- Do we spread our operational information and knowledge as widely as is beneficial?

- Do we identify and target other knowledge from diverse places throughout the upstream network?
- Do we process all of this knowledge, using it for strategic purposes?
- Is higher-level knowledge shared to good purpose throughout the network?
- What are our major competitors doing regarding all of these questions?

Finally, think about the security of your extended organization. Ask yourself these questions.

- Who has full access to all of this information and knowledge? Is it all of our upstream collaborators? All of their collaborators? All of the employees within all of these entities?
- Do we have proper security systems and procedures in placc?
- Does everyone throughout the upstream network have similar security?
- How do we evaluate which of our upstream partners is ready for a closer, knowledge-sharing relationship?

Think about whether your upstream knowledge strategy is optimal. Do you act to develop and share knowledge assets as appropriate to the KM Risk circumstances? And do you protect those assets as appropriate to the CI Risk circumstances? As you consider those questions, let's turn to the other side of the Value Chain, the downstream collaborators, and consider the opportunities and risks you might face from that part of the network.

Intelligence Across the Value Chain: Downstream

Give the people what they want.

—Ray Davies

As noted in the last chapter, close relationships and knowledge sharing with supply chain partners, R&D partners, manufacturing partners, and others upstream along the Value Chain are not necessarily new ideas. These relationships, however, have been enhanced by the new tools of the Internet. As a result, the amount of operational information shared is exponentially greater than what we have seen in the past. And the symbiosis that develops between collaborators can also lead to levels of knowledge sharing, including strategic knowledge that is closely linked to competitive advantage, that is unprecedented.

The same phenomenon is occurring on the other end of the Value Chain, in relationships concerning activities such as outbound logistics, marketing and sales, and service. Once again, information technology and the Internet are the drivers, although, once again, knowledge sharing and closer relationships are actually the critical factors enhancing competitive advantage. Organizations need to consider whether they are using all forms of knowledge to their fullest extent in downstream e-networks. They also need to worry about the security of any knowledge they share.

General Electric is a firm that was somewhat late to the Internet, as was the case with some firms we discussed in earlier chapters. The firm had long been committed to information technology in its supply chain (*Economist* 2001). GE Information Services (GEIS), dating from the 1980s, provided electronic data interchange connections that connected 100,000 firms in GE's network and included over one billion annual transactions. The hype of the dotcoms, however, didn't register with GE managers who saw it more as a consumer phenomenon not necessarily as relevant for its largely business-to-business relationships. In 1999, however, Jack Welch had his famous revelation concerning the Internet, terming e-business to be "priority one, two, three, and four" for all of GE and installing the "destroyyourbusiness.com" plan for moving different SBUs toward the Web. GEIS became GE Global eXchange Services (software and exchanges) and GE Systems Services (EDI networks). The firm is now at the forefront of e-networks.

But more recent changes at GE are of even more interest to us. After his ascension to CEO in late 2001, Jeffrey Immelt launched a campaign to make those with customer contact obsessed with helping their clients (Brady 2002). Part of the emphasis of this initiative was to provide customers with whatever they needed from GE, including management help. More recently, this GE concept has evolved into the "At the Customer, For the Customer" (ACFC) program (Brady 2003). The intent of ACFC is to make all the assets of GE, including knowledge assets, available to customers in order to help their businesses. ACFC comes down to sharing knowledge with close customers. And, of course, few firms can bring the range of knowledge assets to the table that a conglomerate like GE can.

So if customers want market research or R&D knowledge, GE can make it available to them. If they want access to programs such as Six Sigma (quality) or Work Out (empowerment), they can get it. If they want management training at GE's legendary Crotonville site, it's there. Or if they want knowledge about farflung operations, including outsourcing or doing business in a particular country, GE can also provide that. As an example, GE Aircraft Engines was able to perform a Six Sigma action for Southwest Airlines, cleaning up persistent quality problems with a component made by a non-GE supplier. University Community Health System not only got help with setting up the technology in a new hospital and research center, it was given insights into what would soon be coming out of R&D in GE Medical Systems as well as leadership development and workplace design. GE has taken the standard KM formula of cataloguing and sharing the key knowledge assets of the firm and has extended it well into its downstream e-network. Part of this is the e-network that allows close coordination with customers, but the relationships also involve access to many of the firm's key competitive advantage knowledge assets, going far beyond operational information. Imagine the possibilities for an NBC advertiser that can tap into the resident knowledge of all of GE's various businesses, and the advantages that will accrue to that advertiser (and, eventually, GE).

GE has learned to manage its knowledge assets strategically (the firm also is well aware of the CI implications and protects its knowledge, too). In this chapter, we'll focus on the downstream part of the Value Chain and how organizations need to think about strategically managing the knowledge they share with distribution channel partners, marketing partners, customers, and others. We'll also discuss the protection aspects of managing these downstream knowledge relationships. Finally, we'll take a look at the full e-network and the implications of connecting the full network, both upstream and downstream, through knowledge sharing.

The Value Chain: Downstream

Integrated, communication-rich distribution channels are an increasing source of competitive advantage.

The most obvious use of the Internet in downstream applications is for customer orders and associated order processing/fulfillment functions. CRM applications include such activities but also enable core firms to gather information on customer likes and dislikes, leading to customer knowledge—essentially traditional KM collaborative capital on steroids. The data mining capabilities of CRM add to the ability of firms to get to identify, know, and understand their best customers, but the basic concept is still the same.

But e-networks do far more. Going back to the Value Chain, the downstream functions also include outbound logistics, marketing and sales, and service. The outbound logistics, efficiently moving the product through distribution channels, include tying together channel partners (distributors, wholesalers, retailers) as well as managing transportation, warehousing, and other logistical functions. Channel partners are almost by definition external to the core firm, and logistics partners such as UPS, Fedex, and DHL are taking over more and more duties as well. A great deal of operational information is shared between such partners, as is a good amount of knowledge, including high-level intentions such as marketing strategies (pricing and promotional plans, for example).

Marketing and sales responsibilities are also shared along the downstream Value Chain. Once again, channel partners can be involved, as when a retailer handles marketing communication functions for a core firm (local advertising, sales promotions, selling). A car dealer, for example, typically performs such duties for the car manufacturer, advertising model availability, executing promotions such as rebates, and conducting personal selling. More and more, such activities are coordinated from the central firm and supported by the Web. Other outside collaborators such as advertising and IMC agencies, marketing research firms, and other marketing service providers can also be plugged into the e-network, sharing knowledge concerning marketing strategies and communication plans.

Service responsibilities can also be present downstream. Again, automobile dealers are a good example, handling routine maintenance, repairs, and recalls of the manufacturer's product. Plans to use services to competitive advantage, recurring service problems and/or solutions, and other such knowledge can be shared through e-networks.

Finally, customers are also part of the equation. CRM programs, in particular, can gather information regarding end consumers or industrial customers (as well as reseller or channel partners). Customer identities, descriptive information (demographics, psychographics, usage levels), product preferences, price sensitivity, preferred purchasing locations, favored communication mechanisms, and other such information or knowledge are all available and potentially valuable as a competitive weapon. With CRM systems, especially when combined with downstream programs, e-networks are capable of transferring information and knowledge from the customer all the way to the most remote supplier (and back again).

As noted throughout this book, this information and knowledge can be used to even further strategic advantage through purposeful collection, analysis, and forwarding to key decision makers. As with the downstream functions, the breadth and diversity of information and knowledge can add to the knowledge assets of the core organization and the rest of the e-network. And again, an intelligence approach that better distributes and better manages the knowledge is only enhanced by this new wealth of sources and targets.

And, of course, so many more points of contact along the e-network with access to so much more information and knowledge pose security threats. When these additional partners are collaborative firms, the issues are serious enough. When those holding the knowledge are totally outside the collective, as is the case with customers, the potential problems are really multiplied, since the core firm and its network literally have no control over what such individuals and organizations might do.

In the rest of this chapter, we'll illustrate some of these issues by looking at the knowledge sharing that takes place in downstream e-networks. The nature of participants and the type of information or knowledge collected, analyzed, and passed on is instructive to any organization thinking of optimizing its own knowledge strategy.

Similarly, the type of knowledge at risk and how different parties place it at risk is also of interest. We'll deal with each in turn.

KM Risk and Reward: Downstream

Distribution channels and customers offer rich opportunities for knowledge sharing.

So what examples do we have of how knowledge assets can be managed downstream in e-networks? And what can we make of them? One important point to make, once again, is that the technology is not the key, it's what can be done with the technology in terms of communication and knowledge asset development. The information technology, the ease of use, the ease of coordination, and the storage capabilities act together to create tremendous opportunities for firms seeking to better leverage the knowledge contained in their e-networks.

Freightliner, for example, has installed a backward SCM system that helps its dealer network better manage their orders to Freightliner and existing inventory (Nairn 2003). The truck maker's parts catalogue totals 160,000 units. Based on sales histories from the entire network and computer-generated forecasts, the i2 software handles ordering for Freightliner's dealers. So Freightliner is able to share important operational knowledge downstream with its collaborators, making its ordering more efficient and minimizing both overstocks and stockouts. This knowledge flows from both collection (sales histories) and analysis, illustrating an intelligence approach.

Similarly, the outsourcing of increasingly sophisticated parts of production to suppliers (as, for example, in the auto industry where suppliers often make entire components rather than just parts these days) has generated a practice termed "bundling" (Tejada 2003). To insulate themselves from pure price competition, some suppliers seek to use knowledge to sell more value-added products, combining either multiple parts or parts with service. Timken, for example, makes more than 90,000 bearings. The firm has found it difficult to compete on price with other bearing manufacturers, particularly overseas, that concentrate on basic products. Timken has leveraged its expertise and knowledge to tailor customized solutions to customer problems.

Based on what it had learned, for example, about combining friction reduction and lubrication components in automotive bearings, the firm was able to offer similar products (friction-reducing bearings combined with lubricating flaps) for the low-volume dumptruck and windmill markets. Timken has created a number of bundles of products and components that incorporate its own knowledge about bearings combined with knowledge about customer needs. The firm is also able to add organizational knowledge concerning ancillary services in building bundles that include installation, maintenance, and engineering to the basic bearing.

Outsourcing can also involve staff functions (downstream or at a coequal level). IBM has substantially expanded its service offerings, taking over entire computing functions for clients, up to and including computing-on-demand for customers who only wish to lease computing time (Ante 2004). IBM is taking over more and more of the support functions of firms that don't see themselves as having a core competency in information technology. In 2003, for example, IBM arranged to take over Procter & Gamble's human resource systems (throughout the Value Chain). In addition to taking over P&G's hardware and staff, IBM is also acquiring the consumer goods firm's customized SAP system and Web interface. The deal should allow P&G to lower its costs and raise service levels by taking advantage of IBM's accumulated knowledge. But IBM will also benefit from P&G's knowledge assets, as it intends to combine the P&G assets with its own expertise in order to better customize services for other customers.

Another downstream knowledge application is found in logistics. We've already touched on the topic in the upstream chapter, and inbound logistics can certainly be important. But logistics in distribution channels particularly demonstrate the point.

Third- and fourth-party logistics providers have proliferated in recent years, ranging from transportation firms to fully integrated "consolidators" who help core firms better manage their entire supply and distribution lines. Perhaps the best example of the trend is found in the companies that used to be simple parcel services (UPS, Fedex, DHL) that now optimize entire logistics operations for clients.

Modern logistics deals with "three parallel flows: physical goods, information, and finance" (*Economist* 2002). Whereas logistics outsourcing has long included transportation of goods (e.g., freight forwarders, parcel services) and finance, the sharing of information and knowledge is newer but is growing rapidly. With information in hand, the logistics providers have found they can transport goods and help with scheduling and integrating delivery as well. Marten Transport, for example, has taken to applying technology so as to better communicate and coordinate with customers (Machalaba 2003). By working with customers (and, indeed, rewarding those that cut wait times, loading times, and other such factors), Marten has been able to cut downtime, keeping drivers on the road and fixed assets such as refrigerated trailers in use. The only way to do so is to share information. Customers let Marten know production plans and the best times to deliver (so the client is prepared and ready to help unload). Marten lets customers know when arrivals will happen, when delays occur, and other such factors. By analyzing the information/knowledge, Marten can further streamline the process, developing intelligence about customer needs and installing appropriate pricing policies.

Similarly, "pure logistics companies" such as TPG and Exel often don't even own their own transportation assets anymore, simply using their expertise to optimize supply chains and distribution channels for clients (*Economist* 2002). TPG, for example, works with Ford, coordinating with the carmaker's operations to schedule 800 daily deliveries from 300 different suppliers. Exel works with clients such as Maxtor, a disk-drive manufacturer. Exel, which has sold off its own shipping and trucking assets, gets Maxtor products from

Asia and into the production processes of Dell and HP (both in the United States and in Asia). Exel's CEO claims "we analyze and optimize the supply-chain for the company and so create value." As with our other examples, the key to being able to do so is being plugged into the information systems of both sellers and receivers, and not only using the information to better work operations but, through analysis, to create knowledge and even intelligence about how to improve the performance of the entire network.

Another growing outsourced function that demands knowledge sharing is reverse logistics. The term has been with us for a number of years, generally referring to the handling of merchandise returned by customers (Mason 2002). Just as it is possible to outsource distribution, so this backward distribution can be handed over to a third- or fourth-party logistics provider. With the rise of Internet retailing, in particular, outside reverse logistics firms have seen demand swell (more goods are returned after Web purchases, principally because they can't be handled or tried on until after receipt). Environmental concerns have also raised interest in reverse logistics, as firms look to reuse packaging or take back the product at the end of its useful life (as is now required for many goods in Europe). This is a specialized area, and the Web systems that exist to help manage it must be customized, since the nature of the goods and their individual destinations are hard to forecast. Even so, handling returns or reusables and processing this information can provide insights into what is happening at the core firm (are there patterns in terms of returned products? are there patterns in the reasons for return?). 3M, for example, takes back not only its own overhead projectors but those of competitors. The justification is that the competing products are very similar, with parts that can be reclaimed regardless of manufacturer, and the move also raised the volume of reusables high enough to make the process economically feasible. But, in addition, 3M, and any third-party collaborators, will also gain knowledge concerning the life expectancy of all types of competitor projectors, as well as common problems that tend to bring about projector retirement.

As a final downstream example, let's look at knowledge obtained from and used for consumers. Tesco is the market share leader in the U.K. grocery market (which now includes Wal-Mart) and one of the most successful retailers in the world. The firm's Clubcard and related programs are interesting examples of how customer relationship management works and how the resulting knowledge gains can be used for the benefit of the firm and its e-network (Spethmann 2004). Tesco's systems also illustrate the nature and level of the information and knowledge that flow through such structures.

Tesco starts a bit ahead of the game compared to U.S. grocers in that the U.K. market tends to contain more loyal consumers and the store brands are more powerful, allowing the retailers to have a bit more bargaining power with manufacturers. Tesco has taken these factors even further by developing a very close relationship with its customers. The Clubcard is similar to grocery loyalty cards seen in other stores but is not just a "discount" card but rather denotes club membership with associated rewards, including a 1 percent rebate. The rebate is delivered in a quarterly mailing to customers. The key to the system, however, is the processing of the consumer information. Tesco uses its customer purchase information to develop intelligence about who its customers are and how their relationship with the grocery can be deepened.

One part of this relationship is found in a segmentation system Tesco refers to as "rolling ball." Top products are rated on a number of attributes (fresh/not, high/low fat, needs preparation/ready to eat) so as to develop a picture of both the product and its customer. As related combinations of products are discovered (the rolling ball), they are added to the description of the customer who buys such things. Eventually, the firm can come up with a picture of customer segments and the baskets of products they tend to buy. This deep understanding has several useful applications. Initially, the quarterly mailings can include highly targeted promotional offers. Given the stability of Tesco's customer pool, the firm concentrates on selling up (higher-priced items than the consumer already buys) or additional items (which should appeal to them based on their rolling ball characterization). Tesco claims to be able to send up to 4 million distinctly different offering mixes to its 10-million-home customer base, customizing each promotional piece to the household. The firm has also been able to establish and target subclubs (such as Babyclub for families with infants) as well as launch other appropriate services. Tesco Personal Finance, for example, already has 3.5 million customers, and Tesco Talk served 500,000 phone subscribers in its first year of operation. Tesco also shares customer information and knowledge with manufacturers, extending the CRM application further up its own Value Chain.

The point with Tesco and all the other examples listed in this section is that CRM and other operational systems, especially those on the Internet, have become integral parts of contemporary firms. Valuable information and/or knowledge flows through such systems and all can be further developed through analysis and application. Tesco's customer data is important in and of itself. But once it is subjected to the depth of analysis that Tesco applies to it, and once the grocer acts on it, sometimes in partnership with other members of its e-network, this information and knowledge can become intelligence. Programs such as Clubcard or third-party logistics work because firms are recognizing the value of knowledge, the value of better using such knowledge, and the value of extending such knowledge assets throughout their own companies and on to Value Chain collaborators. Yet again, the bottom line is that downstream e-business applications are granting competitive advantage. Firms that fail to execute knowledge management as well as their competition does will find themselves left far behind, the victims of KM Risk.

CI Risk and Reward: Downstream

Distribution channels also offer increased vulnerability.

Just as with upstream applications, firms need to be aware that the amount of information and knowledge flowing throughout the downstream portions of e-networks can put them at serious risk. The logic is similar, as firms building Internet-linked distribution channels and customer relationships, by definition, are putting a lot more operational and marketing information out into the big wide cyberworld. And once again, the even closer relationships that come from such linkages often result in knowledge development and sharing that goes beyond simple exchanges of the basic information. The digital, distributed wealth of knowledge available to so many more partners, including customers, is a very tempting target for competitors practicing CI.

Consider some illustrative examples. Initially, digitized customer data is a concern in and of itself. The outright theft of such information for purposes of credit card fraud and such is something that all firms need to worry about, even if competitive threats are minor. Hacking is generally not practiced by legitimate CI operatives, especially not for the purpose of outright theft, but firms still need to be alert to such activity. Even the U.S. Navy, for example, had credit card information (from its internal purchasing accounts) taken from its IT system (Latour 2003). More to the point of customer data, Best Buy had to shut down its WiFi network when testing revealed that someone sitting in the parking lot outside of any individual store could tap into the system (Green & Elgin 2002).

In a business-to-business situation, the stakes are just as high. The small software firm Niku found that someone had obtained access to a number of its system passwords and entered its secure IT system over 6,000 times (Kersey 2002). Niku accused a competitor of directing the break-in and obtaining critical downstream company knowledge including "upcoming features, lists of potential customers, pricing, and customizations for clients."

Business partners can be another source of concern, as was the case with upstream networks. Microsoft was accused of "theft of intellectual property" after working with Sendo to develop a smart phone, a coequal product development relationship (Reinhardt & Green 2003). Sendo worked on the hardware side, and Microsoft was to deliver a version of Windows appropriate to the phone. After glitches, which both sides blamed on each other, a third party, High Tech Computer Co. in Taiwan, introduced a smart phone that beat Sendo to market. Given that High Tech had little development experience in the area but ties to Microsoft, Sendo drew the conclusion that the huge software firm had passed along some of Sendo's proprietary knowledge (a charge Microsoft vigorously denies). Whatever the outcome of the lawsuit, the general framework of the episode vividly illustrates the gravity of the shared knowledge issue.

Other business partner examples include service companies. The Apollo Group's University of Phoenix was accused of appropriating the trade secrets of its placement testing provider, Chariot Software (Golden 2003). Chariot's complaint claimed that Apollo gave access to Chariot's proprietary software code to a third firm that replaced it as the contracted supplier. A celebrated dumpster diving incident in 2000 involving Microsoft and Oracle was actually conducted at the site of a nonprofit institute that seemed to be conducting public relations activities for Microsoft (Oracle employed the investigative firm actually digging through the trash) (Simpson & Bridis 2000). Indeed, nonprofit organizations involved with Microsoft seem to be attacked as a matter of course, perhaps because the core firm is seen as being a harder nut to crack. Besides the Independent Institute just noted in the dumpster diving incident, Citizens for a Sound Economy (stolen laptops), National Taxpayers Union (leaked internal documents, suspicious visitors), and the Association for Competitive Technology (cleaning crews offered cash for trash) are all perceived Microsoft allies targeted by someone conducting CI (Simpson 2000). Finally, a 2001 case involving an advertising agency ended with the firm being required to bar some personnel from working on a Coca-Cola account because they had previous experience working with Pepsi, and access to some proprietary Pepsi marketing plans (McKay & Vranica 2001).

Consumers can also be a problem. When Palm launched a major competitive intelligence effort against Microsoft in 2000 as the latter sought to enter the handheld market, it particularly targeted users for information (Tam 2000b). Palm monitored Web sites and chat rooms for what enthusiasts were saying about what Microsoft might be up to in developing its Pocket PC product, especially the software. The real coup came, however, when the firm learned that Microsoft was demonstrating the prototype to groups of potential customers. Palm was able to place an employee at one of those meetings, learning what Microsoft's "talking points" were concerning its handheld—allowing Palm to anticipate the features that Microsoft would be pushing in terms of its marketing.

One of the most frustrating issues with consumers, however, is that sometimes the most enthusiastic and loyal customers can be the biggest threat in terms of letting out important information. Message boards, chat rooms, and fan Web sites all have the potential to let out key information or knowledge about a company and its products. During the past two Christmas seasons, FatWallet.com and other Web sites have managed to obtain and post the pricing and promotional plans of major retailers (Waldmeir 2002). If Wal-Mart intended to drop the price on a DVD player next week, for example, such information might end up on the Web site. Obviously such knowledge is to the benefit of customers, but it can also impact the earning power of the firm and/or provide competitors with key insights. Similarly, companies such as Apple, with its famously loyal customers, can find themselves the subject of fan sites such as macintouch.com, macosrumors.com, and appleinsider.com (Tam 2000a). In 2000 Apple filed suit against an unknown "John Doe" who had obtained and posted proprietary information concerning upcoming new products. Once more, the information was important to Apple and not something it wanted revealed to the competition, but a firm has to be careful with how it approaches customers with fanatical brand loyalty.

To summarize, downstream entities, from distribution channel partners to sales and marketing collaborators to customers, have increasing access to operational information. The closer relationships often lead to the sharing of even more information and knowledge. As a result, many more points of attack now exist for competitive organizations seeking to obtain this proprietary information or knowledge. And, of course, the core firm will find it harder to maintain the internal controls it might have in place once Value Chain partners are involved. Firms may face much higher CI Risk because of these trends, and those that fail to recognize the danger and react will find themselves at a tremendous competitive disadvantage.

Value Chain Redux

One firm's upstream is another firm's downstream: Who's in your extended network?

One final thought before we leave the topic of the Value Chain, information technology, and how closer relationships and greater knowledge sharing is affecting the KM Risk and CI Risk situations of organizations. Throughout the discussion in the last three chapters, we have repeatedly referred to a core firm as an anchor to what is happening upstream and downstream from it. Managers need to recognize, however, that Value Chains interact. As a result, that third-tier supplier far upstream from core firm A is, in fact, a core firm itself with its own upstream and downstream collaborators. And the distributor downstream from core firm B is also a core firm of its own Value Chain with further upstream and downstream partners. The Value Chain for any organization includes its own collaborators as well as all of those who make up the Value Chains of these collaborators and their collaborators and their collaborators, and on and on. While these far extended Value Chains offer incredible opportunities for identifying, harvesting, and sharing knowledge, they also pose formidable knowledge protection challenges.

Consider an example. LeapFrog, the educational toy maker, is at the center of a number of interconnected Value Chains spanning the globe (Fowler & Pereira 2003). We noted in earlier chapters how the supply chains of consumer goods retailers (e.g., Zara, Li & Fung) have tightened up in recent years, with six-month or even nine-month lead times declining to just a couple of months or even a matter of weeks. LeapFrog is one of the firms in the middle of this shift, benefiting from tighter Value Chain integration in both directions.

Traditionally, Christmas orders for toys were placed early in the previous January or February, requiring toy makers to guess in terms of what products would be most popular the next holiday season. Celebrated shortages such as 1993's Mighty Morphin Power Rangers 600,000-unit supply in the face of potential demand of 12 million illustrate what can be left on the table if the firm has a bad forecast. At the other extreme is unsold inventory, also a major problem.

LeapFrog, however, is plugged into the supply chain management systems of major retailers such as Wal-Mart and Toys-R-Us. As a result, it receives overnight sales figures. The firm also has background knowledge in terms of individual store sales and related demographics, as well as promotional details such as current advertising, discounts, displays, and other such variables that might affect the sales. Armed with such information, LeapFrog's management is able to analyze the sales figures, effectively developing intelligence about what is happening with its products in the marketplace. From worldwide sales levels as low as 360 units, the firm can extrapolate, forecasting sales far into the future, including the Christmas season.

In 2003, LeapFrog's LittleTouch LeapPads were introduced in early August. Based on the first week's sales and sales distribution, LeapFrog management projected 700,000 units would be needed for the Christmas season, double the prelaunch estimate. That early forecast of 350,000 units had taken a full year to manufacture and feed into distribution channels. Now, LeapFrog sought to source the same number and deliver them to U.S. stores in the four remaining months before Christmas.

Capable Toys of Zhongshan, China, was the manufacturing partner for LittleTouch's. After seemingly completing the year's production, the firm had to turn around and try to meet LeapFrog's new demands. Besides taking care of sourcing issues (raw materials, microchips, and specialized paper), hiring more workers, and obtaining more tooling so as to create more assembly lines, Capable sought to apply its manufacturing expertise to the situation, improving the process so as to increase capacity further. Capable's knowledge base, as well as its own supply chain connections, enabled the firm to meet LeapFrog's demand requirements.

The point, of course, is that the interlocking Value Chains needed to share information and knowledge in order to ensure an adequate supply of Little Touch's—everyone from Wal-Mart and Target, and all of their collaborators, to LeapFrog and all of its collaborators, to Capable and all of its collaborators. Does Wal-Mart necessarily recognize that its sales figures are being funneled to a U.S. book printing firm that was chosen to supply Tyvek to Capable? Wal-Mart probably does, but would all firms? Would your firm? The scale and scope of sharing throughout all these supply chains and distribution channels is not immediately apparent, even to the most savvy of managers. As noted before, the potential of fully developing the knowledge assets throughout all associated networks is not always appreciated, but neither is the competitive intelligence risk.

Back to the SPFs

Our initial anecdote concerned GE, a company that is at the forefront of applying technology to its network relationships. Indeed, the firm has recognized that it has not only operational information but core knowledge that can be of value to it downstream partners, including end customers. Sharing competitive advantage knowledge such as Six Sigma quality programs or management training systems could be invaluable to GE as it tries to offer unique value to customers, and, of course, its network partners could use such knowledge to improve their own operations, becoming even more valuable collaborators or users of GE products.

GE must certainly realize the competitive intelligence risks of such approaches, but it seems to have confidence in its protection systems, as well as those of its partners. In making such an assessment, we believe GE management likely considered the full range of factors that affect the KM Risk and CI Risk levels that face the organization. And these factors are important. GE recently faced an opportunity to expand its power generation business in China. In return for the $900 million contract, however, GE had to agree to share manufacturing processes and the underlying technology embedded in some of its most advanced turbines (Kranhold 2004). While U.S. government regulations on technology transfer barred the sharing of some key elements, GE was still essentially being asked to train its future competition. In making the decision to take the deal, GE had to balance the benefits of sharing critical knowledge with the competitive risks involved. The firm decided to take the deal. Other firms, such as Intel, have decided against bringing their most advanced manufacturing processes and technologies into China.

GE's dilemma illustrates once again how a firm's particular circumstances will determine its unique risk environment. The more national variables favor sharing knowledge downstream from the core firm, through laws and regulations, investment in IT systems, or a culture of cooperation, the more KM Risk the organization will face if it fails to develop modern e-networks and ever closer relationships. Similarly, if the industry is headed toward more collaboration and sharing through CRM and related systems and/or if the individual firm and its main competitors have particular strengths or weaknesses in these areas, the KM Risk will again increase. Firms with attractive scenarios for knowledge asset development based on the combination of national-, industry-, and firm-specific variables facing them will find themselves in high-KM-Risk scenarios such as SPF 15 (800-pound Gorilla) or SPF 45 (Cold War).

On the other hand, if circumstances do not favor establishing formal CRM and/or IT-rich distribution channels, or if even closer relationships are not likely to develop (with knowledge sharing beyond operational information), then the situation is much different. Again, firms need to pay attention to national variables affecting upstream relationships, industry practice, and the firm's own relative strengths and weaknesses. If the firm fails to benefit from sharing operational information or downstream-related knowledge, then it faces low KM Risk. As a result, depending on CI Risk levels, it will find itself in SPF 5 (Brilliance) or SPF 30 (Glass House) situations.

From the CI Risk perspective, an organization with downstream knowledge that means little to competitors or is unavailable to them will face low risk levels. Discerning such a situation depends again on reviewing the relevant risk factors, including how much protection exists in national law (e.g., U.S. technology transfer restrictions in GE's case) or how closemouthed the national culture makes downstream partners. Similarly, the industry situation in terms of CI practice and the firm's circumstances are factors. If CI efforts are limited or the firm has particularly strong protection systems, for example, CI Risk will be lessened. With low threats at all levels, firms will find themselves with overall low CI Risk and classified in SPF 5 (Brilliance) or SPF 15 (800-pound Gorilla).

Alternatively, with a national environment encouraging CI (e.g., China in the GE case), extensive industry CI activity, and poor firm or network structures for preventing disclosure, firms will find themselves subject to higher CI Risk. Their downstream operational information systems, as well as any knowledge sharing that comes from closer relationships, will be at greater risk. With high scores on all three levels of variables, organizations will face high CI Risk and SPF 30 (Glass House) or SPF 45 (Cold War) scenarios.

Looked at another way the prototypical SPF 5 (Brilliance) firm will likely not benefit too much from advanced operational systems in its distribution channels or customer relationships. Information or knowledge is not easily shared or particularly beneficial when it is. And competitive intelligence is muted because competitors are prevented from effective efforts or simply not interested. SPF 15 (800-pound Gorilla) organizations do need to have more cutting edge systems in order to communicate with distributors, retailers, marketing partners such as advertising agencies, customers, and so on. For a variety of reasons, however, the key information and knowledge shared through such systems and/or through closer relationships isn't sought by competitors—again, either because it is not worth the effort or is not easily applied to a different, competing firm's processes.

SPF 30 (Glass House) firms will tend to limit knowledge sharing, finding that downstream partners and/or customers don't have much to offer in terms of information or knowledge. What limited proprietary knowledge there is can be extremely important, however, so it is kept close to the core firm and is not widely distributed. Competitors are very interested in such knowledge, so it is not shared with many downstream collaborators. And SPF 45 (Cold War) companies will need to extensively develop their downstream systems, collecting and sharing information and knowledge throughout their e-networks. Such systems are almost a requirement for competing. Even with such wide development of knowledge assets, however, these firms need to carefully monitor use, as CI efforts are also extensive. So important knowledge is out there in the hands of retailers, marketing communication agencies, and even customers, but it needs protection systems to accompany it, since it is subject to great incursion risk.

One last note is that the front to back nature of interlocking Value Chains demands that firms understand not only their own SPF standing but those of collaborators as well. A firm such as Gucci might be currently considered SPF 5 because of the personal nature of its core competitive knowledge. But as Gucci increasingly competes with firms that utilize the interconnected retail to sourcing networks represented by Zara, H&M, and Li & Fung, it may find that knowledge assets about operations, upstream and downstream, do come to be important. And even if its own situation remains SPF 5, that of its upstream (supply chain) or downstream (retail, marketing) partners may be quite different, falling into SPF categories with much higher KM Risk or CI Risk levels.

Summary

The downstream portion of the Value Chain includes activities that occur postoperation in the core firm of an e-network. Outbound logistics, sales and marketing, and service are considered primary activities in this part of the chain, supported once again by secondary activities such as technology and human resources. Just as in the upstream case, these downstream activities are increasingly integrated, particularly by means of contemporary information technology tools such as customer relationship management systems. End consumers, retailers, distributors, and others feed their demand requirements into the system, and the e-network reacts to ensure appropriate sourcing, inventory levels, and production take place. The downstream systems ensure that the supply then gets to the right places, at the right times, in the right amounts. Getting it right means sharing a lot of operational information among a lot of network partners.

This sharing deepens as other collaborators are brought into the mix, such as advertising agencies and other marketing communication partners, lawyers, staffing firms, and others. We can also observe that partners connected by e-networks often develop closer relationships that involve the sharing of not just operational information but core knowledge assets, those that may be key to competitive advantage. The trend in a lot of industries is toward networks enabling greater dispersal of more and more information and knowledge, some of it quite important to participating firms. All organizations need to get a grip on this wide field of information and knowledge, understanding just how much is out there, how critical its identification, harvesting, and distribution is to competitive advantage, and whether a plan exists for managing all such knowledge assets. Through strategic management of these assets, many firms could improve performance. Whether by identifying knowledge gaps, by discovery through analysis, or by simply ensuring key knowledge gets to decision-makers, an intelligence approach can ensure better use of the wealth of assets available.

But, of course, the threat of incursion is always there as well. So an intelligence approach further mandates that executives understand all the places their most precious knowledge assets are headed. How widely is operational information shared? How widely are more core knowledge assets shared? Do all collaborators have appropriate protection systems in place? Are you aware of the protection capabilities of the full e-network with which you deal? How does one better manage knowledge in this new environment? And how does one protect it?

Executive Moment

In thinking about how you handle your downstream relationships, ask yourself the following questions.

- How tightly integrated are our downstream operations?
  - ☐ With distributors or retailers?
  - ☐ With logistics providers or other outsource partners?
  - ☐ With end customers?
- How tightly integrated are our downstream staff functions?
  - ☐ With advertising agencies or other marketing communication partners?
  - ☐ With other service providers such as HR agencies or lawyers?
- How prevalent are CRM or other cutting edge information technology systems in the countries and industries within which we compete?

With a sense of the systems and practices you have in place in your organization, you can begin thinking about matters such as the following.

- Do we recognize all the information and knowledge flowing through our downstream relationships? Is it all part of our KM plans?
- Could we better manage all of this information and knowledge by
  - ☐ Identifying key information or knowledge?
  - ☐ Supplementing it with targeted collection, if necessary?
  - ☐ Analysis?
  - ☐ Better systems to ensure it gets to key decision-makers?

And from a protection point-of-view, ask these questions.

- Do we treat all information and knowledge as proprietary organizational assets?
- Could we better protect this information and knowledge by
  - ☐ Identifying and separating key information or knowledge?
  - ☐ Installing appropriate protection processes?
  - ☐ Designating different levels of access for employees, network partners, and customers?

Think about these questions and how they relate to your firm. We've covered the situation that we see facing most organizations, and you should now be able to get a sense of the challenges in front of your particular organization. Keep those in mind as we now turn to some ideas on how to better address those challenges.

Part 3 Wrap-Up:
Knowledge to Intelligence Across the Enterprise

The nature of knowledge is subject to change, and the pace of change seems to have picked up in recent years. The traditional view of useful knowledge and what to do with it has become somewhat limiting for a number of reasons, many of which we have covered in earlier chapters. But a major shift in the last decade has been the move to the Internet by firms seeking to better coordinate their Value Chain, from supply to after-sale service. Computerized systems to better manage the supply chain, enterprise resource planning, and customer relationships have existed for quite some time, but the Internet has made such systems more inclusive and easier to connect. As a result, many more individual firms (including very small ones) and their disparate systems can now participate in extended, interconnected Value Chains.

As a result, the wealth of information flowing throughout these extended Value Chains has exploded. Much of this information is important beyond just the everyday running of the firm. Indeed, it can become knowledge: knowledge about how to develop and source products, about how to deliver them efficiently, and about what customers want and need. Further, the close relationships that these systems cause to develop often lead to sharing of other, nonoperational knowledge as well. With an intelligence approach including purposeful search, analysis, and delivery to decision-makers, all of this nontraditional knowledge can become intelligence. As such, it also requires protection.

In the grand scheme of what we have been discussing, these implications are important because they affect the KM Risk and CI Risk conditions of firms. They can enhance the potential of knowledge throughout the firm and its entire Value Chain—increasing KM Risk as competitors employ them but decreasing KM Risk for organizations that can effectively install and use such systems. Alternatively, they can increase CI Risk, simply on the basis of the spread of so much key knowledge into so many hands. The firm can manage these risks by taking some care about how far to scatter its knowledge assets, and we'll discuss some specific prescriptions in the next section. Internet systems affect KM Risk and CI Risk and thus are a matter to consider when identifying an SPF and reacting accordingly. Consider some general observations.

SPF 5: Brilliance

In this scenario, KM and CI Risk are low to moderate. A firm operating in a Brilliance risk scenario is one with little need to manage knowledge assets electronically or share them with collaborators. These types of firms, whether reflective of individual talents or a unique culture, do not gain value from developing ERP, SCM, or CRM systems. Further, they are less likely to network with partners. Because their business models are transparent or based on a hard-to-copy star system, the threat from competitive intelligence is minor. There is just little to motivate developing Web-based Value Chain systems and little concern about infiltrators.

SPF 15: 800-Pound Gorilla

The 800-pound Gorilla firm is more concerned with developing its knowledge assets and less concerned with CI Risk. Here, the Value Chain is fully supported by digital systems likely to include a number of network partners. The key driver behind SCM, SRM, and ERP systems is efficiency. Operational knowledge is used strategically to determine whether and how to outsource and create relationships. Knowledge of end users gleaned through CRM not only supports downstream marketing and sales operations but also feeds back to the supply chain. CI Risk is low to moderate, indicating that the firm's priority is likely to be knowledge development and sharing, with only secondary consideration given to competitor incursions. Although the digital systems and increased sharing can make the organization more vulnerable, its advantages remain hard to copy or of little value to competitors not operating in the same manner or same niche.

SPF 30: Glass House

KM Risk is low to moderate, whereas CI Risk is high, a transparent scenario. Competitors have a clear vision of each other's actions. Advantage is built on developing certain knowledge assets, held close to the vest, and relying on external networks and collaborators very little if at all. Digital tools are going to focus on internal operations and may provide copious amounts of information concerning customers and their needs, but true knowledge insights to be gained from it all may be limited. What few insights there are need to be fiercely guarded. Even within the firm, certain information may not be available to a wide range of employees. Patented processes, trade secrets, and customized product offerings can all provide a source of competitive advantage for the transparent firm, and all are likely to be aggressively pursued by competitors. Knowledge rarely remains proprietary for long, so firms push for first-mover advantage through innovation. In this tough environment, Glass House firms should employ electronic capabilities and manage resulting closer relationships carefully, purposefully, and tightly.

SPF 45: Cold War

A Cold War firm has highly developed knowledge assets and collaboration across its Value Chain. It also competes in an industry with rampant competitive intelligence activities. Technology across the Value Chain, upstream and downstream, helps manage the enterprise, run the supply chain, and serve customers. Firms in the Cold War operate in industries with intense rivalry and knowledgeable end users. Risks of not employing e-business systems or developing the resulting close relationships can be substantial but must be balanced against the equally imposing risks of letting critical proprietary information and knowledge outside the network. In order to compete, Cold War firms likely need to install and use SCM, ERP, and CRM systems to their fullest extents while also looking to develop closer, knowledge-sharing relationships with collaborators and customers. While doing so, however, they need to give substantial attention to protection systems, trying to ensure that this wealth of valuable knowledge flowing throughout the e-network remains proprietary.

Part 4: A Blueprint for Shifting from Knowledge to Intelligence

Installing the Intelligence Program: Structure

They always say time changes things, but you actually have to change them yourself.

—Andy Warhol

Back in the first chapter, we discussed what makes an intelligence approach different from standard knowledge management practice. While an ongoing program for collecting, storing, and sharing all the knowledge assets of the firm can be invaluable, intelligence can offer so much more.

Initially, intelligence recognizes that all forms of information and all knowledge, internal and external, are potentially useful, including competitive and operational knowledge. We've already covered, to a large extent, the reasons why and how the collection and use of such knowledge can help a firm. In this chapter we'll return to how intelligence-gathering systems are structured so as to take advantage of all these potential assets. Second, intelligence goes beyond a programmed collection of knowledge to a more purposeful search. Strategic use of knowledge includes identifying where gaps exist and what can be done to fill those gaps, allowing management to operate with the fullest possible set of assets. In this chapter, we further explore how purposeful search can be established and managed as part of an intelligence program.

Third, an intelligence approach analyzes existing knowledge, adding to the asset stock through learning and by drawing new insights from processing the assets. So we'll also dwell for a bit on common analysis tools that can be usefully applied to knowledge assets. Finally, intelligence suggests that key knowledge gets into the hands of decision-makers, be they executives setting strategy or those lower down in the organization charged with making tactical choices.

All of these matters can help with better use of potential knowledge assets, but intelligence also brings the understanding that knowledge resources need to be protected. Once we've established the types of processes that can better manage knowledge, we'll also discuss how organizations can better protect their new, enhanced assets.

Turning knowledge into intelligence requires an architecture, aside from software products, to facilitate the synthesis and analysis of information and knowledge across function, structure, and time zone. In addition, unfiltered, timely analysis needs to serve executive decisions, keeping decision-makers abreast of changes in the competitive arena. While traditional KM systems have evolved to become decision tools, they have yet to reach outside of the firm's storehouses of information.

An intelligence process takes all of these considerations into its design. An intelligence system can build competitive landscapes by piecing together a jigsaw puzzle of disparate sources of information. It can provide early warning of competitive shifts and help calibrate the impact of actions. Furthermore, as part of its design, an intelligence system can build a counterintelligence process to protect the knowledge assets and analyses it works so hard to create. Protection is a key consideration in a competitive intelligence world, especially for firms that need to develop their knowledge assets across their Value Chain and work across networks and alliances.

This chapter provides an overview of key considerations for building an intelligence system. It begins with some thoughts on extending the capabilities of knowledge assets and concludes by addressing what counterintelligence is and how to design this capability into the fabric of the firm.

Establishing an Intelligence Framework

How do you know what you think until you see what you say?
—Karl Weick

An intelligence framework is purposeful. It begins with a need, question, problem, or challenge that is tactical or strategic in nature. In the CI frameworks we have adapted for our broader intelligence system, the popular CI practitioner question of senior executives is "What keeps you up at night?" The answer then informs purpose. Common CI applications include shadowing competitors, assessing the impact of environmental changes on the firm's strategies, and developing new products and processes as sources of sustainable advantage. Regardless of the assignment, an intelligence process deliberately seeks out and puts to use information and knowledge from primary and secondary sources, internal and external to the organization.

One of the keys of an intelligence system is flexibility. Each decision problem will demand a different research approach, with unique knowledge needs. While KM processes concern themselves with capturing and cataloguing knowledge in established spheres, intelligence processes can be focused around any topic of current concern. The intelligence director and/or team deliberately seeks out information from existing knowledge bases, internal HUMINT, consultants, network partners, and anywhere else that may be useful. Appropriate information and knowledge can then be forwarded to existing or special-purpose teams and/or individuals able to integrate the knowledge and make sense of it. They may also direct more knowledge collection in order to fill in newly identified gaps. This individual or group can also make decisions about what knowledge will be added to the readily available asset base of the organization (and when, if the knowledge is sensitive).

So how does one design an intelligence process that is capable not only of the KM tasks of capture, codification, and distribution, but also this more flexible approach? How is the more flexible intelligence system structured, enabling managers to deal with all sorts of knowledge, purposefully fill in gaps, analyze the knowledge base, and direct key findings to decision-makers? Consider the basic architecture.

Designing the Intelligence Process

Of the people, by the people, for the people.

—Abraham Lincoln

Like a KM system, the intelligence system's primary ingredients are human. Technology is the tool for capturing and moving information but not the key driver. People are the fuel that powers the system. The intelligence system will only succeed if the firm's employees contribute what they discover and know. Thus, the basics for creating the intelligence system rely on four processes—the same four identified in Chapter 1 for building a competitive intelligence system (Gilad 1994; Gilad & Gilad 1988).

- Easy grass-roots access so that employees are willing to contribute at any time from any place.
- Experts, both inside and outside the organization, who help validate, discern patterns, and analyze collected knowledge. Particular experts may be portals around key knowledge areas, driving purposeful collection when gaps are identified. These should be individuals who have volunteered for this duty and will often perform this function in addition to their everyday line or staff responsibilities such as the "T-shaped managers" used at British Petroleum (Hansen & von Oetinger 2001). Unlike KM systems, experts are not in charge of static knowledge but are actively involved in identification, collection, and analysis of potentially useful knowledge assets.
- A storage system allowing secure gathering of and access to knowledge assets. Ease of use for employees in the field, ranging

from procurement specialists to salespeople, is absolutely necessary, as is the flexibility to organize around a new topic of
interest. Commercial systems are available for both KM and CI
that can be easily adapted to intelligence purposes.

- Convergence points, so that key learnings get to the right
  people at the right time. This is one of the key differences
  between intelligence and KM, with the provision that intelligence must be funneled to the highest levels of the firm if it is
  to be useful. The convergence point, the CI facilitator or team,
  can be particularly effective if given executive cabinet status.

Managing the Intelligence Process

Nuts and bolts.

Convergence is at the core of the system. All analyses flow to the CI
facilitator, who becomes the focal point for senior management
needing questions answered, analyses conducted, and/or early warnings provided. The facilitator also serves to keep the intelligence
system flowing within and across business units, gathering programmed knowledge as a matter of course and purposeful knowledge as needed.

Multiple intelligence projects may be ongoing at any point in
time. Having a convergence point provides the opportunity to discover patterns in the flow of knowledge, to build a landscape of
evolving issues, and to serve as a communication process among
teams who may be unaware of how other projects relate to theirs.
While technology helps by cataloguing analyses and team directives,
a member would still need to think about checking the directory.

Centralized information flow, for example, is a key component
to Ericsson's intelligence process (Ormerod 2002). Tactically it has
streamlined the purchasing process to avoid duplicate expense.
Strategically, analysts have dramatically improved efficiency through
training and networking. By guiding analyses and requesting

specific information, Ericsson can capture information and knowledge from employees who might never have thought to share it in the first place.

As noted in the first chapter, the CI facilitator will often oversee shadow teams organized around particular competitors or other important competitive issues. Shadow teams are a different beast than the communities of practice or strategic communities (Storck & Hill 2000) employed in a KM system to enhance learning. They are cross-functional and can be formed to work within and across business units. They engage the KM system, seek out HUMINT, and work in coordination with the expert ring and facilitator. They also report their findings directly to the executive who asked the question and/or makes the decision. Having a team present its findings to senior management helps ensure that content isn't edited and also provides the team with one of the greatest rewards: visibility with top executives.

Cross-functional membership is a key ingredient to creating a successful team. Cummings (2004) conducted a field study of 182 cross-functional and structurally diverse work groups at a Fortune 500 telecommunications firm, discovering that teams that share knowledge both internally and externally perform better. Similarly, Hayashi (2004) found that external knowledge sharing and performance increased with team diversity.

In addition to being cross-functional, intelligence teams should be populated with individuals who are analytical, willing to think outside the box, and have the courage to communicate their findings and beliefs, even if they are not what senior management wants to hear. Team membership should be voluntary and not motivated by political purposes. Participants should be recommended because they have the right stuff and not because they provide visibility for a certain manager or division. This is not a beauty contest. If team members are there for the wrong reasons, they will compromise the team's objectives.

How many members should be on an intelligence team? The short answer is "It all depends." The needs of the investigation should guide size. In our experience a team will often have eight to ten members, although only two or three actually do any work. We recommend a different structure, similar to the intelligence structure itself, including a small core team of internal cross-disciplinary members, enough to ensure all pertinent knowledge sources are represented. A small expert ring could also contribute, on an *ad hoc* basis, bringing additional insights.

A minimalist approach ensures a core intelligence team composed of those people who really believe in the intelligence function and have the "fire in the belly" for analysis. As noted earlier, in larger teams, a few people will often be the only consistent contributors anyway. Using this structure avoids slothful members, members who are attending for political purposes, or members who just enjoy having an audience. The *ad hoc* expert ring members participate because they like being consulted but also like not being bothered with the time and work commitments of team membership. The expert ring can also be brought in when analyses are complete to find weakness prior to presentation to senior management.

There are many ways to designate actual team numbers or full-time-equivalencies and allocate time spent on team efforts. In any case, buy-in from members' superiors is mandatory. In some firms, intelligence teams are created to engage in continuous cycles of shadow and project activity, a practice that almost guarantees management support as participation is a permanent part of many positions. Regardless of the details, contributions to intelligence teams need to be evaluated in the employee's annual review. (For more information on building shadow teams, see Rothberg 1997).

Basic Structural Considerations

Location, location, location.

Traditional KM systems are often managed by a specific department such as production, human resources, or information technology. Just as KM is dependent on IT systems that get it slotted into the latter group, intelligence could be as well. And the reasons may be very compelling. Products such as Microsoft's (2004) SharePoint are capable of collecting and sharing knowledge across department, division, and even company lines. IT would tend to have a big role in choosing and installing such a system, but the software is not an end in itself. Intelligence employs IT only as a tool. The system is not the core of its mission. Intelligence operations access the KM, operations, and security systems, but then they go well beyond with further information collection and integration. So where should an intelligence operation be located?

Having it reside in a specific functional area such as marketing or business development may constrain the type of analyses that are conducted. In addition, and more important, setting it in a functional discipline creates another layer of management. And creating layers of reporting between an intelligence director or team and executive decision-makers has the potential to filter or prevent analysis from getting to where it is needed when it is needed.

Gilad (1994) suggests, and we concur, creating the "Office of the President" for managing the flow of intelligence. The intelligence facilitator or team would be part of the Office and have direct access to senior executives. It would enable the development of relationships so that the intelligence function is woven into the fabric of strategic decision making. In the best-case scenario, the intelligence group has space in the executive suite where it can interact daily and directly with decision-makers.

The configuration of the intelligence process is dependent on the structure of the firm. In an organization where there is one executive decision-making group, one facilitator and an expert ring may be all that's needed. In a multidivisional firm, competition takes place on the business unit or divisional level. In such a case, a facilitator and expert ring for each separate unit is probably best. Each facilitator is responsible for his or her business unit and also participates in corporate-level intelligence generation (as with the BP/T-manager example cited earlier). At the corporate level, there would be an additional intelligence process facilitator, capturing analysis from the business level units and building a broad competitive land-scape. Although actual intelligence operations would be division specific, all contributors would have access to all knowledge assets across the corporation (at least those without security concerns).

We've also spent a great deal of time in this book talking about how many firms are looking beyond their borders, involving more and more collaborators up and down the Value Chain in their knowledge activities. Our prescription for intelligence operations would include such partners as well. Everything that goes for the inside of the core organization goes even further for the entire e-network. All network members need access to the system (so the IT tool needs to reach beyond company borders). Diversity helps. Facilitators or teams need to monitor and manage knowledge collection, purposeful projects, and use. Committed network participants and experts need to analyze the available knowledge. And at some point, the results need to get to decision-makers at the center of the network. Later we'll discuss whether stipulations have to exist concerning making all knowledge available to all network members on the same basis (definitely not), but at a very basic level, the infrastructure should at least reach throughout the network.

Analysis

Now that we have all this information, what do we do with it?

Another key distinction of an intelligence process is that it concerns itself with analysis. Analysis fails when it becomes a document in a drawer or is actually read but not used. The challenge is to collect the right knowledge and conduct the right analysis at the right time for the right executive. Doing so requires an understanding of what analysis actually is and what it should accomplish.

Business intelligence, KM processes, and CI tools are not analysis. Table 10.1 provides an overview of select tools for analysis. There are two well-known handbooks with more complete lists for those interested in further depth: *The Art and Science of Business*

Table 10.1 Analytical Tools for Intelligence

Type of Tool	Brief Description
Competitor Analysis	Competitive Analysis Model (Porter 1980). Dynamic comparison of competitors. Information is gathered on goals, assumptions, capabilities, and strategies to answer intelligence questions: Is the competitor satisfied? What are the competitor's likely moves? Where is the competitor vulnerable? What is likely to cause the competitor to retaliate? Competitor Profiling (Kendrick & Blackmore 2001). Asks ten questions about competitor business models, Value Chain, and positioning.
Early Warning Analysis	This is a process for tracking competitor actions to assess what they are likely to do and whether their actions indicate a shift in strategic focus. It is a control system designed to prevent surprise (Page 1996). In general early warning analysis identifies competitor or competitive scenarios replete with crucial indicators for monitoring shifts. When shifts occur, additional intelligence is gathered, driving additional analysis to determine the severity of change. Warnings are issued as an intelligence brief to senior management. Endemic to competitive surprises are poor assumptions that impeded interpretation of tailored indicators and poor communication systems to distribute the warning. A critical factor in successful early warning systems is the ability to identify patterns in information (Mathey 1996), draw inferences from spotting process anomalies (Hoyt 2002), and feedback to the intelligence team regarding changes in firm actions as a result of the warning (Sawka 1998).
War Gaming	War gaming is a simulation process that integrates multiple analytical tools such as scenario management (Fink & Schlake 2000), multiple scenario planning (Gilbert 2000), and contingency planning and issue analysis (Fleischer & Bensoussan 2003). It can be proactively employed in strategic "issues management" with a two- to three-year time frame, or reactively as responses to competitive surprises (Underwood 1998). Typically, teams are created around competitors, new product opportunities, or emerging regulatory scenarios. Using all available information, scenarios are constructed from multiple perspectives by each team. Teams present their scenarios and then retreat to create new scenarios based on what was learned. A very sophisticated war game simulation

Continued

Table 10.1 Analytical Tools for Intelligence—cont'd

Type of Tool	Brief Description
War Gaming *(cont.)*	calibrates the universe of competitive moves against a database of pertinent competitive information such as the competitor's competitive positions, customer preferences, loyalty and switching costs, and cost structures. Different competitive scenarios are run through this computer model producing quantitative comparisons (Reibstein & Chussil 1999). These techniques identify potential competitor and competitive alternative strategic paths and reaction dynamics, and thus assist the firm in crafting effective competitive strategy.
CI Benchmarking	Benchmarking is a "continuous, systematic process for evaluating the results, products, services, distribution, and work processes of organizations that are recognized as representing best-practice for the purpose of organizational improvement" (Berlage & Sulzberger 1996). CI benchmarking gives meaning to differences discovered in benchmarking processes, providing insight into competitor and firm comparative capabilities.
Psychological Profiling	This process discovers information about key competitor executives (Vella & McGonagle 2000), including publicly available information as well as information gathered by interviewing people who have worked with and are close to them, and psychologically profiling them using various typologies, such as the Meyers Briggs, to predict how they will move and react strategically to various competitive and competitor shifts.

Intelligence Analysis (Gilad & Herring 1996) and *Strategic and Competitive Analysis* (Fleischer & Bensoussan 2003).

These tools provide a methodology guiding information and knowledge collection and organization. They can also provide the bedrock for drawing conclusions. The skill sets required for using collection tools or conducting analyses differ. Information gathering and classification tools require good investigative and organization skills. Analysis tools require a good mind: knowledgeable, integrative, lucid, and instinctive. An intelligence director and an intelligence team should have requisite skills to do both.

Analysis entails a process in which information and knowledge are subject to "systematic examination in order to identify relevant facts, determine significant relationships and derive key findings and conclusions" (Herring 1998: 14). Herring, a veteran of the CIA and pioneer in the CI community, considers analysis the "brain" of an intelligence perspective, synthesizing collected information, identifying key relationships and links, and producing clear, concise insights that can propel executive action.

Ben Gilad, another CI pioneer, would add that analysis serves internal and external purposes. Externally, intelligence analysis creates meaning from market signals or answers "so what" questions to provide the firm with strategic guidance. Internally, analysis can break long-established paradigms and expose "business blindspots." According to Gilad (1994), firms develop "competitive sclerosis," a condition rooted in their unchallenged assumptions, corporate myths, and corporate taboos. Exposing these conditions through analysis can determine whether the firm is still competitive.

Analysis can be either purposeful or ongoing, driven by a clear question, current need, or strategic process. It is framed according to level (tactical or strategic) and type of action (reactive or proactive). Table 10.2 presents this typology. Tactical analysis focuses on discrete activities, usually within a specific Value Chain function, with a limited time perspective (one to two years). Strategic analysis is future-focused and can impact the entire enterprise. Reactive actions are in response to outside forces such as external environment threats or competitive moves. Proactive actions anticipate and predate such threats or moves.

Table 10.2   Intelligence Analysis Typology

Action		Depth	
		Tactical	Strategic
	Reactive	Defend Territory	React to Change
	Proactive	First Move	Chart the Course

Defending the Territory refers to a tactical and reactive analysis. It is a response to a threatening environmental change or competitor action. Imagine a competitor entering a category with an equivalent offering. There are many response alternatives: should the firm strengthen the brand with new features, enhance marketing communications, lower the price, or reposition another product against one of the competitor's other offerings? Analytical tools such as comparative financial ratio analysis and competitor profiling can help identify the competitor's capability set, likely responses, and the firm's ability to act effectively.

First Move concerns tactical, proactive analysis. A firm may be thinking of changing its tactics, including positioning, targeting, product design, distribution, pricing, advertising, or other such short-term decisions. This organization might use tools from the previous example as well as war gaming to determine whether consumers would be likely to accept the firm's new posture, how well a competitor could manage a price war, and what other competitor reactions might be. Firms should also monitor competitor capabilities and consumer preferences to detect shifts in the underlying assumptions behind actions and to identify new opportunities. While tactical moves rarely create sustainable competitive advantage, they can provide short-term advantage and may lead to something more permanent. If some firm can benefit from an immediate opportunity, it might as well be yours.

React to Change is reactive, strategic analysis. A change has occurred threatening the firm's ability to compete. Kodak's decision to leave the film business and focus on digital imaging is a case in point. The firm was slow to react to a disruptive technology, digital cameras, and now the stakes are high as the firm tries to reposition itself in an already competitive marketplace. Analytical tools such as Value Chain analysis can clarify firm competencies, while comparative SWOT analysis can determine whether this strategic shift fits with environmental challenges and the competitor field. In addition, these tools, brought together in a diagnostic analysis can help identify the blindspots that led the firm to this situation in the first place.

Chart the Course refers to proactive, strategic analysis. This is the apex of analysis, the kind that can usher the firm into a brighter future. It brings together many tools to piece together the competitive landscape as it exists and where it is going. Early warning analysis assists in preventing competitor surprises. SWOT analysis, forecasting, competitor dynamics, and war gaming synthesize and integrate the best of the firm's KM and CI practices to arrive at intelligence-driven strategic options. Sometimes firms can change their strategic positioning, as was the case with FedEx's decision to focus on logistics management and Nokia's decision to participate in the development of its own cellular operating system (rather than Microsoft's). Proactive strategic analysis also keeps an eye inward, looking for blindspots and strategically developing new capabilities that match the firm's environmental circumstances.

In general, the goal of analysis is to move from reactive to proactive states. Employing knowledge assets in an intelligence perspective makes this possible. A variety of tools can be used for any of these analytical types. The challenge is to not create paralysis through analysis but instead use a small set of tools focused enough to gather only relevant knowledge yet broad enough to recognize all that is relevant. As analysts employ these tools, they may discover additional strategic frameworks, providing a clearer picture of available options. Focused, integrative analysis that answers executive questions or offers solutions to competitive challenges facilitates strategic actions.

Review

Intelligence is not a library function. It is not a help desk where people call to obtain information or request cursory analyses. These can be a component of intelligence but are not at the core of what we have been describing.

An intelligence process will only succeed if it is supported and used by senior management. Employees need to be encouraged and recognized for their contributions. Intelligence team members need to be supported by their superiors. The facilitator, as well as the team, needs to be able to collect knowledge and information across the firm and its network, both vertically and horizontally.

Unfiltered intelligence needs to be honestly presented to executives by its authors. Senior management needs to refrain from shooting the messenger if it doesn't like the news.

An intelligence process is not a KM system. KM can and should be a component, but intelligence builds on it by bringing in external information, using operational information and knowledge, and including competitive knowledge. Intelligence is also purposeful, seeking out information and knowledge from beyond the bounds of the KM catalogue. Intelligence processes can feed and complement the KM system by contributing tools and analyses while extending its capabilities.

Protection: Counterintelligence

Wake up and smell the coffee!

We've been making the argument that turning knowledge into intelligence is a risky business. The risks have been identified as coming from national-, industry-, and firm-related factors. KM Risk—not developing knowledge assets when competitors are developing theirs—poses an obvious competitive challenge. However, developing knowledge assets also opens the possibility of their disclosure to competitors. But isn't it worth the risk to develop capabilities and reap their rewards even if there can be consequences? If so, what's all the fuss? Does CI Risk really pose a credible threat to a firm's bottom line? The answers are yes and yes. Yes, it is worth the risk to develop knowledge assets as competitive conditions warrant, and, yes, one must really consider the impact of not putting effort into protecting them. And the answer is not just in technological solutions. Firewalls and passwords are not enough. Firms must consciously address the vulnerability of their information, knowledge, and intelligence.

CI Risk can come from either legal (competitive intelligence) or illegal (espionage) sources, and can include activities driven by both firms and nations (Ahart 1993). The accepted wisdom in CI circles is that 80 to 90 percent of the information or knowledge sought is available publicly and can be collected ethically and legally by means of the techniques covered at length in Chapter 1. But espionage can be a consideration, too, and that last 10 to 20 percent may be the key to your competitor putting together an effective analysis.

And it is a growing problem. As reported earlier, the Office of the National Counterintelligence Executive estimated the loss of proprietary information by U.S. firms to foreign incursions to be $300 billion (NCIX 2002). Foreign governments themselves are often involved in these activities, and the number, of course, doesn't even include domestic CI or espionage. A survey of 643 U.S. organizations jointly conducted by the Computer Security Institute and FBI report that the average loss of information through theft cost approximately $1 million per incident (Robinson 2001). The NCIX report identified the openness of U.S. society and the growth of the Internet in business activities as key vulnerabilities. Seventy-five countries with public and private sponsors target U.S. technologies with a gamut of CI or espionage techniques, ranging from information requests to foreign visits (i.e., all the tools covered in our CI primer in Chapter 1).

Over the years, militarily critical technologies have been the most popular target for foreign governments, with the massive U.S. export control system growing to bar the leakage of such knowledge (Erickson 1997). Increasingly, other information technologies are also being targeted, including biotechnology, aerospace, telecommunications, computer software/hardware, transportation, engine technology, advanced materials and coatings, energy research, and semiconductors (Helms, Etkin & Morris 2000). Any information that firms would not willingly share with competitors can be of interest, such as research and development plans, marketing plans, and cost and pricing data (Binnie 1994).

High-technology companies are cited as being particularly exposed to foreign exploitation. Motivations include profit, as many believe this to be the only way to compete against U.S. firms and/or gain access to markets, an increase in stature for the individual who comes up with the goods, or revenge from former employees. Foreign governments often support such actions, believing they will enable their firms to leapfrog scientific hurdles, create military parity with the United States, give their industrial base competitive advantage, or increase the nation's power and influence. Whether the motivation is to benefit a nation, industry, or firm, the financial and competitive impact is astounding.

In 1994 Johnathan Binnie, the Supervisory Special Agent of the FBI, sounded the alarm, declaring that economic security was akin to military service in preserving overall national security (Binnie 1994). The FBI has an "Awareness of National Security Issues & Response Program" (www.fbi.gov/hg/ci/ansir) to advise firms of when and how they are being targeted. Its Web site specifically cites such espionage techniques as "dumpster diving"; commercially available listening devices; "social engineering" (the art of gleaning information from conversation with unwitting targets); and gaining access to cache chips, fax, and photocopy machines that digitally store documents.

Given the e-network trends, increased globalization, and closer collaborator relationships detailed in the preceding chapters, CI Risk today is growing faster than ever. Strategically managing knowledge asset risk has become as important as developing and using knowledge assets in the first place. Firms need to be as astute in designing their counterintelligence programs as they are in designing their intelligence structures.

According to the U.S. Department of Defense (1991), counterintelligence includes "those activities which are concerned with identifying and counteracting the threat to security posed by hostile intelligence services or organizations or by individuals engaged in espionage, sabotage or subversion." Counterintelligence programs are designed to protect competitive information, plans, and projects from adversaries.

Operation Security, or OPSEC, is a counterintelligence discipline that focuses on keeping key knowledge assets out of the hands of infiltrators. OPSEC identifies critical information needing protection, threats, and vulnerabilities, and thereby serves to safeguard knowledge through investigating, advising, and training (DeGenaro 1996). The following discussion will introduce the essentials of counterintelligence operations and is based largely on DeGenaro's work. Greater detail can be obtained there or through the additional cited sources.

By employing counterintelligence, a company can minimize the threat of competitive intelligence being used against it. Obviously, preventing espionage is one major goal. But effective counterintelligence can also minimize the threat of standard CI operations by decreasing the widely available information and knowledge floating around out there. So keep in mind the dual purpose of using knowledge with care while also halting the cloak and dagger stuff as you consider the following strategy.

Critical Knowledge

The first step in developing a counterintelligence program turns on understanding what information actually needs protection. We've spent the past nine chapters detailing a very broad view of the valuable information, knowledge, and intelligence assets of the firm. Operational information, tactics, and strategies from all parts of the firm and its extended network (upstream, downstream, and anywhere in between) hold potential value for competitors. If an organization has done a good job in identifying and managing its knowledge assets, it is a long way down the road of understanding what knowledge is critical.

Threat Analysis

Threat analysis deals with understanding adversaries. This should be one of the goals of collecting competitor knowledge and developing competitive capital. Shadow team design readily lends itself to this aim. Its purpose is to understand competitors, to see the firm through the competitor's own eyes (DeGenaro 1996; Pattakos 1998). Counterintelligence experts commonly suggest using the law enforcement model "MOM" to conduct a threat analysis.

- *Motives* are determined by conducting competitor capability analysis. Where have competitors fallen short in the past? Have they been more reactive than proactive in the marketplace? Are they behind in developing necessary technologies or product innovations? Competitors will seek information to strengthen their own Value Chains. For instance, they will engage what they discover to preempt your product release, challenge your pricing strategy, advance their research and development relative to yours, or make an acquisition to keep it from you.

- *Opportunity* requires an understanding of the target firm's vulnerabilities. How readily can competitors gain access to the firm? Can employees be used? Can competitors, for example, acquire information about leadership and project leaders from administrative staff? Infiltrators can learn a lot about a firm by calling unwitting employees and requesting information. Does the firm provide site tours (increasingly risky in the days of camera phones), does it fail to stamp its documents "confidential", or do employees work on sensitive documents in airports or other public places? All of these and many other behaviors are indicators of a firm with a weak protection program. Once a competitor learns that there is a loose counterintelligence structure, the firm can become an open book.

- *Methods* can be determined by understanding the competitor's culture and its likely collection activities. Does the competitor have a history of dumpster diving, hiring ex-employees, or pumping supply chain partners or customers for information? There are legal and ethical, illegal and unethical methods that drive CI Risk. Some are legal yet subtle, such as hanging around a trade show booth, eavesdropping at hotel and airport bars, and engaging retirees in conversations about their careers. Other legal methods are more overt, including attending patent hearings and tracking regulatory filings and executive speeches. Legal yet unethical practices including some misrepresentations and dumpster diving. Illegal methods are such obvious actions as hacking, electronic surveillance, trespassing, and breaking confidentiality agreements.

Threat analysis helps the firm understand a competitor's intent and ability to obtain the firm's knowledge assets. Forewarned is forearmed.

Vulnerability Analysis

Vulnerability analysis is concerned with identifying the firm's points of entry. The issue here is through what mechanism(s) is the firm most vulnerable? Vulnerabilities are inherent in business processes such as regulatory filings, public relations activities, and corporate communications disclosures. Digital tools such as wireless laptops or cell phones can also be a target.

Adding to this mix, the firm itself is a composite of relationships and communications between "insiders" and "outsiders" (DeGenaro 1996; Pattakos 1998). Insiders are people with direct access to critical information. They may or not be employees, as external players such as bankers, joint venture or alliance partners, board members, interns, auditors, and even family members may be insiders in terms of knowledge access. Indirect insiders can extend the web even further, including tangentially involved partners such as vendors, suppliers, subcontractors, and employment agencies. Insiders may have access only to bits and pieces of information, but they can still provide value to a collector. Their disclosure of information can be deliberate or unintentional. Outsiders include casual acquaintances such as friends and neighbors, customers, trained personnel such as reporters, academics, information brokers, and competitors.

Vulnerability venues span across the firm's reach and include all firm and network locations and systems, travel, conferences, trade shows, courtrooms, public meetings, academic institutions, neighborhood gathering places, and social events. "Cultural blindspots" are another source. Clever collectors find or create what appear to be harmless opportunities for gathering information. DeGenaro (1996: 133) offers this actual case: A competitor was interested in another firm's secured manufacturing process. The interested competitor hired a consultant to encourage a local grade school teacher to schedule a field trip at the target firm's facility. The consultant went along on the trip as a chaperone. The children posed for dozens of photographs in front of interesting backdrops. The target firm could have never considered that this trip was really a cover for information collection.

In short, vulnerabilities abound. The lesson here is that a firm needs to really look at its operation and realize that by developing knowledge assets, by just engaging in business, it is opening the firm to CI Risk. The greatest vulnerability is to keep one's head in the sand, like an ostrich, and not manage this risk intelligently.

Assessing Risk: What to Look For

Once you have identified critical information, analyzed threats of competitor infiltration, and considered the firm's vulnerabilities, you need to ask whether infiltration is likely. Again, the firm's own CI activities should provide it with insights in terms of competitors who may be targeting it.

There are a variety of activities to sound the alert that CI is being conducted against the firm. Here are some things counterintelligence managers should look out for.

- Suspicious phone calls or other contacts
- Requests for regulatory filings (at the firm or the agency)
- Outside contacts with employees or retirees (surveys, headhunters, etc.)
- Outside contacts with collaborators
- Lost laptops, PDAs, cell phones, and so on
- Surveillance
- Hacking

Look for activity patterns, especially in the obvious places, such as hacking or missing electronics. Less obvious are ordinary activities engaging unsuspecting employees. The telephone is a notorious collection tool. Infiltrators will ask for validation of incorrect information, use employee names as references, and/or misrepresent themselves as headhunters and interviewers. Other common techniques are requests for interviews, white papers on research topics, and benchmarking studies. Regardless of method, infiltrators are often skilled, smooth, and believable. Employees can share information with competitors and never know it.

Nearly all counterintelligence specialists will agree that having a well-developed human network is a primary ingredient to a good detection program. Employees need to be coached on what to look for and updated frequently about any suspicious events. In addition, vendors, administrative people working in regulatory filing offices, distributors, and suppliers all have contact with you and with competitor firms. They can be asked whether information inquiries about the firm are being made, by whom, and how often.

Counterintelligence Programs

Building a counterintelligence program starts with an honest assessment of the firm's current protection capability. It is one thing to identify vulnerability but quite another to understand the depth of risk it presents to the organization. Sometimes the intelligence threat comes from unlikely sources conducting everyday business. Former National Security Agency member Ira Winkler (1997) talks about salespeople who will provide sensitive information to an account to seal a deal. Key to this process is a deep understanding of not only competencies but also business practices across the firm.

A counterintelligence program is grounded not only in findings by shadow teams conducting threat analysis or an intelligence team cataloguing critical information and vulnerabilities, but also in the firm's Human Resources department. Espionage often comes from its own employees. Human Resources can assess the level of employee naiveté, morale, and disenchantment. Employees who feel disenfranchised by the firm can be less loyal and more likely to disclose information. Those who have experienced downsizing, divestiture, and dismissal are key targets for savvy competitors. HR can put procedures in place for access and disposal of company documents, computers and files, and exit interviews. HR can also play an integral role in developing and delivering awareness programs to existing employees and as part of new hire orientation.

Counterintelligence training needs to occur at every level and across every function of the organization. There are four segments to a sound counterintelligence training program.

- Corporate Policy
  - *Does the firm have a clear policy defining which types of documents, electronic or paper, are considered confidential?* Strategic plans, research and technology plans, marketing plans, plant designs, machine engineering, and chemical formulas are examples of documents that should be stamped "confidential." Any information that the firm deems to be linked to its creating and sustaining competitive advantage needs to be clearly marked. And employees should be well aware of how seriously the firm takes this distinction.
  - *Are corporate filings comparable to competitors?* The firm should never give more information than is needed in any public document. Comparing these documents with competitors will reveal whether the company is overcomplying.
  - *Do key personnel have clear guidelines as to what information can and cannot be shared in public forums?* The corporate communications executive needs to clarify the type of interviews and panels in which managers and executives can participate. Information that can and cannot be shared also needs to be clearly delineated. This also holds true for what researchers, scientists, and technicians share at conferences and symposiums. Marketers participating in trade shows need guidelines on what pipeline information stays out of

their booths, regardless of client relationships. Employees who travel need guidelines regarding what they should not work on in public forums, such as airplanes and eateries, as well as what they should not discuss at hotel bars and conferences. Finally, all employees need to be sensitized as to what they shouldn't talk about outside the confines of the organization.

☐ *Does the firm have sufficient nondisclosure and noncompete policies?* Relationships with outside vendors and alliance partners need to be defined in legal documents. (Specific guidelines for managing knowledge transfer between partners will be discussed later in this chapter.) Employees privy to sensitive information should be limited in working for competitors for a period of time should they choose to leave the firm. Finally, the creation of new knowledge during an employee engagement needs to be clarified as belonging to the firm and therefore not to be shared with new employers.

☐ *Does Human Resources consider counterintelligence issues in exit interviews?* Human Resources professionals need to assess the level of disenchantment of exiting employees. They need to remind departing employees of their legal commitments in content and in principle. They also need to track their impressions of such interviews.

- Training
  ☐ *Do employees know the firm's counterintelligence policies?* Some believe that much of what we have mentioned thus far is common sense, that employees know what sensitive information is and how to handle it. Our professional experiences suggest this is not true. One author of this book had a consultancy in "grain country," an area in the Midwest that hosts three major cereal companies. Competitors shared a common airport hub, and two were literally across the railtracks from each other. On more than one flight, I sat next to a person busily working on a chemical formula. On

another occasion I overheard employees talking about the threat of a trucking strike against a competitor. When asked how they knew this, I was told they overheard it in the neighborhood bar. In the airport's restroom I overheard two people discussing a senior management shakeup and how the new person coming in was going to head a new competitive initiative. Smart, well-meaning employees are not necessarily CI Risk savvy.

☐ *Do employees know what to do with suspicious phone calls and e-mail queries?* Do they even know what to be suspicious about? As mentioned previously, the telephone is often the weapon of choice for infiltrators. DeGenaro suggests that employees never hang up on suspicious callers because they can find another way in. Instead he suggests "leaving the door open—just a crack" (1996: 137). Callers using employee names as references for credibility may ask for information. Or they may cite purposefully wrong information or even factual information to establish credibility. A good rule of thumb is to ask for a number where you can get back to the caller with the information they seeking. This provides an opportunity to verify the caller's authenticity and to direct them to the appropriate person. Requests for interviews and papers should be handled similarly. Ask for a letter on letterhead and then follow up to see if the request is authentic. E-mail inquiries need similar scrutiny. Check out the institution or firm the person claims to represent. See if he or she is employed there and in what capacity. Initiate a phone call to determine whether the request for information or interviews is valid. Ask that such requests be made formally on letterhead.

☐ *Do employees know how to secure documents and technology when they travel?* Any confidential document or electronic file needs to be kept in the hotel's safe when the employee is not in the room. Hard drives should never leave the employee's side, unless they can be placed in the hotel safe. Cell phones, PDAs, and Blackberries also need to be kept on the person at all times.

- ☐ *Do employees know what to do with their suspicions?* It is essential for employees to track all suspicious calls and inquiries. It is also imperative to have a central place where this tracking is reported. Developing activity patterns assists in identifying where the infiltration is coming from and whether it is part of a bigger incursion process. Human Resources personnel can also share their exit interview impressions. Shadow and intelligence teams dedicated to this activity are one possibility; a corporate security officer is another. Whatever the structure, the key is to track this activity and, like a puzzle, piece together the story it tells.

- Finding the Holes, Plugging the Leaks
  - ☐ *Do you know where the firm is still vulnerable?* Steps 1 and 2 have been completed. You have identified your critical information and you believe the firm's knowledge assets are secure. You think you understand your competitors and the methods they are likely to use to discover the firm's secrets. Your vendors and alliance partners have signed nondisclosure agreements. Your employees have signed noncompete documents and have been sensitized and trained. The firm is ready for the final examination. Plan to test the system by calling employees in different parts of the organization, across level and function, and requesting information. See if those answering the calls leave the door open, and see if the event gets reported.

    Serious implementers of counterintelligence programs run "Red Team" attacks. Bill DeGenaro (Center for Operations and Business Intelligence, www.the-center.com) is a master of this trade. The Red Team is given three days to discover any information or knowledge that the firm believes is secured. Using ethical and legal techniques, the Team sets forth to find the prize. Executives who have used this method report that DeGenaro's Red Team has a superb success rate in finding holes.

- Monitoring the Program
  - □ *Do you make the right counterintelligence adjustments?* Finding and plugging holes is an iterative process. As competitors, industries, and global economies change, so do counterintelligence needs. The time it takes to develop and implement a protection program is well spent. It is easier to provide infiltrators with information than one would think. Keeping the counterintelligence program relevant is the best defense against CI Risk.

Building knowledge assets takes resources and in exchange provides the bedrock for competitive advantage. Not having a secure and appropriate protection program in place is like letting a kid (infiltrators) run loose in a candy shop.

Counterintelligence and the Environment

We'll soon consider KM Risk, CI Risk, and the SPFs and how they fit with constructing intelligence teams and counterintelligence programs. But before discussing those types of general issues, it's important to note how these structures and processes can be arranged to take advantage of a given environment and, perhaps, change it.

The best way to frame these comments is probably in the form of an example. We mentioned earlier in the book that the United States passed a law, the Economic Espionage Act (EEA), in 1996. The effect of the act was to tighten and make a national standard for the protection of softer intellectual capital assets such as trade secrets (as opposed to intellectual property, often protected by patents). Interestingly, the driver behind the Act was concern over economic espionage by foreign firms and nations.

The key provisions of the EEA stipulate that if (a) a piece of knowledge has value to a firm and (b) it then takes steps to protect it, then the knowledge is covered as a trade secret under the law. If left in the open, competitors can still take it, but if kept secret, it is protected knowledge. This has several important connotations for firms considering intelligence and counterintelligence systems.

Initially, the act of identifying the knowledge as a corporate asset may make it a protectable trade secret. Again, the first step is establishing value, so treating it as a valuable asset may get you there. An intelligence capability for managing knowledge can help to make your knowledge assets more protectable, since a big part of it has to do with managing all information and knowledge as the important assets they are. Second, establishing a counterintelligence system to protect them should seal the deal. Indeed, the recommended compliance standards for EEA read like the counterintelligence structure we just covered.

- Audit the firm's intellectual capital.
- Determine the value.
- Conduct a risk assessment of the likelihood of theft or contamination.
- Implement an appropriate level of security (Fraumann & Koletar 1999).

The key point is that this single national law has created a new environment for managing both KM Risk and CI Risk. Firms operating in the United States can structure both their intelligence systems and counterintelligence systems accordingly to take advantage of the new reality.

The devil is in the details, of course, and protecting at the level required by EEA will necessitate close compliance to all counterintelligence standards (e.g., "confidential" notation on all paper and electronic documents, controlling access, passwords and firewall, encryption, document destruction policies, monitoring public filings and comments, restricting access to facilities, and so on (Powell 1994; Schwab & Porter 1998; Wingo 1997). Sloppy execution could lead to the determination that the firm did not effectively protect the assets, making EEA immaterial. Network relationships also have to be considered. If one shares knowledge with network partners, then it has to carefully consider what parts of its knowledge asset base will be shared, with whom, and how the partners will protect these secrets. A collaborator compliance system can be effective (Carr, Erickson & Rothberg 2004) in satisfying EEA and helping to manage knowledge and protection. Under such a program, collaborators are evaluated for their counterintelligence systems. Only with passing scores do such collaborators qualify for deeper levels of knowledge sharing. If a partner can't be trusted to handle it appropriately, the partner doesn't get the most critical knowledge.

Again, the point of this aside is to illustrate how intelligence teams and counterintelligence are both decisions made under the rubric of the SPF structure we've constructed in this book. Know your environment, and make the knowledge and protection decisions accordingly. Doing so can help you operate at the appropriate risk level given your SPF. It may also help you to drop your own KM Risk or CI Risk levels as your firm gets better at planning and executing knowledge management and counterintelligence schemes.

Protection of Networks

Part 3 of this book spent a good amount of time detailing how modern business is more closely linking with network partners. Strategic alliances and looser collaborations are becoming mainstream in the business landscape. They bring together firms to achieve business purposes. They also provide the opportunity for knowledge transfer and learning, both intentional and unintentional. Companies need to recognize that they are trading mounds of information or even knowledge with outside partners on a daily basis. Without a counterintelligence design, a firm can share more than it even knows.

Alliances give partners access to each other's competencies and skills (Kogut 1988). Knowledge transfer can be experiential where "learning is from the alliance experience" itself, such as when implementing technology capabilities. Knowledge transfer can also be vicarious, where learning "the other partner's skills" (Tsang 1999) or absorbing strategic and deeply embedded knowledge (Hamel 1991) is the objective. Key to vicarious knowledge transfer is management involvement, especially in inexperienced firms (Tsang 2002). The organization's absorptive capacity (Shenkar & Li 1999), the complexity and tacitness of knowledge, and cultural differences between partners (Bhagat et al. 2002) will impact knowledge transfer success.

That said, how does a firm protect knowledge assets that are not designated as contributions in alliances or less formal arrangements? We asked this question to people engaged in alliance relationships across multiple firms and borders in the pharmaceutical and semiconductor industries. Our discussion offers both an executive and a midlevel management perspective. While we do not claim this discussion to be inclusive or representative of all strategic alliance experiences, it does provide food for thought.

The executive perspective focuses on designing the legal contract between partners to delineate what gets transferred and what does not. Attorneys are engaged in every stage of the relationship, from negotiating and drafting the contract to attending key meetings. When attorneys are not present at meetings, participants are supposed to meet with them later and share what was exchanged. If knowledge outside the agreement is acquired, even if it has competitive implications for the firm, it cannot be passed further on into the partner firm and used.

The executive perspective suggests staffing alliance teams with experienced people who have not worked for the partnering firm. This helps avoid cognitive issues regarding what can be learned in the alliance and what may have been learned in an employment situation. Visits from partners to facilities need to be contained to a room outside of sensitive areas. "No raiding agreements," where employees cannot change camps in the midst of a contract, are essential.

Knowledge transfer is bound to occur outside of contractual guidelines. Just by conducting business together lessons will be learned. Joint studies of markets and competitors can serve to educate less sophisticated partners about marketing techniques, research, and analysis. The contractual negotiation itself can also be a learning experience. The executive perspective stresses understanding the partner's succession plans for the alliance team and senior management. While this might not be an issue on the partner's agenda, it becomes one after being raised in the negotiation and continues to play a role in future contracts.

Also challenging are the cultural differences between firms. Compensation and bonus policies can differ, overrewarding one firm's sales group while underrewarding the other, for example. This issue might not have been considered during the negotiation. How, then, do you identify the less obvious issues? Here's where an intelligence team can be used. The executive perspective is to form a cross-functional team to discover and brainstorm the different potential issues that can arise in a knowledge transfer situation from different operational groups. They ask the question "What if?" This provides the opportunity to make the alliance contract more inclusive and/or effectively adapt it as issues arise.

The midlevel manager perspective is different. It recognizes that a contract exists and defines the terms around what knowledge gets shared and what does not. However, in actual practice, as the work is being done, a different story can emerge. This is because either the contract is not clearly understood by all, it does not address specific issues that arise, or not everyone understands the strategic importance of protecting knowledge assets. Either way, it is a different reality from the executive perspective.

Let's take the case of engineers who are the key players in a strategic alliance around the development and implementation of a manufacturing technology. Their charge is to get the project done. Oftentimes, they care little about the contractual document. They need information to complete their work, and it is information they will seek. And sometimes they will seek it "under the table" from people outside the alliance team. There are time pressures and dead-lines. What else can they do?

Working across multiple firms with foreign partners, engineers can be asked to share knowledge outside the scope of the contract. If they do not share what is requested, they may not obtain the knowledge necessary to accomplish what they need to do. Knowl-edge becomes a bargaining chip—one that is played again and again. As one middle manager puts it, "It's part of the game." Sometimes knowledge exchange is less deliberate and takes advantage of a less sophisticated partner's representatives. They may not be as familiar with the conditions in the contract. "If you develop relationships and they share things they shouldn't, that's their problem. Some-times you actually rely on this."

Sometimes the under-the-table approach is required when alliance partners refuse to share what is in the negotiated contract. There is an inherent strategy in some alliances that you sign the con-tract and share as little as possible while you learn as much as you can. In this case, you have to rely on relationships to move forward. This is especially true when these relationships have soft knowledge (the ability to know that equipment isn't working right by the sound of the machine) such as human capital.

Whatever the case, knowledge transfer among alliance partners can readily stray from contractual guidelines. Counterintelligence training for alliance team members is essential. Our interviews suggest that often the specifics of contracted negotiations are not clearly communicated across level and function to all involved. It doesn't appear to be enough to have an attorney assigned to the rela-tionship or to have executives from each partner agree on knowl-edge transfer guidelines. The people actually engaged in doing the work need to understand the legal and competitive ramifications of under-the-table trading. In addition to the legal side, they need to understand the competitive side, the big picture for the firm that wants to protect knowledge assets in a competitive intelligence world.

While there will always be unintentional sharing of knowledge between partners, there can be stronger control over the transfers, intentional or not. This brief look at strategic alliances in particular highlights the dangers inherent in working with outside partners. In order to effectively manage CI Risk, organizationwide training, execution, and monitoring must be installed. It's the only way to keep your valuable knowledge assets where, and only where, you want them.

Back to the SPFs

Diagnosing a firm's SPF is a complex task, bringing to bear national, industry, and firm variables. The design and protection of an intelligence process is responsive to SPF conditions. Firms finding themselves in low-KM-Risk situations (SPF 5, Brilliance, or SPF 30, Glass House) have limited prospects for developing their knowledge. Their knowledge may be difficult to transfer, may not be applicable in different situations, or may simply not be required given the competitive situation. Networks and outside partners may not be important to success. As such, the intelligence structure we highlighted in the first half of this chapter should be applied carefully, as the benefits may not justify the expense or trouble. On the other hand, carefully managing the knowledge assets and identifying those that may have an impact could lead to competitive advantage.

Those organizations facing high KM Risk (SPF 15, 800-pound Gorilla, or SPF 45, Cold War) will often need to expansively develop their knowledge assets in order to compete. Full development may establish competitive advantage. Alliances or other network relationships, with attendant knowledge sharing, can be the price of admission to participating in the market. As a result, installing intelligence teams with purposeful gathering, analysis, and clout can be extremely important. They will need to be structured to gather and share information and knowledge across the extended networks, as needed. Knowledge assets are the key to competitive advantage and need to be managed carefully, through intelligence systems, in order to be fully exploited.

In situations of low CI Risk (SPF 5, Brilliance, and SPF 15, 800-pound Gorilla), competitive incursions are not a major threat. Either knowledge is unimportant to competing or it just won't benefit the capturing firm in the same manner it does the target. Networks and alliances may or may not be important, but the availability of useful knowledge throughout these structures is limited. Counterintelligence should not be ignored, but the full-fledged system detailed in the second half of this chapter may not be necessary. Some thought still needs to be given to protection, but the main purpose of the counterintelligence operation is to identify critical knowledge and protect it—recognizing that the vast mass of noncritical knowledge doesn't warrant the same amount of attention.

On the other hand, for firms looking at high CI Risk (SPF 30, Glass House, or SPF 45, Cold War), CI activities are likely to be rampant. Knowledge is critical to competitive advantage and either so plentiful or so rare as to warrant major initiatives to obtain it from key competitors. Alliances or other network relationships again may be present or not, but whatever outside collaborations exist, they need attention. A substantial counterintelligence operation needs to be constructed, monitoring knowledge assets, their use, and their distribution. Formal procedures need to be in place to detect and counter CI efforts, and adherence to the procedures must be carefully policed. In these cases, an effective, comprehensive counterintelligence function can be the key to competitive advantage.

Across each SPF, counterintelligence issues prevail. There are multiple ways for sophisticated operatives to learn about supply chains (discarded packing slips), internal processes (through job posting interviews), the creation of new strategic initiatives (by tracking new hires), and research agendas (through telephone interviews or white papers). Weaving counterintelligence processes into the firm's intelligence architecture recognizes that developing knowledge assets as well as protecting them are key sources of advantage in competitive industries.

Specific SPF classifications require a deep look at the nation, industry, and firm indicators. Here is some food for thought about the interplay between SPF and implementing intelligence and counterintelligence processes.

SPF 5: Brilliance

In this scenario, KM Risk and CI Risk are low. Knowledge assets are developed around talent, charisma, or a unique business idea. Even in a competitive industry, this scenario indicates that if advantage is won, it will be through an intangible asset. The intelligence process in this scenario is concerned with shadowing competitors, scenario planning, possible changes in regulatory and economic conditions, or identifying what the next cultural opportunity may be. The structure can be simple: a person with an expert ring, for example, or teams created on an *ad hoc* basis. Counterintelligence concerns revolve around determining if knowledge assets can become tangible, creating policy for protecting them, and awareness programs for employees. And depending on the size of the firm and the nature of advantage, counterintelligence programs may not be needed at all.

SPF 15: 800-Pound Gorilla

In this situation, KM Risk is high and CI Risk is low to moderate. Relationships are built with network partners across the Value Chain and perhaps across national boundaries. The intelligence structure can enhance KM systems with external knowledge and analytical capabilities and focus on issues that competitively impact the supply chain and distribution channels. Players in this scenario are going to be concerned with gaining structural knowledge from the Gorilla or challenging support firms in becoming part of the Gorilla's network. Shadow team activity would track such firms across segment lines and national borders. Also, intelligence teams can provide cost/

benefit analysis on conducting business with partners in different countries taking into account all national as well as financial and competitive data. An integrator or director would build the landscape of competitive challenges and opportunities across the Value Chain. Protection is focused on knowledge transfer between the firm and partners, specifically as it relates to process. The New Balance example cited earlier in the book concerned a number of higher-level KM Risk and CI Risk issues but also had an element concerning operational knowledge. The Chinese contract manufacturer transferred manufacturing knowledge and began competing with its partner. An intelligence team may have predicted that outcome. Counterintelligence activities also focus on the honoring of contractual agreements, the impact of disgruntled employees, and the protection of digital processes for managing the enterprise.

SPF 30: Glass House

This landscape has low to moderate KM Risk and high CI Risk. KM systems manage client and firm product information. Chase Manhattan (Greenemeir 2001) and Fleet (Zaino 2003), for example, rely on their relationship management capabilities to understand their customers, conduct analyses, and provide an optimum portfolio of services. Their competitive focus is insular, on their own process for increasing revenue and customer satisfaction. Designing this system into an intelligence process would include competitor analysis and monitoring of regulatory and demographic changes. In this regulated environment, competitive moves are transparent and readily copied. Proactive tactical analysis can create first-mover advantage. It is important to know competitor capabilities in order to react or to preempt the firm's strategic posture. If this scenario holds for a multinational firm, then an intelligence design of a facilitator and expert ring should exist in each location. A facilitator on the corporate level can keep a real-time global landscape. Protection centers on maintaining client relationships and proprietary firm processes. Thus, nondisclosure agreements, noncompetes, and awareness training, especially for digital devices, are key.

SPF 45: Cold War

This environment is challenging in that both KM Risk and CI Risk are high. These firms often engage in strategic alliances and joint ventures to develop new technologies or to enter markets with which they are unfamiliar. It is not unusual, for instance, for pharmaceutical firms to partner with Johnson & Johnson or Procter & Gamble when switching a previously patented drug to over-the-counter. Pharmaceutical firms, technology firms, and even old economy firms entering new markets rely on partnering. Automobile manufacturers entering China, for example, have only been allowed to own 50 percent of a facility. In this SPF, intelligence systems and counterintelligence systems have to be part of the fabric of the firm and executive decision process. All forms of analysis are likely to be conducted here, but the goal is to be proactive and quick in implementation. The intelligence structure should mirror the structure of the firm, and an Office of the President should be created at the corporate level. It is wise to staff this function with a facilitator and dedicated intelligence team. Counterintelligence activities are as essential as analytical activities. SPF 45 requires the firm to engage in a full counterintelligence program. Partnering across borders, industries, and firms requires *a priori* understanding of partner firm and national cultures. Deep intelligence is required when heading into a contractual process, and it's necessary to monitor the transfer of knowledge and its impact. The firm should subject all employees to a counterintelligence awareness program as well as create well-communicated corporate policies about documents, practices, and the importance of protecting knowledge assets for the firm's survival.

Summary

An intelligence process can build on existing KM systems. It contributes to the practice of gathering external information and knowledge resources in conducting analyses to answer specific executive questions. As a direct link to strategic planning and implementation, the intelligence function provides unfiltered, timely analysis. Using a variety of models and active tools, an intelligence process can explain current situations, identify strategic opportunities, and model the impact of different decisions on the competitive landscape. Structuring the organization to engage in these activities is not costly. It requires identifying energetic and capable people who are knowledgeable and willing to share what they know, access their personal networks, and dig in analytically.

Just as important as creating an intelligence growth process is installing a system to protect knowledge assets. Information and knowledge theft is a very real and costly phenomenon. The transfer of knowledge outside of contractual agreements is a very real phenomenon. Taking the steps to understand what needs to be protected and then protecting it is a necessity in a competitive intelligence world. Given that some information loss comes from ignorance and not malevolence, an awareness program can begin to stem the tide of knowledge leakage. More formal and more sophisticated countermeasures can be put in place with higher-level threats.

Executive Moment

Intelligence and counterintelligence programs can be built into the firm's existing structure. Some executives believe that their KM systems are intelligence systems. Let's see.

- Can strategic questions be answered in an unfiltered, timely way? This is not the same as a library function. It assumes that analysis takes place and that think-tank capabilities exist.
- Is there a central location where competitive information is continuously evaluated for importance and analyzed to identify patterns, impact, and challenges? Having a repository in the KM system for analyses is not the same as continuously conducting and using analysis.
- Is there a person you can turn to who monitors information that is important to you and can answer "so what" for you? A

well-trained intelligence facilitator will know what you need and why you need it and how it fits into ongoing strategic concerns. This is not the job of a corporate librarian or information search expert.

- Is there a person in your organization who will always tell you the truth?
- When was the last time a competitor did something that came as a surprise? If this happens, then your current intelligence function is not working.
- How often have you been prepared, in advance, for changes in the regulatory, demographic, technological, or social environment? Early warning analysis and scenario planning are key activities in an intelligence capability. If you underestimated the impact of a change, then your intelligence process isn't working.
- What tools do you use when engaging in strategic analysis and decisions? Do you combine them into analytical frameworks to answer questions?

If you have partners in your Value Chain:

- How much due diligence was done on the partner's soft factors before contractual negotiations? Do you understand the personalities of the negotiating and work teams? Do you understand the partner's culture, the competitiveness of its industry, and its nation's history in honoring legal agreements?
- Does anyone really know what type of information is shared "under the table"? Who is talking to the people in the trenches?
- Is anyone conducting analysis on your partner's capability to compete head-to-head with you as knowledge is transferred?

As for counterintelligence, the key point is that most firms are unaware of how their everyday practices can open them to infiltration. If you answer yes to any of these questions, you may want to carefully think about how you are protecting your assets.

- Do you have well-articulated and well-communicated corporate policies on confidentiality, trade secrets, nondisclosure, noncompetes, and so on?
- Are your employees aware of what the firm believes is sensitive information?
- Have laptops, PDAs, cell phones, and other digital devices been stolen or misplaced?
- Would you even know if your computer network was breached?
- Do salespeople, purchasing agents, research personnel, or any others dealing with outside entities know what information they shouldn't share?
- Do people know how to manage telephone requests?
- Have you briefed retirees on what components of their jobs they shouldn't discuss?

Installing the Intelligence Program: Culture

For whatsoever a man soweth, that shall he also reap.

—Galatians 6: 7–8

A key ingredient in shifting from knowledge to intelligence, or for any process that depends on people sharing what they know, is the firm's culture. "How we do things around here," what is expected, what is rewarded, the stories shared, the celebrations and demonstrations of what's valued: All are going to weigh more heavily in creating a successful learning environment and intelligence process than having the right technology or written procedures. Ultimately, employees take cues from each other and from their superiors, who take cues from executives, who take cues from presidents and CEOs. For knowledge to become intelligence, the firm's leaders, both formal (through position) and informal (through opinion) need to walk the walk. Through their actions, the cultural shifts that can create a practice of knowledge sharing, analysis, and action can be born.

Social Capital

Building bridges.

An intelligence-friendly culture is built on trust and the social capital that forms from it. While there are many definitions of social capital, we adopt the one offered by Cohen and Prusak (2001: 4): "Social capital consists of the stock of active connections among people: the trust, mutual understanding, and sharing of values and behaviors that bind the members of human networks and communities and make cooperative action possible." The development of social capital is also dependent on the absence of fear. Close relationships dissolve fear and distrust, making people feel safe enough to "explore unknown territories" (Krogh, Ichijo & Nonaka, 2000: 45), a key driver in intelligence processes.

Social capital feeds an intelligence perspective. Social capital refers to established relationships that can become organizational assets. A deep understanding between an employee and a supervisor or between a salesperson and a client, built up over time, because of similar backgrounds or simply because they "hit it off," provides each party with something of value. Social capital supports networks of relationships and people in cooperative engagements. It congeals teams, harbors communities, and fosters the sense that members participate in organization life together and can impact its vibrancy. In short, social capital is the fabric around which knowledge and intelligence activities spin, where its threads are "advise, trust and friendship networks" (Prescott 2003). The deeper the levels of social capital among members, the more likely knowledge and information will be shared.

Whether teams or experts, intelligence facilitators or grassroots contributors, citizens of the organization's community need to believe that participating is important. They need to feel participating is vital to the firm's future, that it will not be a waste of time, that executives care, and that the integrity of information and analyses matters more than the delivery of good news. This is a tall order. It requires a culture that encourages openness, risk-taking, and the support of communities. The ingredients are obvious but not simple. For social capital to grow, it needs various forms of leadership and a climate free of fear and infused with trust.

Social capital also affects the protection aspects of intelligence. We'll discuss some of the more specific issues in the coming pages, but the depth of the relationship among executives, managers, and employees in terms of protecting the knowledge assets of the firm will influence how widely things can and should be shared. While the obvious concern is what happens if critical knowledge flows down the organizational hierarchy (will employees at increasingly lower levels understand the need to protect it and act accordingly?), the same things can happen as it moves upward. Managers or executives can also leave the firm or inadvertently spill the beans, leaving employees wondering to what extent they can reveal their own critical insights about the firm. And when people who work together develop close personal ties, it can become harder to differentiate between what should be shared and what shouldn't. We'll return to these issues as we develop the cultural considerations important to building an intelligence perspective.

Leadership

Walking the walk.

Leaders set the tone for the firm's culture. They inherit existing cultures but still drive the emergence of new ones through their vision and direction. Their actions are more meaningful than words. Through expressed vision, budgets, reward systems, and installed practices, leaders establish the values the organization's community members recognize and to which they respond.

There are distinct leadership requirements if an intelligence process is to work. CEOs and presidents need to communicate their beliefs in the value of the intelligence process and recognize employees as a vital component of knowledge growth, development, and protection. Their support for the intelligence process clarifies the firm's policy for contributing knowledge, discovering information, and sharing what is found. Clear standards will help avoid some of the gray areas to be discussed in the ethics chapter. By means of such direction, knowledge-sharing actions can be built into job descriptions, reward structures, and recognition ceremonies. And most importantly, leaders seek out and use the unfiltered, timely, action-oriented analyses that are the products of such efforts. In short, they are "knowledge-conscious" leaders, both teachers and learners (Stewart 2001).

A senior level executive is also needed to champion the intelligence cause. Intelligence activities are only valuable if they are responsive to executive needs and if executives use intelligence in their decision processes. A champion will help the facilitator and intelligence teams get audiences with executives in order to identify intelligence projects, gather knowledge, and present analysis.

Leadership is also an attribute of intelligence facilitators. It is up to these people to build the expert ring, intelligence teams, and network of external sources. Recruitment, rapport, and organization are key. Facilitators develop credibility, having access to executives and the ability to cut across functions and levels to gather information. They are involved with training, yet provide space for teams and experts to conduct analysis. With executive support, facilitators create the climate for intelligence, establishing a buzz about how people can add value by contributing what they know and participating in decision processes. The most critical element for these leaders is the ability to develop rapport so people want to participate and share their resources. Facilitators get people to participate because they want to, not because they have to. They can engage with individuals throughout the disciplines and functions of the organization. The best ones have considerable social capital of their own and actively participate in building and harnessing the social capital of the entire intelligence structure.

The final leadership need is on the team level. Much of this book stresses using intelligence teams to engage in shadowing, discovery, and analysis. Knowledge work in general is increasingly team-based, resulting from complex new economy realities and employee desires to make meaningful contributions (Pearce 2004). This shift in how work is structured warrants a commensurate shift in leadership. Pearce suggests moving from vertical to shared structures embodying fully empowered teams. Shared leadership "entails a simultaneous, ongoing, mutual influence process within a team that is characterized by 'serial emergence' of official as well as unofficial leaders" (48). Shared leadership is relevant in situations when membership is interdependent, creative thinking is necessary, and the task is complex. Intelligence teams meet these criteria. Their cross-functional structure makes them interdependent, while their investigative tasks and integrative analyses are both creative and complex.

How does shared leadership work? Instead of management or the intelligence facilitator appointing a leader, different team members assume leadership of different projects as they emerge. Designation would be dependent on expertise, network contacts, time constraints, and/or desire. At times, the experts themselves may become intricately engaged in a specific project or analysis and become emergent leaders. While this process requires additional training, the benefits to an intelligence capability outweigh the costs. More employees become experienced in leadership opportunities, develop an understanding of the challenges of different roles, and hone their skills in getting people to contribute knowledge and effort. The value is found in having depth on the bench. If an intelligence facilitator or intelligence team leader leaves her position or the organization, there are others with skill and experience to step up to the opportunity.

And as has been suggested about the role of leadership in developing and benefiting from an intelligence capability, executives need to lead by example. They do so by fostering a shared-leadership culture. In addition to supporting training and developing reward structures, Pearce (52) suggests that they take the first step in empowering teams by asking, "What do you think?" This is a big cultural step. It involves executives bringing the intelligence facilitator and/or team members, people at lower ranks, into their trusted circle. Here, value is placed on expertise and frankness. There are two distinct cultural challenges. One is for executives to be open to unfiltered analysis and opinions that may run contrary to their own beliefs and assumptions. The other is for employees to feel "safe" in presenting such information. One of the greatest benefits in this relationship can be in identifying firm blindspots, missed in an insular, unquestioning culture or for some other short-sighted reason. But the fear is that in pointing out the blindspot, the messenger can get shot. Core to creating an intelligence culture is an environment not permeated with fear, one that is instead nourished by trust.

Leaders also need to set the tone in terms of protection. They should establish formal procedures that employees see as sensible. Communication, through policy and action, sends the message that adherence to protection standards is important and will be rewarded. Leaders set an example by being careful in their own activities (e.g., public appearances and speeches) and welcoming input from counterintelligence and other individuals about organizational vulnerabilities. In short, an intelligence approach won't work without leaders taking an interest in and demonstrating commitment to the process.

A Fearless Space

Rewarding the messenger.

Any knowledge, intelligence, or learning process is dependent on people sharing unabridged versions of what they know. This can require that people take risks. Sometimes, contributed information can turn current perceptions and realities on their heads. Instead of receiving validating information, those seeking input may receive morsels that do quite the opposite, perhaps even debunking deeply held assumptions and beliefs, identifying missed warning signals, or upending grand strategies. If so, what's in it for the contributor? Maybe his knowledge is an ingredient that feeds a new perspective, or maybe it's so disruptive that there's a new person on the unemployment line.

In their book *The Knowing-Doing Gap*, Pfeffer and Sutton (2000) suggest that an atmosphere of fear and distrust are deterrents to capturing knowledge and turning it into action. It's simple: When employees don't trust their bosses or work for people who use fear as a motivator, they are less likely to share knowledge and information. Even worse, they can hide bad news or lie. Fearful gatekeepers can screen negative information for leaders, providing a rosier picture of reality than actually exists. Such inaccurate images can again create blindspots that result in improper actions or actions not being taken. Pfeffer and Sutton cite NASA's mistakes in the *Challenger* shuttle disaster as a case in point. Fear is a reckless management technique for firms that rely on knowledge assets. It can drive people to focus on short-term results and themselves instead of the good of the organization.

Employees also fear the consequences of being wrong. Instead of infusing creativity and innovation in their thinking and contributions, they play it safe and stick to what they know works. While this approach may not lead to loss, it also doesn't lead to maximum gain. If baseball players are heroes when they get hits 30 percent of the time, why are employees in the doghouse when they are wrong sometimes in the challenging and complex world of business? Instead of something to be punished, can't failure also be an opportunity to learn? Permission to fail is common in highly innovative organizations and its parameters can and should be extended to firms that want intelligence's innovative approach to knowledge assets.

Power is another aspect of a fearless culture. Knowledge is often seen as power, and one challenge of establishing KM systems has always been how to convince employees and managers to give up their personal, powerful knowledge assets, granting access or ownership to the collective of the firm. This is also critical in an intelligence environment, where individuals share operational and competitive insights or contribute to analyses. Once again, this will not happen in an environment of fear. As individual knowledge or insights are harvested, those individuals have to feel that their personal power will not be diminished but enhanced—that they will be seen as even more valuable (and rewarded) because of their contributions. Further, by sharing, they need to be reassured that their positions remain valuable and they won't become redundant once the firm captures what they know.

An intelligence process will fail in a culture of fear and distrust. There is no way around it. If the purpose of turning knowledge into intelligence is to help make better executive decisions, then executives have to create a climate of honesty, acceptance, and development. It's hard enough for members of intelligence teams to conduct analyses without their own bosses trying to spin their work. Executives need not fuel this fire by sending signals that they are selectively open to analyses that substantiate their existing points of view. Instead, they need to be willing to create a climate where analyses may also identify their own blindspots, either internal to the firm or lurking in the competitive landscape. Finally, not all inferences or predictions flowing from intelligence analyses will be true. And that's okay. Better to have a climate where what is believed to be true can be shared openly than for the emperor to discover he is naked when competitors are eating his clothes and shareholders are holding a mirror in front of him.

In terms of protection, some degree of fear may not be a bad thing, but it needs to be carefully managed. Clearly, giving away the store is something that can't be tolerated, and systems need to be in place to detect and rectify such problems (hopefully before they occur). Executives, managers, and employees all need to follow accepted protection procedures. On the other hand, all individuals need to have faith that they have been properly trained in protection standards and that if they follow the standards, they should have no fear of retribution (e.g., if a manager without clearance is refused access to some piece of knowledge, the employee should be rewarded, not punished). Further, in the "don't shoot the messenger" vein, individuals should be recognized for bringing to light any vulnerabilities that exist. Indeed, enthusiastically accepting input into how to make the system stronger in any way, including protection, fuels intelligence.

Trust

A revolutionary way to build trust: Tell the truth.
—Thomas Stewart

Trust is central to developing social capital and building intelligence-generating cultures. Trust suggests confidence in a person or situation, a belief in another's tendency to do the right thing. It is a societal cornerstone. It is a function of reputation, expertise, and integrity. In their book *In Good Company*, Cohen and Prusak (2001: 28) see trust as the "essential lubricant to any and all social activities, allowing people to work and live together without generating a constant, wasteful flurry of conflict and negotiations." To them, social capital depends on trust. Why? Trust builds upon itself, cuts transaction costs, supports cooperation in organizations, and offers people intrinsic rewards. They view trust as situational, however, a function of relationships and circumstance, as a person can be trusted in one situation and then not another. Trust can be fickle, based on factual judgments or intuitive interpretations of first impressions. In organizations, trust will be influenced by whether a person is perceived as an insider or outsider, has come recommended by others that are trusted, or has earned a reputation. Trust can be fragile and volatile or strong and widespread. When it exists, the organization will be more successful in collaborative and creative work. When it doesn't, the firm will tread water.

Trust fuels the intelligence process. Without it, people are less likely to voluntarily share of their knowledge, networks, and time. Without grass-roots contributions, the work of experts and the support of managers, the intelligence process itself will have difficulty developing the trust of the very executives it is designed to support. Employees have to trust that their inputs are being used to good purpose and will be rewarded if valuable. Teams have to trust the knowhow of their members and that their analytical efforts are meaningful. The intelligence facilitator has to trust the intentions of teams, competence of experts, and executive relationships. Senior decision-makers have to trust that the analysis they receive is unfiltered, timely, and impartial. In this model, trust begets trust. Having teams present their findings to senior management and/or having a facilitator who can walk into the president's office with intelligence news creates visible and valued reinforcement. The more people believe that what they do matters, the more they will trust in the process, and the better the process will generate meaningful intelligence.

For executives, trust of others can change as they move up the ranks. As people get promoted, and their responsibilities and points of reference change, their focus on what is important changes. As a result, so may their relationships with previously trusted confidants. In the senior ranks, executives need to now seek advice from informed yet impartial people. Joni (2004) calls this phenomenon "structural trust." She suggests that executives create a "kitchen cabinet" of advisors external to the firm who can offer insight and provide a "third opinion" with no conflicts of interest or agendas.

We also recommend structural trust. We further recommend that senior level executives have a method for gaining information that is trustworthy, unfiltered, and willing to push the limits of internal politics and policy. And we believe that the intelligence facilitator and intelligence teams have an important role to play in this mix. When the process is structured effectively, these people have full access to the firm's knowledge resources. They can go to any person at any level anywhere in search of information and expertise. They also can access a kitchen cabinet of their own, the expert ring of indifferent, experienced, and knowledgeable consultants and external network sources. One of the mandates for turning knowledge into intelligence is to provide executives with unfiltered, timely analysis. The facilitator and teams are poised to offer knowledge and intelligence that is rich, deep, and honest. They also have the advantage of anonymously leveraging perspectives from across the enterprise, something to which an external kitchen cabinet or executives may not be privy.

Effective protection is centered on trust. An organization that doesn't trust its systems or its people to keep things to themselves can't afford to do much knowledge sharing of any kind. Trust needs to be built up over time, but once systems are in place, standards are implemented, and people trained, the firm needs to start seeing how well it works. Once the players demonstrate that they understand and follow appropriate procedures, more and more knowledge can be processed throughout the organization. And again, the trust issue goes in both directions. Individuals passing knowledge up the chain want to be able to trust higher-ups not to leak it inappropriately, as well.

The development of trust is two-way. People engaging in the firm's intelligence process have to trust that their honest contributions matter and that they can participate without retribution. Executives have to trust that the intelligence facilitator and teams are providing them with unfiltered, unaltered, frank analysis. Executives may not like what they hear, and intelligence may not always be right. For firms where advantage can be gained or lost on the application of knowledge assets, however, this is a necessary and manageable risk. You just have to trust it.

Making It Happen

It would be hard to disagree that a firm's culture should encourage the development of social capital by building trust, dissolving fear, and demonstrating leadership. Getting it done is another story. All of the authors cited in this section have written books or articles on exactly how firms built such cultures, and such a rich choice of offerings wouldn't exist if the process were easy. As a short guide, we offer some of the common themes expressed.

Prusak and Cohen (2001) make the argument that executives need to deliberately invest in social capital. They suggest that the policies making it happen will acknowledge employee value by means of retention, promoting from within, facilitating personal contact, sending clear signals about trust and cooperation through reward policies, and communicating clearly.

Nucor built such policies into its "social ecology" (Gupta & Govindarajan 2000). British Petroleum did so, too, in their SBU management structures (Hansen & von Oetinger 2001: Pfeffer & Sutton 2000). Both of these firms communicated the importance of knowledge sharing across units, stressing its importance if they were to remain competitive. They made it clear they expected management to ensure that this happened and built reward policies to support the process. Knowledge hoarders were not rewarded; knowledge sharing was. Honest mistakes became learning experiences, and knowledge networks and communities were created. Business units and departments routinely distributed performance data. They also built supporting structures—coaches and peer groups that engaged across business units at BP, and intra- and inter-plant transfers at Nucor. While the organizations created the initiatives, provided the funding, and built the structures and processes, members of each firm began to willingly participate after a time. Actual gains became tangible between the advantages of learning from across the firm's expertise, and the goodwill developed through social capital. Both firms used formal mechanisms to get the process rolling. The mechanisms themselves supported the tenets that information is transparent, rewards are driven by learning, and people and their relationships are the focal points for success.

In short, senior management has to develop the infrastructure to support an intelligence capability. Just as importantly, it has to reinforce the organization's culture by participating in it and using what it generates. Ultimately, when executives include the intelligence facilitator and/or teams in their kitchen cabinets and employ this capability to investigate and facilitate decisions, then the message will be heard loud and clear that senior management values the knowledge of its people. The same issues again apply to protection. When executives make clear the importance of protection, the importance of training, the importance of following procedures, and other such issues, they will get the necessary cooperation.

Across the Network

Social capital, leadership, fearlessness, and trust also matter outside the core firm.

As with the infrastructure, all these considerations need to be reviewed in light of the realities of modern e-networks. Social capital exists not just at the personal level but also between organizations. Collaborators from all parts of the Value Chain build ongoing relationships with the core firm of a network, increasing social capital as they establish that they are valuable partners. As the relationships deepen, everyone will feel more comfortable sharing their knowledge assets to ever greater degrees, trusting they will be used appropriately, effectively, and without leakage.

The core firm, and perhaps longer-serving collaborators, need to provide leadership if the network is to work. That central organization has to show its own willingness to share knowledge assets, to apply its partners' knowledge assets properly, and to protect everyone's collective insights. It has to provide appropriate analysis, again not shying away from hard truths that might become obvious from the perspective of one of its external partners. It also has to champion knowledge as a critical success factor of the entire network and treat it as the priority it needs to be.

Within the network, partners have to be fearless, providing accurate, unfiltered insights. Collaborators need to feel comfortable contributing any kind of knowledge to the collective pool, without fear of being ostracized if that contribution doesn't fit the agenda of the core firm or some of the larger partners (e.g., a retailer reporting back quality problems, especially versus a particular competitive offering). While network partners do need to fear losing access to collective knowledge if they fail to protect it appropriately, they also need to be able to identify vulnerabilities without worrying about retribution.

Trust needs to develop throughout the network. As with employees, not everyone is going to be treated the same, and as collaborators build relationships over time and show an ability to protect knowledge, they can have access to more and more of the collective intelligence. We discussed collaborator compliance earlier, and we believe that the appropriate structure for many networks will involve tiers. The collaborators who have built up the most social capital, and especially trust, will have access to the most collective knowledge. Those at the fringes or who have not had the opportunity to build social capital and trust will have access only to the most basic operational information. As such a partner moves further into the network, it will gain access to ever more critical knowledge, including competitive advantage knowledge if it achieves the highest levels. And some networks may have quite a number of tiers between the extremes. The procedures for gathering and sharing knowledge and the procedures for protecting knowledge can be reviewed with current and potential collaborators, and networks can establish performance standards for admission to ever higher levels of knowledge collaboration. Again, it may take some time for a newer entrant to establish the necessary social capital to become a full participant in the network. The whole point of the exercise, remember, is to take an intelligence approach, making strategic decisions about how much to spread knowledge around and how carefully to protect it.

Back to the SPFs

From one perspective, the importance of having a rich culture and extensive social capital is SPF neutral. Clearly, strong relationships and trust among people who work with each other are key for a firm to run smoothly and productively. Leaders will set the tone of how much honesty and knowledge sharing occurs. Policies that encourage certain behaviors and recognition, whether monetary or symbolic, will reinforce them. The extent to which cultures buy in to an intelligence process will be reflected in infrastructural support and the belief that it will make life better.

From another perspective, the cultural aspects are critical with regard to the different SPF situations and the resulting strategies. When KM Risk is high, getting that culture established and working is absolutely imperative. When KM Risk is low, a more leisurely approach can likely work. Similarly, when CI Risk is high, getting the protection aspects of culture ingrained has to be a high priority. When low, the importance is less. In addition, KM Risk and CI Risk are not immutable. By buffing up its own knowledge capabilities relative to its potential and/or that of competitors, a firm can change the nature of its KM Risk curve (remember that firm resources and experience help to determine the position of that curve). Similarly, with a better counterintelligence culture in place, an organization can change the position of its CI Risk curve. So only part of the decision is reacting to circumstances; part of it is also doing something to, perhaps, change those circumstances.

SPF is about creating a balanced approach to risk. Building an intelligence culture is crucial in situations where KM Risk is high. For SPF 15 (800-pound Gorilla) and SPF 45 (Cold War), the seat of advantage comes from developing knowledge assets fully, across the Value Chain and networks of collaborators. Many of the works cited in this chapter (Cohen & Prusak, Pfeffer & Sutton, Stewart) provide rich examples of companies like British Petroleum, Xerox, and GE, which built and then nourished knowledge-sharing cultures that spanned business units and geographies. Gains in both the richness of social capital and business outcomes are noted. Teams are empowered and rewarded. Managers share knowledge to build goodwill. Process innovations improve the bottom line. A rich knowledge-sharing culture, a necessary ingredient for an intelligence process, has its roots in leadership and supportive climates.

When KM Risk is lower, the depth of social capital and knowledge-sharing activities can be lower. The impact of a strong culture, however, can leave its mark nonetheless. In SPF 5 (Brilliance), it is the talents of a star or the depth of cultural norms that will influence success. Social capital may be strong, but its purpose is not to share knowledge as much as it is to share the experience of membership to the firm (e.g., Southwest Airlines' upbeat employee culture). In SPF 30 (Glass House), knowledge assets are developed and shared only very deliberately to create advantage in the face of high CI Risk. Here, social capital may be less important than the development of proprietary processes and relational capital with clients. Sharing turns on common product offerings and not usually on client knowledge across units. Chase Manhattan's relationship management system (RMS) is a case in point. The RMS helps account managers provide customers with high-value portfolios by accessing multiple databases across the organization. Managers share knowledge with the system so that it can create best practice recommendations. It is not the knowledge of specific clients that is shared but instead the totality of transactions that made for the best relationships. (*Knowledge Management Review* 1998). Fleet's CRM system goes a step further. Although a business advisory platform, it also provides a services portfolio system based on rules to manage risk (Zaino 2003). In both of these cultures, sharing turns on the recording of best practices and the use of algorithms to mine the universe of transactions in different databases. But sharing about client portfolios does not seem to be in the offing. Transaction information is shared, and the systems do the rest. This requires little social capital and more willingness to input into the system.

The following SPF scenarios provide an introduction for considering the development of an intelligence culture.

SPF 5: Brilliance

With KM Risk and CI Risk both low, there is little need for an intelligence culture. The charisma of the leader will be reflected in "how things are done around here." Social capital can develop as a function of the size of the firm or nature of its culture. Information sharing will turn on publicly available documents or easily discovered competitive indicators. Trust is born of personal interactions and leadership behavior. Looking forward, however, firms that develop sharing cultures may be able to find ways to capture, share, and protect currently difficult knowledge assets, preparing themselves for the future as they move to different risk levels.

SPF 15: 800-Pound Gorilla

KM Risk is high and CI Risk is low to moderate. A strong intelligence culture will demonstrate high levels of trust in the social capital that evolves from the networking of the firm across its Value Chain and with collaborators. Essential to this culture are structures of teams and/or knowledge-sharing communities that engage people across functions, divisions, and geographies. Leaders rely upon teams or intelligence focal points for their competence, honesty, and clarity. In addition to supporting executive decisions, knowledge of all sorts is shared across organization members, supporting their decision processes.

SPF 30: Glass House

When KM Risk is low to moderate and CI Risk is high, there can be a tendency for a star system to emerge. Internal competitiveness can run counter to the need for the firm to develop positioning in an industry where first-mover status and reputation are the few sources of advantage, but it still happens. It is incumbent upon leaders to develop reward systems that not only encourage innovation but also the sharing of best practices and knowledge of all sorts. Social capital is more likely to develop within divisions than across, making structural supports for knowledge sharing essential.

On the competitive side, the culture is responsive not only to predicting competitor actions, but also to being careful about the products of intelligence activity. Culturally, it is wise to try and manage turnover, preventing the exit of proprietary knowledge and legally protecting the firm from those who do leave. This is a challenging culture for developing an intelligence capability. Competitive in all spheres, success will turn on the right combination of policies and reward structures, as well as leaders setting a tone that resonates across the orchestra and not in just a few sections.

SPF 45: Cold War

Both KM Risk and CI Risk are high. The intelligence culture in this scenario needs to have depth and strength. The firm's cultural footprint mimics an SPF 15 with the added dimension of operating in an industry awash in CI activity. Trust and social capital become ever more important as competitive landscapes require the input of competitive knowledge from across the enterprise. The intelligence facilitator and teams have to be able to present analyses to executives that may fly in the face of their competitive and positioning assumptions. The stakes for ego winning out over truth here are high. The motivator in an SPF 45 is winning the competitive war, not the fear of reprisal or being shot. Another cultural consideration in this scenario is the need to protect knowledge from unwanted transfer to partners. Whether this happens or not is also a cultural issue. Do employees understand the source of the firm's competitive advantage and the importance of the knowledge they may be sharing? A key concern, then, is the frequency and depth of communication between senior management and everyone else concerning the firm's vision, advantage, and commitment to an intelligence culture.

Summary

Building an intelligence culture takes will. We say this because people will be asked to do things that may be outside of current cultural norms. Take disagreeing with an executive, for example, or discovering that a current program is losing money, is noncompetitive, and seems to be a pet project of little value. Once senior executives begin asking questions and providing a safe haven for truth, there's no telling what will be revealed. Of course the desire for warts-and-all analysis and actually doing it are quite different things. And this sometimes includes, as Ben Gilad would say, "breaking china": identifying blindspots that may harbor sacred cows (Gilad, 1994). This willingness to break china can be one of the most valuable norms of all.

In addition to supporting the firm's success, a key reward of an intelligence culture is the engagement of the firm's most critical assets, its people and their minds. Organizations need people with different skills because of the complexities of business. People want to feel they do meaningful work and contribute to their organizations because of the depth of the human soul. A strong intelligence culture can bring these complexities together, forging a path that satisfies both conditions.

Executive Moment

Instilling a culture that supports an intelligence capability takes the firm beyond one that supports knowledge sharing. It requires people to not only contribute what they know, but to also become involved in discovery, analysis, and application. Senior executives need to open their kitchen to employees from different ranks and develop trust in a facilitator and teams whose charge it is to tell the truth, no matter what. Is your firm ready to evolve to embrace an intelligence culture? Let's see.

When was the last time you did the following?

- Assembled a group of employees outside of your trusted ring and asked, "What do *you* think?"
- Had people challenge your closely held assumptions and beliefs?
- Bring you news you didn't want to hear?
- Bring you news you didn't want to hear before it was too late?
- Wanted someone to investigate issues that keep you up at night?

These first few questions reflect levels of desire and trust. If you always rely on the same trusted few, then you are missing the opportunity to discover what your firm really knows. If your viewpoints are usually supported, either you are very smart or very lucky, or the people around you are too afraid to play devil's advocate and may be twisting information. The final question is about having a person who can respond to your needs in a swift, apolitical, and honest way.

When was the last time you did the following?

- Rewarded people for sharing what they know?
- Punished people for hoarding information?
- Created an opportunity for people with like interests to get together?
- Gave someone who made a mistake a second chance?
- Used a failure as an opportunity to learn?

These items turn on policies that create an environment of either trust or fear. They communicate what you value and what you don't. They also suggest that you know people are people, that no one is perfect, and that learning from honest mistakes is an opportunity. These messages can help ensure that the emperor has new clothes.

In addition, we are evaluating whether opportunities for people to meet, greet, and learn from each other have been supported. While some of this may occur spontaneously, institutionalizing the practice lets people know it is valued.

When was the last time you did the following?

- Communicated your vision?
- Appointed or supported a champion to encourage intelligence activity?
- Asked for help?
- Created different structures for leadership opportunities?
- Actually used recommendations from a white paper or strategic analysis from outside your kitchen?

Here is where the rubber meets the road for a leader. While all of the questions reflect on leadership, these last few really indicate whether you are only talking the talk or ready to walk the walk. It takes a paradigm shift to really build and use an intelligence capability. Are you ready?

Ethics of Intelligence: Keeping Your Hands Clean

Joanne Gavin, Marist College

Do the right thing.

The development and use of intelligence can be critical to the long-term survival of many organizations. Gaining knowledge and effectively turning it into intelligence has been the focus of this book so far. This chapter offers guidance on how to legally and ethically collect and use this intelligence.

Determining the shape of intelligence's ethical landscape can be a challenge for many employers and employees, especially regarding the conduct of competitive intelligence activities. Consider the case of a brand manager for an international consumer products company who was contacted by one of his customers and offered the full marketing plan of a rival company. The brand manager was elated because in the past such information allowed his company to successfully challenge its competitor's marketing strategies. Believing that upper management would welcome his good fortune, he excitedly passed the marketing plan to his superior. The superior, in turn, passed the report to top management.

In previous years, employees were encouraged to solicit their contacts, gaining bits and pieces of knowledge that were passed to superiors. The superiors would assemble the bits and pieces into reports that would be used to develop competitive strategies. Employees successfully extracting rival marketing strategies were frequently praised, and some had received bonuses and promotions. The brand manager, with such knowledge in hand, thought he was following accepted company procedure and would be rewarded. What he didn't realize was that the top management had changed its position regarding the acquisition of competitive intelligence. Instead of using the report, his president contacted the president of the rival company, explained what had happened, and returned the marketing report without ever looking at it. Instead of receiving praise, compensation, and/or a promotion, the brand manager was reassigned to a dead-end position signifying the end of his career with that company.

What is unfortunate about this story is that the brand manager lost his promising career because of his failure to understand top management's shifting view of competitive intelligence. In hindsight, he clearly should have told his customer to not even bother him with the rival's marketing plan. But what if the customer had merely mentioned, in general conversation, what the rival had planned for the next year? Would the brand manager have been rewarded, or not?

Why Focus on Ethics in Intelligence?

The ethics of gathering and using knowledge assets, particularly competitive knowledge, is an important issue. The greatest fonts of knowledge mean very little if no one will collaborate with an untrustworthy firm or if employees are going to wind up in jail. This chapter focuses largely on the CI side of ethics. This is not to say that important ethical issues don't exist relating to KM and its applications, but they are less volatile than the pursuit of knowledge external to the firm explicitly focusing on learning about competitors. Further, we've already talked about some of the key ethical concerns in the last chapter where we focused on "people" issues in intelligence—how employees and network partners must be treated if they are to buy into the system and share valuable knowledge.

But before focusing on CI ethics, let's at least touch upon the ethics of managing knowledge assets. From our perspective, we suggest managers think about two things: (1) organization–individual relationships and (2) organization–organization relationships. Knowledge asset development occurs when individual employees share what they know, cooperate in keeping their eyes open and collecting further knowledge, and/or participate in analysis. In terms of ethics, managers need to do things like establish clear guidelines as to what is individual knowledge and what is organizational, put fair reward systems in place that encourage employees to contribute their individual knowledge to the collective, and give credit to employees for valuable contributions. They also need to communicate clear policy when it comes to sharing confidential or sensitive documents that are not available to the organization's population. Essentially, KM systems are ongoing exchanges, and if they are to work, employees need to be clear about what can be shared, and firms need to ensure that employees get something of value back in return for contributing to the system.

The same idea applies to firm-to-firm relationships. The exchanges between e-network collaborators also involve giving up knowledge in return for something else (often other knowledge). In this instance, managers need to ensure they are perceived as valuable collaborators who give as much as they take. Managers also need to be clear about what type of knowledge is not to be shared in the definition of the collaborative agreement. Network partners that don't contribute their fair share will not be seen as attractive collaborators in the future. Consider Microsoft. While a great and successful company, it has had increasing difficulty in finding collaborators as it tries to enter new markets. Potential partners have seen what has happened elsewhere, where Microsoft has been able to lock up more than its fair share of profits (in PC software, for example) while earning a reputation as a prickly supplier. As a result, in the newer field of mobile phones, Symbian was launched by large hardware makers specifically so that Microsoft couldn't lock up the software market (Harvey 2003). A company that gains a reputation as difficult will find itself trying to manage a knowledge network consisting of itself while competing with more agreeable firms that are able to establish wide-ranging networks. So ethical considerations deserve a nod when talking about managing knowledge assets. In particular, however, gathering competitive knowledge rates substantial attention.

Unethical Behaviors Can Expose a Company to Legal Liability

The primary reason ethics are so important to those engaged in competitive intelligence is legal. Lawyers are becoming more and more engaged with the practices of companies and individuals using competitive intelligence (Ehrlich 1998). The following standards are drawn from court cases in this area, and there are four activities currently under scrutiny: identity misrepresentation, bribery, covert surveillance, and outright theft of property.

Of these four issues, identity misrepresentation probably has the largest gray area regarding ethical behavior (Ehrlich 2000). For instance, if a person legitimately has a number of identities such as graduate student, manager of a rival company, and part-time member of the city council, can that individual be selective as to which identity is used when collecting competitive intelligence? When approaching the rival company as a student or city council member, can the position as a manager of a competing company be kept quiet? Current ethical guidelines suggest that such an omission may be an act of fraud. Also, the legal profession sees this as an area warranting litigation.

While one might argue that every company is responsible for preventing the dissemination of its own important information, the courts are also holding responsible those who fraudulently obtain that information. The standard used to determine misrepresentation comes down to the question: "Would the targeted employee have divulged the important information if he or she had known the complete and true identity of the person seeking the information?"

Further, there is the liability assumed by the person asking the question regardless of whether there is intentional misrepresentation or not. This may be a grayer ethical area than misrepresentation, but the responsibility is squarely on the seeker's shoulders. The questioner is assumed to be knowingly seeking confidential and important information.

While companies cannot guarantee that every employee is ethical and will act in an ethical manner, they do need to establish policies on ethical behavior. By clearly communicating such a position, a firm will not only instruct employees in avoiding inappropriate behaviors but will also limit organizational liability in the event of an employee's unethical behavior. According to the Federal Sentencing Guidelines an "effective program to prevent and detect violations of the law" that is in place prior to any offense, can mitigate a corporate defendant's potential sentence significantly (Young 2000).

Unethical Behavior Can Also Damage a Firm's Reputation

In addition to creating legal risk for an organization, a lack of ethics in competitive intelligence can seriously damage a company's reputation. Both consumers and organizations with strong ethical foundations will choose to do business with reputable companies. Although it may take some time to see the effect that unethical behavior has on a company, in most cases there will eventually be a negative impact. As an example, one need look no further than the recent demise of the Arthur Andersen Company. A series of highly unethical and questionable actions led to the complete dissolution of the firm and the loss of over 30,000 jobs.

Ready examples also exist of organizations significantly impacted by unethical employee behaviors. Both Texaco and Denny's encountered considerable market share losses after claims of racial discrimination. Nike, after being accused of unfair working conditions in Southeast Asia, found itself doing damage control (Schwartz, 2000). Even Wal-Mart had to scramble to defend itself after charges of sexual discrimination in its promoting policies.

The apparent risk to both large and small organizations is that consumers are becoming more and more aware of the ethical reputations of the companies with which they do business. The informed consumer wants to spend her money and place her loyalty with companies that respect the customer, the community, and the environment. Business partners, current and potential, will also have concerns about having relationships with firms seen as crossing the line in terms of unethical CI activities. Whether a supplier, vendor, or customer, collaborators will want to see tight, well-executed procedures for dealing with competitive knowledge. Sloppiness could affect an entire e-network, and no one will want to be part of a high-profile episode. This, along with the legal ramifications, has changed the way many companies are doing business.

To illustrate, consider what happened to Boeing in 2003 (Lunsford and Squeo 2003). Among the series of scandals that eventually resulted in the resignation of CEO Phil Condit, the most serious breach of conduct was the discovery of proprietary documents from competitor Lockheed Martin (Daniel 2003; Pasztor and Squeo 2003; Squeo and Pasztor 2003). Boeing originally got some kudos for conducting an internal investigation in 1999 concerning a 1998 rocket contract with the U.S. government. The investigation revealed that three employees had knowledge and access to the Lockheed Martin documents (one was a former Lockheed employee); two were fired and one retired. Other employees were later disciplined as well. By summer 2003, however, it became clear that the two documents found in 1999 were only the tip of the iceberg, with Lockheed Martin claiming almost 45,000 pages of documents still at Boeing. Boeing was accused of a systematic program to obtain and use the documents in order to obtain the rocket contract. The Air Force yanked $1.1 billion worth of the rocket contract as the allegations came to light, and a separate suit by Lockheed is still pending.

The key question with Boeing is whether this episode was a misguided but isolated action by a couple of employees or an incident suggesting a widespread ethical breakdown in the firm. In acting so quickly to pull part of the contract, the Air Force reportedly also considered past behavior by Boeing, including inappropriate possession of Department of Defense documents in the eighties and nineties. And, of course, once a further ethical breach came to light with the hiring of a government procurement specialist, the CEO had little defense against suggestions of a corporate culture allowing too many ethical lapses.

A firm needs to think about where it sets the bar in terms of ethics. Even if one buys the "few bad apples" theory, shouldn't an organization anticipate such things, establishing ethical standards for CI such that slight breaches of the standards still leave it with defensible positions? If the corporate policy is too close to the line on CI ethics, then overeager employees may easily push the entire firm into places it doesn't want to be. An appropriate policy, tightly enforced, will keep the firm clear of the law and in the good graces of collaborators and customers.

Making Ethical Decisions

Choosing Between Black and White

All engaged in competitive intelligence activities can readily agree that certain behaviors breach ethical standards. Blatantly stealing trade secrets, accessing confidential information, fraud, and invasion of privacy are among the most serious and obvious of these behaviors. No one need tell us that the break-in at the Watergate Hotel to steal the Democrats' campaign information was unethical. It was not only unethical, it was illegal.

Until recently, we guided our competitive intelligence activities by these legal standards. If it was illegal, most organizations chose not to engage in the activity. Today, however, more companies are choosing to examine the full ethical implications of their competitive intelligence practices, not just the legal ones.

The Gray Areas of Competitive Intelligence

Trade Secrets

While it is somewhat easy to declare that stealing trade secrets is strictly off limits, what happens when trade secrets are acquired by accident? Unlike patents, where the knowledge is protected regardless of how someone else acquires it (even independent invention is no defense), trade secret protection is based on how the knowledge is discovered. There are a number of seemingly gray areas regarding the accidental acquisition of confidential information.

One area occurs when a current or former employee of a targeted company willingly divulges trade secrets in response to your inquiries. While this may seem innocent on the surface, there are a number of ethical problems at work here. First, employees, whether current or former, have a duty to respect the confidential nature of their company's trade secrets. Essentially this means the employee should know what constitutes a trade secret in their company and how such information should be handled. Indeed, many states allow nondisclosure agreements, and they tend to hold up in court. Further, inquiries to solicit trade secrets can be unethical and can land you in ethical and legal trouble. Ethical considerations demand that you respect the trade secrets held by other organizations. This means that even if a targeted company's employee divulges a trade secret, you should not use that information. If publicly available, of course, the trade secret becomes fair game, since the firm in question isn't taking reasonable steps to keep it secret.

Breach of Confidence

The concept of trade secrets may provide a clear picture of what constitutes off-limit competitive intelligence inquiry. However, breach of confidence may not be quite so clear. In many respects, confidential information holds the same degree of importance as trade secrets. Confidential information is generally viewed as a valuable property of an organization. The line is blurring between trade secrets and confidential information, at least in the United States, as the Economic Espionage Act has more widely defined what a trade secret is (economically valuable and kept under wraps), so managers should expect an ever diminishing distinction between the categories.

The issue of confidential information places more of an ethical and possibly legal burden on the inquirer. One may hold that a questioner should know what constitutes confidential information and that current and former employees have a duty not to divulge such information. In reality, the true ethical burden falls onto the shoulders of both the questioner and the employee.

Employees and former employees are required to respect the nature of confidential information and not use or disclose such information. For those parties engaged in competitive intelligence, the ethical question rests on two issues. Initially, is the information being sought held in confidence by the targeted company? Second, have we induced the targeted company's employees to breach that confidence?

Fraud

Intentionally lying to another person for the purpose of getting him to say or do something is obviously unethical. As discussed earlier, one frequent example of fraudulent behavior is lying about one's identity. While it may be the easiest way to get information from another person, it is clearly wrong. As noted there, the simplest test is to ask, "Would the employee give the information requested if he or she knew your true identity?" If the answer is no, then this is obviously a breach of ethical standards.

Are you required, however, to give your identity before you speak to an employee about competitive information? And are you required to offer full disclosure of all the positions you hold? Are attempts to confuse or mislead unethical? The legal answer is that you do not have to volunteer your full identity unless you are asked. The ethical response is that complete disclosure is the only way to know the answer to the questions regarding the employee's true willingness to reveal the knowledge.

Privacy

The issue of privacy has both black and white areas as well as several that are shades of gray. Specifically, the black and white areas consist of wiretapping, computer hacking, and breaking and entering. Clearly these areas are illegal and unethical.

But what about the collection of information when there is no expectation of privacy? Here the lines in the sand become fuzzy and difficult to distinguish. For instance, sifting through a target company's trash is generally not illegal. The same holds for overhearing conversations in a public area. The question becomes, are these behaviors ethical? As CI professionals evaluate these behaviors, more are coming to the conclusion that these activities may be unethical.

Code of Ethics

How should an organization protect itself from engaging in unfair and unethical competitive intelligence gathering practices? One of the first places to look is the Society of Competitive Intelligence Professionals Code of Ethics. The eight principles provide an excellent framework for developing ethical standards (www.scip.org/ci/ethics.asp).

The SCIP Code, however, provides only a generalized outline for defining ethical behavior. To fully embrace a set of ethical standards, an organization must translate these general principles into practical, everyday procedures. It is one thing to say to your employees to be honest; it is more helpful to define what honesty means in everyday behavior in your organization.

To illustrate, honesty means telling the truth about who you are and what you are seeking when somebody asks you. Honesty means properly and completely identifying who you are before you engage in an interview. Honesty means disclosing to your own organization if there are questions regarding how information was obtained. Honesty is avoiding dishonest acts of commission *and* omission.

In addition to creating a culture that clearly identifies acceptable and nonacceptable behaviors, a company needs to clearly state the consequences for violations of these expectations. And because mistakes will occur, companies also need to explain to employees how to rectify inadvertent unethical behaviors. The point is: Give your employees clear, explicit guidelines on how to remedy mistakes when gathering competitive intelligence. This will avoid the "should have known" syndrome that regularly costs good people their careers and organizations legal and public relations problems.

The Ethical Traps Are Sometimes Easily Missed

Companies would do well to address shades of gray in the development of ethical competitive intelligence practices. The more explicit the competitive intelligence rules, the easier it is for employees to follow them. Often, employees find themselves in trouble without any warning. The following are some situations where the uninformed employee may quickly get in over his head (Trevino & Weaver, 1997).

A competitor's employee interviews with your firm and seems very willing to divulge confidential information. Should you take advantage and explore this line of questioning? The simple answer is no, but deciding when you have crossed the line into unethical questioning is not that easy. For instance, neither you nor the candidate may intentionally be seeking to bring out confidential information. However, an innocent question from you leads the candidate to answer with confidential information. While it may have started out innocently, it has now moved into unethical practices. The wise interviewer will constantly monitor both the questions and the answers during the interview. When a question elicits a possibly inappropriate response, the interviewer should redirect the candidate. It may be most appropriate to advise the candidate not to divulge trade secrets or confidential information during the interview.

Information you are seeking can be found through costly and time-consuming research from public domain sources. To save time and money, you decide to pick up the phone and question one of the target company's employees. The issue at work here is whether you fully disclose who you are and the purpose of your inquiry or intentionally misrepresent yourself. Also, a question may arise if the employee is induced into divulging confidential information in the process of gathering other information. Most competitive intelligence professionals would suggest using public domain sources whenever possible. Then there is no question as to whether any ethical lines have been crossed.

One of your suppliers inadvertently sends you a confidential report from one of your rivals. Should you read it? Whether the confidential report was sent by accident or not, reading it is clearly unethical. The safest course of action is to either return the report to your supplier or, if appropriate, to the rival company. Then inform your supplier that you expect a higher standard of ethics from them. The question you should ask yourself is: "Are your marketing plans and confidential information being sent to your rivals?"

You engage someone else to acquire competitive intelligence. One way to avoid questionable practices in intelligence gathering is to engage an outside person or firm to do it for you. The question here is whether you are responsible for the actions of a person who is not an employee or a firm that is supposed to be knowledgeable about professional standards. If you hire a professional competitive intelligence firm, you would expect it to engage in ethically acceptable behavior. Frankly, there is no guarantee of that, and it is in your best interest to find out. Organizations with high ethical standards would question outside firms about exactly what methods they intend to use to gather the information they are seeking. Let them convince you that their practices stand up to your ethical standards. If they do not, find another firm. Even if you gain from their unethical practices, you may still be legally responsible for damages to the target company. And the public relations problems may cost your company dearly.

Developing Your Ethics Policies

There are several different ethical reasoning models that could be used as the standard when developing ethical policies. Some of the more prominent models include Virtue, Rule, Utilitarianism, and Justice. While each of these models has received attention in the academic literature, each presents its own unique benefits and challenges when applied to the workplace.

Virtue ethics focuses on individuals and their capacity to judge and do the right thing in the right place at the right time in the right way (MacIntyre 1984). In an ideal world, this would be the model of choice. Every company would strive to develop each employee's personal character to recognize ethical dilemmas and avoid them. Developing an ethical employee may be the goal of every organization, but it is not realistic in most situations.

Rule-based ethical reasoning states that each individual has a set of inalienable rights and that to protect these rights individual behaviors should be based on a set of rules (Baier 1978). The conventional wisdom in this model is to develop a set of rules that, if followed, would ensure that all employees acted ethically. This may be a reasonable assumption, but all one has to do is examine the lessons learned from Enron and Arthur Andersen to see that it is impossible to design a rule to meet every situation. And even if that were possible, creative individuals would always find the loopholes.

Utilitarianism looks beyond self-interest to consider impartially the interests of all persons affected by an action (Mill 1910). We often hear this model described as making decisions with the "greatest good for the greatest number" in mind. Again, a noble ambition but one that may not sit very well with management and stockholders who feel that the interests of their company should take precedence over that of others.

The final ethical framework is Justice, whose major components are equity, fairness, and impartiality. The two main aspects of Justice Theory are Procedural Justice and Distributive Justice (Rawls 1971). Distributive Justice focuses on the equal or fair distribution of outcomes. In a competitive environment, no organization, ethical or not, is interested in ensuring that all organizations are equally represented in market share, revenues, or any other traditional business success measure. Procedural Justice, however, examines the process by which the outcomes are distributed (Thibault & Walker 1975). The ethical concept here examines if everyone is given a fair and equitable chance to compete in the marketplace. It is this concept of fair processes that CI practitioners should be focused on when engaging in competitive behaviors and developing company-specific codes of conduct.

Back to the SPFs

For the last few chapters, we have examined the circumstances a firm faces when balancing KM Risk and CI Risk. In doing this, we have set out several Strategic Protection Factors (SPFs) under which your organization may fall. Using the concepts of Procedural Justice, we can develop some possible scenarios that CI professionals might face and offer suggestions for deciding the correct ethical behaviors in each situation.

SPF 5: Brilliance

A firm operating in the SPF 5 (Brilliance) quadrant is enjoying relatively low risk in both knowledge management and competitive intelligence. Because of these low risks, there is little intelligence gathering and therefore little risk of unethical behavior. There is also little knowledge sharing of consequence, limiting ethics concerns on the KM side. Organizations operating here even avoid the risk of unintentional unethical behaviors because if information is obtained by accident, it can simply be discarded without concern of loss. This does not mean that the organization and its members are more ethical; it simply means that they are not engaged in activities that may lead to the temptation to act unethically.

SPF 15: 800-Pound Gorilla

Companies operating under SPF 15 (800-pound Gorilla) conditions experience high KM Risks and low CI Risks. Because of the nature of an SPF 15 company, it is often forced to share information in order to develop necessary relationships. These firms need to consider how they develop and share knowledge with collaborators, making equitable exchanges. But since entrance to this environment is often difficult and market leaders are hard to copy, the necessity to gain intelligence on competitors is restricted. For these reasons, the level of work by CI professionals is limited, and most often the necessary information can be obtained from public sources or through very simple and straightforward mechanisms. Although the CI professional is more engaged than one in an SPF 5 organization, the risk of unethical behavior is still relatively low. Even though the threats of unethical behaviors by employees are low, all employees should be educated about the company's ethical expectations for knowledge sharing and intelligence gathering.

SPF 30: Glass House

As we examine a company with an SPF 30 (Glass House) designation, we find it engaging in much more intelligence-protection activity. Effective organizations in this environment will often have limited knowledge development but will strongly protect the knowledge assets they do have. This type of organization is feeling the pressure to gain a competitive advantage through inside knowledge of its competitors. At this level of competitive pressure, it becomes very important to engage in active education of employees about the company's ethical practices. Employees need to understand the parameters under which they may obtain information about others. They should also be fully educated on why and how to make behavioral decisions. Employers should use Procedural Justice Theory as a foundation for helping employees see that if a behavior gives them an unfair competitive advantage over their rivals, it is unethical and unacceptable. The company must also successfully convince employees that this focus on ethical intelligence gathering is serious and real, not just politically correct lip service. Companies must state in words and follow through with behaviors that tell employees that unethically gathering information will be punished.

SPF 45: Cold War

A company operating under an SPF 45 (Cold War) scenario is engaged in the highest levels of both CI Risk and KM Risk. Relationships must be established and developed within and without the organization, so long-term, collaborative knowledge exchanges need to be pursued. Competition is at its extreme, and employees may feel pressure to gather intelligence at any cost. Educating employees in this environment is critical. They must not only understand that the company truly supports ethical behavior, but they must also be given the fundamentals of ethical decision-making to enhance their ability to make decisions on the fly about the ethical appropriateness of any given behavior. This becomes especial important in alliance relationships defined around knowledge transfer. These employees must also be well trained in the Procedural Justice model so they can evaluate the fairness and equity of their CI behaviors. Employees should learn to ask the question: "Does this behavior impinge upon a fair and equal opportunity for all companies involved?" Finally, these employees must trust in the company enough to know that the company will support their ethically based decisions.

Executive Moment

Few companies or executives willfully engage in blatant unethical behaviors. Those who do, expose themselves to legal issues and a diminished company reputation. The real challenge for most executives is how to prevent employees from engaging in behaviors that are less obviously unethical. We suggest that the answer to this challenge is in training your employees to understand both your company's vision for ethically competing and the principles of a fair and just process for all.

We suggest that you ask yourself the following questions.

- Do my employees truly understand the position we take on ethical behavior?
- Do we treat employees and collaborators fairly in terms of knowledge sharing?
- Have we established appropriate procedures for competitive intelligence activities?
  - ☐ Are all employees aware of the procedures?
  - ☐ Do they follow the procedures?
- Do employees trust the company to support and reward them for acting ethically?
- Do they understand that our goal is to ensure a fair and equitable process for all?
- Are they able to use this understanding to make ethical decisions even when competition is at its most fierce?

Part 4 Wrap-Up:
A Blueprint for Shifting from
Knowledge to Intelligence

Moving from knowledge to intelligence is a paradigm shift: from knowledge sharing to strategic action. While an intelligence process accesses the firm's knowledge systems and structures, it also steps outside the firm, purposefully pursuing information and knowledge wherever it exists. In doing so, it creates a more complete picture for building strategic landscapes. And it does so with flexibility, deliberateness, and clarity. Some may say that once knowledge is contributed to the system, it's yesterday's news. We would argue that yesterday's news is a foundation for what tomorrow can be. Learning from past experience while investigating current issues provides insight into what has worked, what hasn't worked, and why. Knowing where the potholes are in the road, that's knowledge management. Knowing how they got there and how to walk around them is knowledge management, too. Knowing which new road to choose instead—that's intelligence. It takes a universe of knowledge, from different functions, levels, and divisions, from as well as networks, different experts, and consultants, to make such choices.

To succeed, the intelligence process must be intricately woven into KM processes and the firm's structure. It also requires a focal point, a facilitator and/or intelligence team, that has carte blanche to gather knowledge across function, level, location, network, and expert contributors. The facilitator and/or team must also deliver unfiltered findings to executives without editing, retribution, or fear.

Good analysis is dependent on two things: good and complete information and good minds. For analysis to be meaningful, it needs the right audience with the motivation to act. Executives are the starting point and ending point for intelligence work. Their belief in the process is demonstrated through their actions. They must create policies that reward engagement, and they should use the intelligence process for making good decisions, keeping themselves informed, and maintaining the firm's competitiveness.

This requires a signature culture rich in social capital and trust. Resilient leaders open themselves to this process. They create a climate in which people aren't afraid to tell the truth, take a risk, or admit that they are wrong. They open themselves up to candid analysis whose purpose is twofold: to drive actions and to identify blindspots. Leaders are motivated to improve shareholder value. Until they are willing to look hard both internally and externally, performance can reach a plateau, tethered by misguided assumptions and beliefs about what the firm and competitors can do. Leaders striving for excellence will do both. They will recognize that a key ingredient in this process is to drink from their well of knowledge assets. They bring the water bearer, the point person, into their kitchen for news from the landscape. They commission analysis that can fly in the face of what is believed to be true. They create a climate in which they may be told the emperor has no clothes. They have foresight because the water bearer has also told them to have an extra garment in their wardrobe. They ask, listen, and then act.

To do this, leaders must clearly communicate, throughout their sphere of influence, the importance of intelligence to the firm. These communications take many forms.

- Internal programs to get grassroots buy-in
- Clear ethical practices for engaging in the gathering and sharing of knowledge
- Rewards structures encouraging sharing, discouraging hoarding, and recognizing strategic contribution
- Directives to executives and managers to support the boundary-spanning activities of the intelligence facilitator and teams
- A budget for training the facilitator, teams, and rings of experts
- Communication concerning the importance of knowledge to the firm's bottom line and the need to protect it

Perhaps the most important communication will be delivered through the leaders' actions. Do they use the intelligence system, has the facilitator become a trusted member of the kitchen, is the messenger rewarded and not shot, are they careful with sensitive knowledge? If leaders provide an example, others will follow.

A lot of effort goes into building KM and intelligence processes. The same amount of effort needs to go into protecting them. Building social capital and trust, developing structures and systems, communicating, and acting do not replace safeguarding. Well-intentioned people can be lured into revealing information to competitors. Uninformed people can trade knowledge in an effort to get a job done, not realizing the gravity of the action. Careless people can misplace or lose sensitive electronics. Naïve people can discuss business in questionable public venues. Trade show reps and salespeople can tell too much. One can go on and on with the vulnerabilities, but the point is that counterintelligence activity requires leadership attention, too. Employees need to be informed about and trained in managing situations where knowledge leakage can occur. Understanding the importance of knowledge to the firm's competitiveness must be core to the culture. And this can be done without creating an aura of Big Brother. It's a matter of informing and providing the correct incentives. If people are aware and motivated, they will follow a well-structured plan.

The challenge in building an intelligence culture is to create the right mix of sharing and protecting, of creatively discovering information and staying on the right side of ethical lines, of being analytically inclusive and economical in presentation, of both leading and following, of teaching and learning. A culture built on trust, where leaders walk the walk and build an infrastructure that fortifies this path, can foster an intelligence climate that keeps people engaged, the firm competitive, and its knowledge assets protected.

Conclusion

Change challenges competitiveness. With endless sources, change is unrelenting. Its recent wave arrived in the wake of digitization, globalization, and the knowledge economy. For the next wave, what's your preference: a good guess or an intelligent wager? Organizations have choices in managing change. They can react once they see which way the current flows, or like Gretsky, they can "skate to where the puck is going to be." The first option requires the firm to mobilize its knowledge assets—the second demands a relentless intelligence orientation. At its core, an intelligence process deliberately engages in discovery to serve senior decision-makers. In so doing, knowledge captures and shares information, and intelligence explores and activates it. While both have viable capabilities of their own, they work better in partnership for managing change.

How can the firm create a dynamic intelligence capability? Initially, it should embrace the credo that knowledge has value and intelligence has power. Knowledge assets, the intellectual capital of the firm, are the bedrock for a learning organization. We have suggested expanding this foundation to include both competitive knowledge as an asset and the practice of gathering information from outside the company's borders.

Knowledge becomes intelligence when activated through synthesis, integration, and analysis of multiple sources of information, creating landscapes of understanding in response to executive needs. Intelligence gets its power from unfiltered, timely scrutiny of the competitive environment and the firm itself. Whether providing operational or strategic value, intelligence can directly impact how and what the firm does. To facilitate this, executives need to articulate an intelligence vision to get people engaged. And, they need to use the intelligence capability to give it meaning.

Second, knowledge and intelligence activities are given meaning only by the people who show up to the game. If people do not contribute information or expertise, if people do not use the system and find value in it for themselves, then the capability will cease to exist. The knowledge architecture then needs to be user friendly for both individuals and teams. The intelligence conversion itself needs to create simple structures that can readily access the firm's knowledge banks and external information. Woven into KM processes, facilitators and shadow teams can build expert rings of knowing inside and outside the firm. Cross-functional in design, intelligence teams provide competing perspectives and analyses infused with information from outside the firm's walls. Facilitators develop close working relationships with executives, intelligence teams, experts, and grassroots contributors. Together, facilitators and intelligence teams operate in a parallel organization structure, becoming a focal point for bringing together the firm's knowledge assets and piecing together the competitive puzzle.

New Economy thinkers and practitioners have recommended that the firm develop its intellectual capital in pursuit of sustainable competitive advantage. To this mandate we have added the need to develop competitive assets and engage the firm's knowledge bank in CI-style analysis. CI is an important component in building the firm's intelligence capability. And all of this is also true of your competitors seeking to become intelligent at your expense. Third, then, is the need to balance the risks of competing in not only a knowledge-driven but also an intelligence-driven economy. The first risk, KM Risk, considers the implications of not developing knowledge assets to their fullest potential when rivals are. The second risk, CI Risk, recognizes the challenges of keeping knowledge assets out of the hands of competitors. To strategically manage knowledge assets, firms need to find the point that minimizes their exposure to both KM Risk and CI Risk. We suggest that firms engage in diagnostic activity to determine their Strategic Protection Factor. This framework is a tapestry of nation, industry, and firm factors, as well as including e-business and network factors. These factors push the firm to consider which knowledge assets should be developed, to what depth, and how far across its Value Chain, internally and externally. In balancing the need to collaborate competitively and protect knowledge assets, the firm's SPF keeps intelligence issues in the forefront while providing insight into the firm's counterintelligence needs.

Fourth, we suggest a simultaneous design of intelligence and counterintelligence structures and processes. Naïveté, loose lips, carelessness, and weak policies are behind many intelligence leaks. Simply recognizing that competitive intelligence is a real threat and creating clear policies and training regarding knowledge sharing can create a significant barrier. This will not only help prevent scientists at conferences, salespeople at trade shows, or administrative personnel on telephones from spilling the beans, but will also stem inappropriate knowledge transfer in alternative business models. A product of the current era of change is the proliferation of network structures across the Value Chain with collaborators and alliance partners. Many of these new relationships seek to create operational excellence and develop new products (upstream) or to create new channels for distribution across products, markets, and countries (downstream). At each turn are opportunities for firms to leak information and for partners to learn more than what was bargained for. Firms may also find that collaborators, perhaps some they didn't even know they had, aren't as careful about protecting knowledge as they are. While legal contracts are drawn to respond to this challenge, they aren't enough. What needs to be added is clear communication throughout the organization about what information is important to the firm's competitiveness and why. This perspective may help employees think twice about revealing information for short-term gain in favor of protecting it for the long run.

Finally, intelligence structures, designs, mandates, and training will only work if the organization invests in sustaining a culture that is rich in social capital. Developing relationships and trust makes the system tick. People need to willingly share what they know, engage in analytical activity, and trust that in sharing expertise they are not sacrificing their power. They have to trust that they can contribute honestly and still have promising career paths, that they will still have jobs if they make honest mistakes. They have to trust that the executives engaging in the intelligence process are doing so because they want to know everything: the good, the bad, and the ugly, about the competitive environment and about the firm itself. Leaders have to be ready to accept that an intelligence capability can build landscapes of change and also identify the firm's impediments to change. Setting the tone and policy for the ethical gathering and use of information, leaders across level and function ensure that people understand their roles and that the process will have integrity.

Strategically managing inevitable change is the firm's greatest competitive weapon. It turns on the quality and use of analysis generated through intelligence processes. How does the firm create a resilient intelligence capability? The recipe has equal parts of these ingredients.

- A simple design that is inclusive, user friendly, and has a focal point
- A culture that gets people involved and engaged in analysis
- An SPF designation that responds to national, industry, and firm factors
- An orientation and process for protecting what you know
- Leaders who, through policy and person, walk the walk

How can firms strategically manage change? They can do it by building an intelligence capability that prepares them for the Next Economy—whatever that may bring.

References

Chapter 1

Behnke, L. and P. Slayton, Shaping a corporate intelligence function at IBM, *Competitive Intelligence Review*, 1998, 9:2, 4–9.

Birkinshaw, J. and T. Sheehan, Managing the knowledge life cycle: Knowledge isn't static, but it often gets managed as if it were, *Sloan Management Review*, 2002, 44:1, 75–83.

Blumenstein, R. and N. Harris, Internet sleuth sends SkyTel on a wild ride, *The Wall Street Journal*, (May 26, 1999), B1, B4.

Choo C.W., Sensemaking, knowledge creation, and decision making. In Choo, C.W. and N. Bontis (Eds.), *The Strategic Management of Intellectual Capital and Organizational Knowledge* (Oxford University Press, New York, 2002), 79–88.

Curtis, J., Behind enemy lines, *Marketing*, (May 24, 2001), 28–29.

Davenport, T.H. and L. Prusak, *Working Knowledge: How Organizations Manage What They Know.* (Harvard Business School Press, Boston, 1998).

Edvinsson, L. and M.S. Malone, *Intellectual Capital: Realizing Your Company's True Value By Finding Its Hidden Brainpower.* (Harper Business, New York, 1997).

Finkelstein, S., *Why Smart Executives Fail.* (Portfolio, New York, 2003).

Friedman, V., The rise and fall of the one-man brand, *Financial Times*, (December 5, 2003), 8.

Fuld, L., *The New Competitor Intelligence.* (John Wiley & Sons, New York, 1995).

Galloni, A., Carreyrou, J. and C. Rohwedder, Stripped of stars at top, will Gucci still be Gucci? *The Wall Street Journal*, (November 11, 2003), A1, A14.

Gilad, B., *Business Blindspots*. (Probus Publishing Company, Chicago, 1994).

Gilad, B. and T. Gilad, *Business Intelligence Systems: A New Tool for Competitive Advantage*. (AMACOM, Chicago, 1988).

Gomes, L., Upstart Linux draws a Microsoft attack team, *The Wall Street Journal*, (May 21, 1999), B4.

Heavens, A., Industrial espionage "likely motive" for Microsoft attack, *Financial Times*, (October 30, 2000), 16.

Kerstetter, J., P. Burrows, J. Greene, G. Smith and M. Conlin, The dark side of the valley, *Business Week*, (July 17, 2000), 42–43.

Mackintosh, J., Ford says it feared loss of trade secrets, *Financial Times*, (December 8, 2003a), 18.

Mackintosh, J., Ford tries to tie up ex-president, *Financial Times*, (December 15, 2003b), 11.

Matson, E., P. Patiath and T. Shavers, Strengthening your organization's internal knowledge market, *Organizational Dynamics*, 2003, 32:3, 275–285.

Miree, C.E. and J.E. Prescott, "TAP-IN" to strategic and tactical intelligence in the sales and marketing functions, *Competitive Intelligence Review*, 2000, 11:1, 4.

Nelson, E. and G. Anders, Wal-Mart, Amazon.com settle fight over recruitment and trade secrets, *The Wall Street Journal*, (April 6, 1999), A3.

Peterson, A., Making the sale, *The Wall Street Journal*, (November 15, 1999), R16.

Rothberg, H.N., Fortifying competitive intelligence systems with shadow teams, *Competitive Intelligence Review*, 1997, 8:2, 3–11.

Rothberg, H.N. and G.S. Erickson, Competitive capital: A fourth pillar of intellectual capital? In Bontis, N. (Ed.), *World Congress on Intellectual Capital Readings*, (Butterworth-Heinemann, Woburn, MA, 2002), 94–103.

Rothberg, H.N. and G. S. Erickson, Competitive capital: A sustainable source for competitive advantage, *Global Competitiveness*, Proceedings of the 1999 American Society for Competitiveness Conference, Atlanta, GA, October 21–23, 1999.

Simpson, G.R. and T. Bridis, Oracle hired firm to probe Microsoft allies, *The Wall Street Journal*, (June 28, 2000), A3, A10.

Solomon, D. and S. Thurm, Lucent files suit to keep ex-employees from disclosing sensitive data to Cisco, *The Wall Street Journal*, (June 21, 2000), B5.

Starkman, D., US kills probe of Reuters' use of Bloomberg data, *The Wall Street Journal*, (July 16, 1999), B15.

Tomsho, R. Medical supplier sues Boston Scientific, *The Wall Street Journal*, (April 6, 2001), B2.

Zach, M.H., Developing a knowledge strategy. In W.C. Choo and N. Bontis (Eds.), *The Strategic Management of Intellectual Capital and Organizational Knowledge*, (Oxford University Press, New York, 2002), 255–276.

Chapter 2

American Society for Industrial Security (ASIS)/Pricewaterhouse-Coopers, *Trends in Proprietary Information Loss*. (ASIS, Alexandria, VA, 1999).

Bennett, J. and B. Mantz, Amgen's patent infringement trial draws rivals' lawyers in search of data, *The Wall Street Journal*, (June 26, 2000), A3–4.

Bernhardt, D., Strategic intelligence: The sword and shield of the enterprise, *Competitive Intelligence Magazine*, 2002, 5:5, 24–28.

Breeding, B., CI and KM convergence: A case study at Shell Services International, *Competitive Intelligence Review*, 2000, 11:4, 12–24.

Cappel, J.J. and J.P. Boone, A look at the link between competitive intelligence and performance, *Competitive Intelligence Review*, 1995, 6:2, 15–23.

Gilad, B., Strategic intent and strategic intelligence. In B. Gilad and J. Herring (Eds.), *The Art and Science of Business Intelligence Analysis*, (JAI Press, Greenwich, CT, 1996).

Hamel, G. and L. Valikangas, The quest for resilience, *Harvard Business Review*, 2003, 81:9, 52–65.

Kahn, G., Invisible supplier has Penney's shirts all buttoned up, *The Wall Street Journal*, (September 11, 2003), A1, A9.

Kontzer, T., The need to know, *Informationweek.com*, (August 18, 2003), 34–44.

Levin, R., A.J. Klevorick, R.R. Nelson and S.G. Winter, Appropriating the returns from industrial research and development, *Brookings Papers on Economic Activity*, (Winter 1987), 783–831.

Office of the National Counterintelligence Executive, Annual Report to Congress, 2002, www.ncix.gov.

Office of the National Counterintelligence Executive, Annual Report to Congress, 2001, www.ncix.gov.

Pepper, J., Competitive intelligence at Procter & Gamble, *Competitive Intelligence Review*, 1999, 10:4, 4–9.

Porter, M., *Competitive Strategy*. (Free Press, New York, 1980).

Pringle, D., Nokia confronts Microsoft head-on in a software battle, *The Wall Street Journal*, (May 22, 2002), A1.

Tam, P-W., Palm puts up its fists as Microsoft attacks hand-held PC market, *The Wall Street Journal*, (October 7, 2003), A1, A14.

Chapter 3

Boyle, M., Wal-Mart keeps the change, *Fortune*, (November 10, 2003), 46.

Christensen, C.M., *The Innovator's Dilemma: When New Technologies Cause Great Firms to Fail*. (Harvard Business School Press, Boston, 1997).

Creswell, J., Options: Trash to treasure?, *Fortune*, (January 12, 2004), 38.

Curtis, J., Behind enemy lines, *Marketing*, (May 24, 2001), 28–29.

Dalton, G., If these shelves could talk, *The Industry Standard*, (April 2, 2001), 49–51.

Dunning, J.H., *International Production and the Multinational Enterprise.* (George Allen & Unwin, London, 1981).

The Economist, How about now: A survey of the real-time economy, (February 2, 2002), 1–20.

Galloni, A., Carreyrou, J. and C. Rohwedder, Stripped of stars at top, will Gucci still be Gucci? *The Wall Street Journal*, (November 11, 2003), A1, A14.

Hill, C.W.L., P. Hwang and W.C. Kim, An eclectic theory of the choice of international entry mode, *Strategic Management Journal*, 1992, 11: February, 117–128.

Kahn, G., Invisible supplier has Penney's shirts all buttoned up, *The Wall Street Journal*, (September 11, 2003), A1, A9.

Nelson, E., The web @ work: Procter & Gamble, *The Wall Street Journal*, (December 31, 2001), B4.

Nelson, E. and G. Anders, Wal-Mart, Amazon.com settle fight over recruitment and trade secrets, *The Wall Street Journal*, (April 6, 1999), A3.

Nelson, E. and A. Zimmerman, Kimberly-Clark keeps Costco in diapers, absorbing costs itself, *The Wall Street Journal*, (September 7, 2000), A1, A12.

Rocks, D., Dell's second web revolution, *Business Week*, (September 18, 2000), EB62–EB63.

Wingfield, N., Amazon takes page from Wal-Mart to prosper on web, *The Wall Street Journal*, (November 22, 2002), A1, A6.

Chapter 4

Belson, K., Asia's internet deficit, *Business Week*, (October 23, 2000), EB105–EB110.

Bontis, N., *National Intellectual Capital Index: The Benchmarking of Arab Countries*, (United Nations Development Project, New York, 2003).

Burt, T., Europe's auto parts suppliers shun web, *Financial Times*, (May 7, 2001), 13.

Dunning, J.H., *International Production and the Multinational Enterprise*, (George Allen & Unwin, London, 1981).

The Economist, Marrying an alien, (July 3, 1999), 56–57.

Edvinsson, L., The knowledge capital of nations, *Knowledge Management*, 2002, April, 27–30.

Ehrlich, C., Liar, liar: The legal perils of misrepresentation, *Competitive Intelligence Magazine*, 2002, 5:2 (March–April), 11–14.

Elizondo, N. and E. Glitman, Cross border competitive intelligence, *Competitive Intelligence Magazine*, 2002, 5:5 (September–October), 31–32.

Helfgott, S., Cultural differences between the US and Japanese patent systems, *Journal of the Patent & Trademark Office Society*, 1990, March, 231–238.

Hill, C.W.L., P. Hwang and W.C. Kim, An eclectic theory of the choice of international entry mode, *Strategic Management Journal*, 1992, 11: February, 117–128.

Hofstede, G., National cultures in four dimensions: A research-based theory of cultural differences among nations, *International Studies of Management and Organization*, 1983, 13, 46–74.

International Business Efficiency Consulting, *The Intellectual Capital of the State of Croatia*. (GIPA, Zagreb, 2002).

Invest in Sweden Agency, Annual Report, 1999.

Khan, G., A sneaker maker says China partner became its rival, *The Wall Street Journal*, (December 19, 2002), A1, A8.

Klemperer, P., How broad should the scope of patent protection be? *Rand Journal of Economics*, 1990, 21:1 (Spring), 113–130.

Kotabe, M., A comparative study of US and Japanese Patent Systems, *Journal of International Business Studies*, 1992, First Quarter, 147–168.

Mackintosh, J. and P. Marsh, Toyota executive backs French workers over US counterparts, *Financial Times*, (March 3, 2003), 1.

Manchester, P., Security fears deter European companies, *Financial Times*, (July 7, 1999), VI.

Marsh, P., Business distrust "holding Europe back," *Financial Times*, (November 22, 1999), 2.

Mitchener, B., EU tells IMS Health to license data system to rivals, *The Wall Street Journal*, (July 5, 2001), A8, A9.

Morrison, S. and R. McGregor, Silicon valley stars in its own spy thriller, *Financial Times*, (March 14, 2003), 17.

Mouritsen, J., H.T. Larsen and P.N. Bukh, Understanding intellectual capital statements: Designing and communicating knowledge management strategies. In N. Bontis (Ed.), *World Congress on Intellectual Capital Readings*, (Butterworth-Heinemann, Woburn, MA, 2002), 179–202.

Mowery, D.C., The US national innovation system: Origins and prospects for change, *Research Policy*, 1992, 21, 125–143.

Mowery, D.C. and D.J. Teece, Japan's growing capabilities in industrial technology: Implications for US managers and policymakers, *California Management Review*, 1993, 35:2 (Winter), 9–34.

Nelson, R. (Ed.), *National Innovation Systems*. (Oxford University Press, New York, 1993).

Organization for Economic Cooperation and Development, Scoreboard 2001—Towards a Knowledge-Based Economy, 2002.

Pasher, E., The intellectual capital of the state of Israel, 1999.

Patel, P. and K. Pavitt, Is western Europe losing the technological race? *Research Policy*, 1987, 16, 59–85.

Rice, S., Public environmental records—A treasure chest of competitive information, *Competitive Intelligence Magazine*, 2000, 3:3 (July–September), 13–19.

Spero, D.M., Patent protection or piracy—a CEO views Japan, *Harvard Business Review*, 1990, September/October, 58–67.

Tomsho, R. Medical supplier sues Boston Scientific, *The Wall Street Journal*, (April 6, 2001), B2.

U.S. Department of the Navy, Knowledge-Centric Organization Toolkit (cd), 2001.

Waters, R., Three Chinese arrested for technology secrets theft, *Financial Times*, (May 4, 2001), 5.

Wheaton, K.J., How to make an embassy work for you, *Competitive Intelligence Magazine*, 2000, 3:1 (January–March), 14–17.

Wilke, J.R., Two silicon valley cases raise fears of Chinese espionage, *The Wall Street Journal*, (January 15, 2003), A4.

Chapter 5

Bennett, J. and B. Mantz, Amgen's patent infringement trial draws rivals' lawyers in search of data, *The Wall Street Journal*, (June 26, 2000), A3–4.

Burns, J. and D. Pilling, Dirty tricks in the international drug industry, *Financial Times*, (May 10, 1999), 6.

Carr, C.A., G.S. Erickson and H.N. Rothberg, Intellectual capital, competitive intelligence, and the Economic Espionage Act, *Journal of Learning and Intellectual Capital*, 2004, forthcoming.

Darveau, L-J., Forecasting an acquisition: 5 steps to help you see it coming, *Competitive Intelligence Magazine*, 2001, 4:1 (January–February), 13–17.

Desrochers, D.M., G.T. Gundlach and A.A. Foer, Analysis of antitrust challenges to category captain arrangements, *Journal of Public Policy & Marketing*, 2003, 22:2 (Fall), 201–215.

Dyer, G., GSK sues Novartis over "stolen bacteria," *Financial Times*, (August 23, 2002), 15.

The Economist, Over the counter e-commerce, (May 26, 2001), 77–78.

Hill, A. and P. Dishman, Countering the threat of disruptive technologies, *Competitive Intelligence Magazine*, 2001, 4:5 (September–October), 19–22.

Kahn, G. Invisible supplier has Penney's shirts all buttoned up, *The Wall Street Journal*, (September 11, 2003), A1, A9.

Kerstetter, J., P. Burrows, J. Greene, G. Smith and M. Conlin, The dark side of the valley, *Business Week*, (July 17, 2000), 42–43.

McEvily, S.K. and B. Chakravarthy, The persistence of knowledge-based advantage: An empirical test for product performance and technological knowledge, *Strategic Management Journal*, 2002, 23:4, 285–305.

Mysore, N. and D. Lobo, Competitive intelligence in the airline industry, *Competitive Intelligence Magazine*, 2000, 3:2 (April–June), 17–20.

Porter, M.E., *The Competitive Advantage of Nations*, (The Free Press, New York, 1990).

Porter, M.E., How competitive forces shape strategy, *Harvard Business Review*, 1979, 57 (March–April), 137–145.

Rice, S., Public environmental records—A treasure chest of competitive information, *Competitive Intelligence Magazine*, 2000, 3:3 (July–September), 13–19.

Squeo, A.M. and A. Pasztor, US probes whether Boeing misused a rival's documents, *The Wall Street Journal*, (May 5, 2003), A1, A7.

Vitzthum, C., Just-in-time fashion, *The Wall Street Journal*, (May 18, 2001), B1, B4.

Wilke, J.R., Two silicon valley cases raise fears of Chinese espionage, *The Wall Street Journal*, (January 15, 2003), A4.

Wing, M., CI in a newly competitive market, *Competitive Intelligence Magazine*, 1999, 2:1 (January–March), 14–16.

Yake, T., Why retailers fail, *Competitive Intelligence Magazine*, 2001, 4:3 (May–June), 15–19.

Chapter 6

Aeppel, T., On factory floors, top workers hide secrets to success, *The Wall Street Journal*, (July 1, 2003), A1, A10.

Ansberry, C., Let's build an online supply network! *The Wall Street Journal*, (April 17, 2000), B1, B10.

Barnett, M., G. Dalton and M.J. Thompson, Wal-Mart's power play, *Industry Standard*, (May 28, 2001), 26.

Beaulieu, P.R., S.M. Williams and M.E. Wright, Intellectual capital disclosures in Swedish annual reports. In N. Bontis (Ed.), *World Congress on Intellectual Capital Readings*, (Butterworth-Heinemann, Woburn, MA, 2002), 135–156.

Boje, D., The storytelling organization: A study of story performance in an office supply firm, *Administrative Science Quarterly*, 1991, 36, 106–121.

Bontis, N., Managing organizational knowledge by diagnosing intellectual capital: Framing and advancing the state of the field, *International Journal of Technology Management*, 1999, 18:5–8, 433–462.

Clark, D., Inside Intel, it's all copying, *The Wall Street Journal*, (October 28, 2002), B1, B4.

The Economist, The Cemex way, (June 16, 2001a), 75–76.

The Economist, Wal around the world, (December 8, 2001b), 55–56.

Edwards, C., Intel, *Business Week*, (March 8, 2004), 56–64.

Gomes, L., Upstart Linux draws a Microsoft attack team, *The Wall Street Journal*, (May 21, 1999), B4.

Lave, J. and E. Wenger, *Situated Learning: Legitimate Peripheral Participation*. (Cambridge University Press, Cambridge, 1991).

Marsh, P., A synchronized swim in the pool, *Financial Times*, (January 24, 2003), 9.

Nelson, E. and G. Anders, Wal-Mart, Amazon.com settle fight over recruitment and trade secrets, *The Wall Street Journal*, (April 6, 1999), A3.

Orr, J., *Talking About Machines: An Ethnography of a Modern Job*. (Cornell University Press, Ithaca, NY, 1996).

Tam, P., High-technology giant duels with nimble knock-off artists, *The Wall Street Journal*, (September 25, 2002), A1, A10.

Thomas, J.C., W.A. Kellogg and T. Erickson, The knowledge management puzzle: Human and social factors in knowledge management, *IBM Systems Journal*, 2001, 40:4, 863–884.

Wenger, E., *Communities of Practice: Learning, Meaning and Identity*. (Cambridge University Press, Cambridge, 1998).

Chapter 7

Ansberry, C., Let's build an online supply network! *The Wall Street Journal*, (April 17, 2000), B1, B10.

Ansoff, H.I., *The New Corporate Strategy.* (John Wiley & Sons, New York, 1988).

Clark, D., Inside Intel, it's all copying, *The Wall Street Journal,* (October 28, 2002), B1, B4.

The Economist, Electronic glue, (June 2, 2001a), 77–78.

The Economist, Link in the global chain, (June 2, 2001b), 62–63.

Ewing, J., Sharing the wealth, *Business Week,* (March 19, 2001), EB36–EB40.

Foremski, T., Doubling up helps chip away at IT challenge, *Financial Times—IT Review,* (November 12, 2003), 3.

Harris, N., "Private exchanges" may allow b-to-b commerce to thrive after all, *The Wall Street Journal,* (March 16, 2001), B1, B4.

Lee-Young, J. and M. Barnett, Furiously fast fashions, *Industry Standard,* (June 11, 2001), 72–79.

Lehmann, D.R. and R.S. Winer, *Analysis for Marketing Planning,* 2nd Ed., (Irwin, Homewood, IL, 1991).

Linsford, J.L., United Technologies' formula: A powerful lift from elevators, *The Wall Street Journal,* (July 2, 2003), A1, A6.

Little, D., Let's keep this exchange to ourselves, *Business Week,* (December 4, 2000), 48.

Porter, M.E., *Competitive Advantage: Creating and Sustaining Superior Performance.* (The Free Press, New York, 1985).

Rocks, D., The net as a lifeline, *Business Week,* (October 29, 2001), EB16–EB23.

Chapter 8

Aeppel, T., Small firms outsource abroad by tapping offshore producers, *The Wall Street Journal,* (November 7, 2004), A2.

Bragg, R. and S. Kumar, Managing supplier relationships, *Industrial Engineer,* 2003, 36:9, 39.

Clark, D., Intel-Xerox teamwork leads to new office-product chips, *The Wall Street Journal,* (September 10, 2003), B5.

Cohen, M. and V. Agrawal, All change in the second supply chain revolution, *Financial Times—Mastering Management,* (October 2, 2000), 8–10.

Daniel, C., Dell seeks new routes for its lean machine, *Financial Times*, (April 2, 2002), 18.

The Economist, Inside the machine: A survey of e-management, (November 11, 2000).

Ericksen, P.D., The extended enterprise: Aim for mutual gain and competitive advantage, *Target*, 2000, 16:3.

Grande, C., Facing up to the new computer world, *Financial Times*, (February 16, 2001), 10.

Hamel, G. and C.K. Prahalad, *Competing for the Future*. (Harvard Business School Press, Boston, 1994).

Konicki, S., "Poor man's solution" saves Kennametal big bucks, *InformationWeek*, (March 18, 2002), 60.

de Lisser, E., Hearing and seeing business travel blab and laptop lapses, *The Wall Street Journal*, (November 8, 1999), A1, A20.

Manchester, P., Keeping check on a vital partnership, *Financial Times—Understanding Supply Chain Execution*, (November 26, 2003), 4–5.

Park, A. and P. Burrows, What you don't know about Dell, *Business Week*, (November 3, 2003), 76–84.

Park, A. and P. Burrows, Dell, the conqueror, *Business Week*, (September 24, 2001), 92–102.

Sanborn, S., Case study: Seeking a better way to buy; Kennametal turns to Tigris to create a better purchasing and sourcing system, *InfoWorld.com*, (August 23, 2002).

Sawhney, M., Use the power of the net to divide and rule, *Financial Times*, (August 18, 2003), 7.

Singer, T., Sharer beware, *Inc. Tech*, (March 16, 1999), 38–48.

Solomon, D. and S. Thurm, Lucent files suit to keep ex-employees from disclosing sensitive data to Cisco, *The Wall Street Journal*, (June 21, 2000), B5.

Steele, M., Purchasing, supply management, and sustainability, *American Society for Competitiveness Conference*, October 11, 2002, Alexandria, VA.

Talacko, P., E-procurement system takes off, *Financial Times—IT Review*, (June 4, 2003), II.

Tam, P-W., High-technology giant duels with nimble knock-off artists, *The Wall Street Journal*, (September 25, 2002), A1, A10.

Thomas, K., Business benefits on both sides of the fence, *Financial Times—Understanding Supply Chain Execution*, (November 26, 2003), 6–7.

Ward, A., Spying fear sparks Samsung phone ban, *Financial Times*, (July 7, 2003), 1.

Wingfield, N., A stolen laptop can be trouble if owner is CEO, *The Wall Street Journal*, (September 19, 2000), B1, B4.

Chapter 9

Ante, S.E., Why IBM called in the consultants, *Business Week*, (February 16, 2004), 62–63.

Brady, D., Will Jeff Immelt's new push pay off for GE? *Business Week*, (October 13, 2003), 94–98.

Brady, D., The education of Jeff Immelt, *Business Week*, (April 29, 2002), 80–87.

The Economist, A moving story, (December 7, 2002), 65–66.

The Economist, While Welch waited, (May 19, 2001), 75–76.

Fowler, G.A. and J. Pereira, Behind a hit toy, a race to tap seasonal surge, *The Wall Street Journal*, (December 18, 2003), A1, A12.

Golden, D., FBI investigates if university stole trade secrets, *The Wall Street Journal*, (July 21, 2003), A3, A6.

Green, H. and B. Elgin, The big boys' mad dash into wi-fi, *Business Week*, (December 23, 2002), 38.

Kersey, J., You're only as good as your password, *Business Week*, (September 2, 2002), 78–80.

Kranhold, K., China's price for market entry: Give us your technology, too, *The Wall Street Journal*, (February 26, 2004), A1, A6.

Latour, A., Keep hackers out, *The Wall Street Journal*, (November 17, 2003), R6.

Machalaba, D., Trucker rewards customers for good behavior, *The Wall Street Journal*, (September 9, 2003), B4.

Mason, S., Backward progress, *IE Solutions*, (August 2002), 42–46.

McKay, B. and S. Vranica, Pepsi wins battle to bar ad agency on work for Coke, *The Wall Street Journal*, (November 5, 2001), B2.

Nairn, G., Big IT projects do not solve everything, *Financial Times—IT Review*, (October 1, 2003), 4.

Reinhardt, A. and J. Greene, Death of a dream, *Business Week*, (February 10, 2003), 44–45.

Simpson, G., Microsoft break-in puts spotlight on investigative firm, *The Wall Street Journal*, (June 19, 2000), A48.

Simpson, G.R. and T. Bridis, Oracle hired firm to probe Microsoft allies, *The Wall Street Journal*, June 28, 2000, A3, A10.

Spethman, B., Loyalty's royalty, *Promo Magazine*, (March 2004), 32–41.

Tam, P-W., Apple sues unknown person over links, *The Wall Street Journal*, (August 3, 2000a), B12.

Tam, P-W., Palm puts up its fists as Microsoft attacks hand-held PC market, *The Wall Street Journal*, (August 8, 2000b), A1, A14.

Tejada, C., The allure of "bundling," *The Wall Street Journal*, (October 7, 2003), B1, B4.

Waldmeir, P., New battle on the web—who owns prices, *Financial Times*, (December 13, 2002), 8.

Chapter 10

Ahart, C.R., Economic espionage versus industrial espionage, *A Digest of Threat Information and Commentary for Security and Counterintelligence Professionals*, (FBI, Washington, DC, 1993).

Berlage, K. and K. Sulzberger, Competitive intelligence and benchmarking practice: A valuable management information instrument for a global universal bank. In B. Gilad and J. Herring (Eds.), *The Art and Science of Business Intelligence*, (JAI Press, Greenwich, CN, 1996).

Bhagat, R., B. Kedia, P. Haverston and H. Triandis, Cultural variations in the cross-border transfer of organizational knowledge:

An integrative framework, *Academy of Management Review*, 2002, 27:2, 204–221.

Binnie, J., Counterintelligence in the 1990s: The threat to corporate america, *Competitive Intelligence Review*, 1994, 5:3, 17–21.

Carr, C.A. , G.S. Erickson and H.N. Rothberg, Intellectual capital, competitive intelligence, and the Economic Espionage Act, *Journal of Learning and Intellectual Capital*, 2004, forthcoming.

Cummings, J., Work groups, structural diversity and knowledge sharing in a global organization, *Management Science*, 2004, forthcoming.

DeGenaro, B., Counterintelligence. In B. Gilad and J. Herring (Eds.), *The Art and Science of Business Intelligence*, (JAI Press, Greenwich, CN, 1996).

Erickson, G.S., Export controls: marketing implications of public policy choices, *Journal of Public Policy & Marketing*, 1997, 16:1, 83–92.

Fink, A. and O. Schlake, Scenario management: An approach for strategic foresight, *Competitive Intelligence Review*, 2000, 11:1, 37–45.

Fleischer, S. and B. Bensoussan, *Strategic and Competitive Analysis.* (Prentice Hall, Upper Saddle River, New Jersey, 2002).

Fraumann, E. and J. Koletar, Trade secret safeguards, *Security Management*, 1999, (March), 64.

Gilad, B., *Business Blindspots.* (Probus Publishing, Chicago, 1994).

Gilad, B. and T. Gilad, *Business Intelligence Systems: A New Tool for Competitive Advantage.* (AMACOM, Chicago, 1988).

Gilad, B. and J. Herring (Eds.), *The Art and Science of Business Intelligence Analysis.* (JAI Press, Greenwich, CT, 1996).

Gilbert, L., Using multiple scenario analysis to map the competitive futurescape: A practice based perspective, *Competitive Intelligence Review*, 2000,11:2, 12–19.

Greenemeier, L., J.P. Morgan Chase extends knowledge management *Information Week*, 2001, 1:834, 97.

Hamel, G., Competition for competence and inter-partner learning within international strategic alliances, *Strategic Management Journal*, 1991, 12, 83–103.

Hansen, M. and B. von Oetinger, Introducing the T-shaped manager, *Harvard Business Review*, 2001, (March), 107–116.

Hayashi, A., Building better teams, *Sloan Management Review*, 2004, 45:2, 5.

Helms, M., Etkin, L. and D. Morris, In-security: The pillaging of corporate America, *Competitive Intelligence Review*, 2000, 11:3, 93–106.

Herring, J., What is intelligence analysis? *Competitive Intelligence Magazine*, 1998, 1:2, 13–16.

Hoyt, B., Early warning: The art of inference, *Competitive Intelligence Magazine*, 2002, 5:1, 10–14.

Kendrick, T. and J. Blackmore, Ten things you really need to know about competitors, *Competitive Intelligence Magazine*, 2001, 4:5, 12–15.

Kogut, B., Joint ventures: theoretical and empirical perspectives, *Strategic Management Journal*, 1988, 9:4, 319–332.

Mathey, P., Early warning analysis: Preventing management surprises. In B. Gilad and J. Herring (Eds.), *The Art and Science of Business Intelligence.* (JAI Press, Greenwich, CT, 1996).

Microsoft, Deploying Microsoft's enterprise intranet portal using Microsoft Office SharePoint Portal Server, white paper, 2004.

Office of the National Counterintelligence Executive, Annual Report to Congress, 2002, www.ncix.gov.

Ormerod, P., How Ericsson turned its workforce into intelligence gatherers, *Competitive Intelligence Magazine*, 2002, 5:1, 27–29.

Page, M., Providing effective early warning: Business intelligence as a strategic control system. In B. Gilad & J. Herring (Eds.), *The Art and Science of Business Intelligence*, (JAI Press, Greenwich, CN, 1996).

Pattakos, A., Threat analysis: Defining the adversary, *Competitive Intelligence Review*, 1998, 9:2, 53–62.

Porter, M., *Competitive Strategy.* (Free Press, New York, 1980).

Powell, D., An introduction to the law of trade secrets, *Colorado Lawyer*, 1994, 23, 2125–2127.

Reibstein, J. and M. Chussil, Putting the lesson before the test: Using simulation to analyze and develop competitive strategies, *Competitive Intelligence Review*, 1999, 10:1, 34–48.

Robinson, M., Competitive information security: Lessons from Los Alamos, *Competitive Intelligence Magazine*, 2001, 4:4, 14–16.

Rothberg, H., Fortifying competitive intelligence systems with shadow teams, *Competitive Intelligence Review*, 1997, 8:2, 3–11.

Sawka, K., Early-warning: The decision-maker's perspective, *Competitive Intelligence Review*, 1998, 9:2, 63–65.

Schwab, A. and D. Porter, Federal protection of trade secrets: Understanding the Economic Espionage Act of 1996, *Pennsylvania Law Weekly*, (August 17, 1998), 14.

Shenkar, O. and J. Li, Knowledge search in international cooperative ventures, *Organization Science*, 1999, 10, 134–143.

Storck, J. and P. Hill, Knowledge diffusion through strategic communities, *Sloan Management Review*, 2000, (Winter), 63–74.

Tsang, E., Acquiring knowledge by foreign partners from international joint ventures in a transition economy: Learning by doing and learning myopia, *Strategic Management Journal*, 2002, 23, 35–854.

Tsang, E., A preliminary typology of learning in international strategic alliances, *Journal of World Business*, 1999, 39, 211–229.

Underwood, J., Perspectives on war-gaming, *Competitive Intelligence Review*, 1998, 9:2, 45–53.

U.S. Department of Defense, *Industrial Security Manual Safeguarding Classified Information*, DOD 5220.22-m. (Defense Investigative Service, Washington, DC, 1991), 9-4-1.

Vella, C. and J. McGonagle, Profiling in competitive analysis, *Competitive Intelligence Review*, 2000, 1:1, 20–29.

Wingo, H., Dumpster diving and the ethical blindspot of trade secret law, *Yale Law & Policy Review*, 1997, 16, 195.

Winkler, I., Corporate espionage, Inc., 1997, 19:8, 91.

Zaino, J., 2003, Fleet sees payoff in CRM, *Information Week*, (August 18, 2003), 47.

Chapter 11

Cohen, D. and L. Prusak, *In Good Company: How Social Capital Makes Organizations Work*. (Harvard Business School Press, Cambridge, MA, 2001).

Gilad, B., *Business Blindspots*. (Probus Publishing Company, Chicago, 1994).

Gupta, A. and A. Govindarajan, Knowledge management's social dimension: Lessons from Nucor steel, *Sloan Management Review*, 2000, (Fall), 71–80.

Hansen, M. and B. von Oetinger, Introducing T-shaped managers: Knowledge management's next generation, *Harvard Business Review*, 2001, (March), 107–116.

Joni, S.A., The geography of trust, *Harvard Business Review*, 2004, 82:3, 82–89.

Knowledge Management Review, Relationship management at Chase Manhattan, 1998, 1:2, 16–21.

Krogh, G., K. Ichijo and I. Nonaka, *Enabling Knowledge Creation: How to Unlock the Mystery of Tacit Knowledge and Release the Power of Innovation*. (Oxford University Press, NY, 2000).

Pearce, C., The future of leadership: Combining vertical and shared leadership to transform knowledge work, *Harvard Business Review*, 2004, 18:1, 47–57.

Pfeffer, J. and R. Sutton, *The Knowing-Doing Gap: How Smart Companies Turn Knowledge Into Action*. (Harvard Business School Press, Cambridge, MA, 2000).

Prescott, J., The social capital of CI professionals, *Competitive Intelligence Magazine*, 2003, 6:1, 33–35.

Prusak, L. and D. Cohen, How to invest in social capital, *Harvard Business Review*, 2001, (June), 86–93.

Stewart, T., *The Wealth of Knowledge*. (Currency, New York, 2001).

Zaino, J., Fleet sees payoff in CRM, *Information Week*, (August 18, 2003), 47.

Chapter 12

Baier, K., Deontological theories. In *Encyclopedia of Bioethics*, Volume 1. (New York, Free Press, 1978), 413–417.

Daniel, C., Boeing to trumpet new rules on ethics, *Financial Times*, (August 25, 2003), 17.

Ehrlich, C.P., A brief CI compliance guide, Part 2: Food lions, lazy mosaics, and fuzzy impostors, *Competitive Intelligence Review*, 2000, 9:3, 54–59.

Ehrlich, C.P., A brief CI compliance manual, *Competitive Intelligence Review*, 1998, 9:1, 28–37.

Harvey, F., A big test for a smart operator, *Financial Times*, (August 20, 2003), 8.

Lunsford, J.L. and A.M. Squeo, Boeing CEO Condit resigns in shake-up at aerospace titan, *The Wall Street Journal*, (December 2, 2003), A1, A12.

MacIntyre, A., *After Virtue*. (Notre Dame University Press, South Bend, 1984).

Mill, J.S., *Utilitarianism, Liberty, and Representative Government*. (Dent, London, 1910).

Pasztor, A. and A.M. Squeo, US probes Boeing rocket executive, *The Wall Street Journal*, (July 23, 2003), A3, A6.

Rawls, J., *A Theory of Justice*. (Harvard University Press, Cambridge, MA, 1971).

Schwartz, P., When good companies do bad things, *Strategy & Leadership*, 2000, 28:3, 4–12.

Society for Competitive Intelligence Professionals (SCIP), SCIP Code of Ethics for CI Professionals, http://www.scip.org/ci/ethics.asp.

Squeo, A.M. and A. Pasztor, US probes whether Boeing misused a rival's documents, *The Wall Street Journal*, (May 5, 2003), A1, A7.

Thibault, J. and L. Walker, *Procedural Justice: A Psychological Analysis.* (Lawrence Erlbaum, Hillsdale, NJ, 1975).

Trevino, L.K. and G.R. Weaver, Ethical issues in competitive intelligence practice: Consensus, conflicts, and challenges, *Competitive Intelligence Review,* 1997, 8:1, 1–22.

Young, M.R. (Ed.), *Accounting Irregularities and Financial Fraud: A Corporate Governance Guideline.* (Harcourt Professional Publishing, San Diego, 2000).

About the Authors

HELEN N. ROTHBERG

Helen N. Rothberg, Ph.D.

Dr. Helen Rothberg has been the principal consultant for HNR Associates "a network of knowledge" since 1987. Her expertise spans strategic planning and behavioral science. Her noted specialties are in the fields of knowledge management and competitive intelligence where she builds "shadow teams" and facilitates strategic change.

Dr. Rothberg is an Associate Professor of Strategic Management, School of Management, Marist College, Poughkeepsie, NY. Her publications appear in a host of academic and practitioner journals, conference proceedings, magazines and business newsletters.

Helen N. Rothberg's credentials include an MBA from Baruch College, CUNY, and M.Phil. from City University Graduate Center, and a Ph.D. in Business specializing in both Organization and Policy Studies from the City University Graduate Center, NY.

Helen resides in the mountains of Orange County, NY with her four legged companions.

G. Scott Erickson, Ph.D.

G. SCOTT ERICKSON

G. Scott Erickson is Associate Professor of Marketing in the School of Business at Ithaca College. He holds a Ph.D. from Lehigh University, MIM from Thunderbird, the Garvin School of International Management, an MBA from Southern Methodist University, and a B.A. from Haverford College.

His research interests include intellectual capital, intellectual property, and other areas in which law and public policy intersect with marketing. He has been published in outlets such as Journal of Public Policy & Marketing, European Journal of Marketing, Journal of Marketing Management, Industrial Marketing Management, International Journal of Technology Management, and American Business Law Journal. He also serves on the Board of Directors of the American Society for Competitiveness.

He has been a consultant for twenty years, including stints with Alexander Proudfoot and Lehigh University's International Trade Development Program. Areas of expertise include technological innovation, operations, and marketing strategy.

Index

800-pound Gorilla (SPF 15). *See* Market domination and risk